BIDIALECTALISM

An Unexpected Development
in the Obsolescence
of Pennsylvania Dutchified English

BIDIALECTALISM

An Unexpected Development
in the Obsolescence
of Pennsylvania Dutchified English

VICKI MICHAEL ANDERSON

Publication of the American Dialect Society 98

Supplement to *American Speech*, Volume 88

PUBLICATION OF THE AMERICAN DIALECT SOCIETY

Editor: ROBERT BAYLEY, *University of California, Davis*
Managing Editor: CHARLES E. CARSON, *Duke University Press*

Number 98
Copyright 2014
American Dialect Society
ISBN: 978-0-8223-6796-3

Library of Congress Cataloging-in-Publication Data

Anderson, Vicki Michael.
  Bidialectalism : an unexpected development in the obsolescence of Pennsylvania
    Dutchified English / by Vicki Michael Anderson.
      pages cm. – (Publication of the American Dialect Society ; number 98)
  "Supplement to *American Speech*, Volume 88."
  Includes bibliographical references and index.
  ISBN 978-0-8223-6796-3 (pbk. : alk. paper)
      1. English language—Dialects—Pennsylvania. 2. Pennsylvania Dutch—Languages.
  3. Bidialectalism—Pennsylvania. I. Title. II. Series: Publication of the American
  Dialect Society ; no. 98.
PE3102.P45A53 2014
427'.9748–dc23   2014009300

British Library Cataloguing-in-Publication Data available

CONTENTS

Acknowledgments   vii

1. Introduction   1

2. Outcomes of Dialect Contact and the Case of Pennsylvania
   Dutchified English   7

3. A Working Description of Pennsylvania Dutchified English
   and South Central Pennsylvania English   19

4. PDE Phonological Features and Their Use: Unraveling
   in Action for PDE Obstruent Devoicing   43

5. Other PDE Phonological Features and Their Use: Further
   Evidence for the Unraveling of PDE   73

6. On the Trail of the Bidialectal   113

7. The Emergence of Bidialectalism at the End of the Life Cycle
   of PDE: A Case Study   129

8. Conclusion   175

   Appendix 1: Sample Tokens from Youngest Monodialectal
   PDE Speakers   179

   Appendix 2: Excerpts from Rachel's Conversations   180

   Notes   185

   References   191

   Index   199

ACKNOWLEDGMENTS

When I was a child growing up in south central Pennsylvania as a speaker of Pennsylvania Dutchified English, I could never have imagined that I would one day have an opportunity to write a monograph on the dialect. In fact, I'm not sure that anyone I knew at that time actually considered the way we spoke a dialect. To most of us, being "Dutchified" meant talking something like the old people talked; to our teachers, our way of speaking was just bad English; to tourists who came to see the Amish, the way we spoke was quaint and laughable. It would not be until I took a graduate Introduction to Linguistics course as a 23-year-old adult that it finally occurred to me that Pennsylvania Dutchified English was a genuine dialect of American English and that as such it was worthy of description and study.

I also could not have realized as I was growing up that I and my age-mates (those born in the 1960s and 1970s) would be the last generation of speakers for Pennsylvania Dutchified English. After all, the old people and our parents were all "Dutchified," and so were a good many of our own age group; it never occurred to us that one day we would have children who would not speak the same way we did and that, due to the lack of intergenerational transmission, the way we spoke would someday cease to exist. No, we who were worried about language preservation were more concerned about the demise of Pennsylvania Dutch—I never heard it called "Pennsylvania German" until I entered graduate school—and many of us wished that we could speak that language, like our grandparents did. Pennsylvania Dutchified English just did not seem to be of much value. This is still the situation in Pennsylvania today: those interested in how language fits with the Pennsylvania Dutch ethnic identity attend events where Pennsylvania German is spoken—festivals, special church services, storytelling galas, and the like—but no one bothers about Pennsylvania Dutchified English. Its decline proceeds unnoticed, and its death—when the last Pennsylvania Dutchified English speakers of my generation pass away—will likely go unheralded by the general public even in Pennsylvania itself.

However, thanks to the support and opportunities I have been given to write about this little-known dialect, it is possible that the death of Pennsylvania Dutchified English will not go unremarked by the academic linguistic community. For that I am immensely grateful. There is no way to save Pennsylvania Dutchified English, but I hope that this little bit I have to offer about my native dialect will make some contribution to the field of linguistics as a whole.

I would not have had even this to offer if it had not been for the support and encouragement of many people, whom I wish to acknowledge here, not just on behalf of myself, but also on behalf of all those who speak Pennsylvania Dutchified English:

To my parents, for encouraging my interest in Pennsylvania Dutch, and for buying me Gates's humorous dictionary *How to Speak Dutchified English* as a Christmas present in 1987. Little could they or I have realized that the end result of having that book would be a manuscript on Pennsylvania Dutchified English.

To my husband, Jon, for patiently acting as my sounding board and for believing that Pennsylvania Dutchified English is an intriguing dialect, even if as a speaker of a more standard American English dialect he has had more than his share of humorous "misunderstandings" when interacting with my family and friends in Pennsylvania.

To Elizabeth Riddle, for patiently showing me during my master's degree work at Ball State University that yes, Pennsylvania Dutchifed English is a real dialect worthy of study.

To Stuart Davis, for his encouragement, guidance, and help in understanding how special Pennsylvania Dutchified English is, for his aid in uncovering some of its complexities, and for his patient advice. His insight and breadth of linguistic knowledge has elevated my work on Pennsylvania Dutchified English far above what it could have been if I had been on my own.

To Robert Bayley and the two anonymous reviewers for their specialized dialectological insight and big-picture perspective of the place of this work in the study of language variety obsolescence and of German dialects in America in particular. And to Charles Carson for his editorial expertise and attention to detail.

To all of you I owe my deepest gratitude.

1. INTRODUCTION

Linguists readily acknowledge today that all languages undergo change and that many language varieties in contact with other varieties eventually undergo obsolescence and die out (see, e.g., Wolfram 2002, 764). Researchers of linguistic contact phenomena have worked to determine exactly what processes lead to language variety change and obsolescence, but the stages through which obsolescing varieties actually pass on their way to extinction are still not completely delineated or understood. Nevertheless, with the exception of cases in which a language dies "intact" because all its speakers are killed off by disease or warfare, language variety obsolescence typically involves two processes, namely (1) simplification at various linguistic levels and (2) restriction in the domains of life in which that language variety is used by a community of speakers as they shift their allegiance from one language to the other. In most communities where language contact takes place, at least one generation becomes bilingual in both the minority language and the dominant language before the final community shift to the dominant language occurs; eventually, however, the original language of the community "dies" (at least for that community). Thus, speech community–wide bilingualism is really a sort of penultimate stage before a language embarks on its final decline toward extinction (Wolfram 2002, 764–65). Most of the studies undertaken to date on this kind of obsolescence have involved language shifts in immigrant speech communities from a shared L1 to the L2 of the larger community into which immigrants have settled (e.g., Dutch migrants in New Zealand [Hulsen, de Bot, and Weltens 2002] or Spanish immigrants in America [Kirchner 1995]). In such language shifts, the scenario often proceeds like this:

As the first generation speakers use their L1 less, the model they provide for the second generation may be a different version in some sense from what they acquired. Not surprisingly, some of its structures may show convergence to the dominant language in the community. For example, while they still speak Spanish fluently, first generation Puerto Ricans in New York may begin to use calques from English (English phrases they translate word for word into Spanish words). Or, they may drop certain grammatical constructions (e.g., the subjunctive). When their turn comes, the second generation may not even acquire the version of the L1 of their elders' generation because of domain loss and attitudinal factors. The result is attrition in the second generation and a new version that is transmitted to the next generation. [Meyers-Scotton 2002, 180]

However, Meyers-Scotton (2002) cautions,

[T]he reality or details of a second- or third-generation shift away from the L1 is not necessarily due ONLY to having a reduced model to follow—even though this is the scenario many researchers sketch. [2002, 180; emphasis mine]

In other words, the processes involved in the demise of a language variety can be significantly more complex than mere attrition in use of language features by individuals in the speech community, and unexpected linguistic outcomes can manifest themselves in the interim period between a community's development of bilingualism and the final demise of the minority language variety. Such is the case for Pennsylvania Dutchified English (PDE), a little-studied dialect spoken today in south central Pennsylvania. (South central Pennsylvania in general encompasses the counties of Adams, Berks, Cumberland, Dauphin, Franklin, Huntingdon, Juniata, Lancaster, Lebanon, Mifflin, Northumberland, Perry, Schuykill, Snyder, and York.) The unique dialect spoken in this region is now in the last decades of its life cycle as the speech community shifts to a regional standard of English, South Central Pennsylvania English (SCPE). As PDE obsolesces, two particular unexpected outcomes have surfaced: First, younger generations of speakers are not simply using dialectal features less and less frequently; they are using those features in different ways, with different linguistic constraints and different manifestations of what it means to "speak PDE." (This phenomenon will be referred to in this work as dialect "unraveling" based on its metaphorical similarities to the unraveling of a rope: just as a rope is no longer a rope after a certain point as it is disentangled strand by strand, so PDE has become unstable in feature after feature to the point where it is impossible to be transmitted as a viable dialect to the next generation.) This monograph explores the unraveling of the PDE dialect through an investigation of a number of PDE phonological variants and their use by a small set of PDE speakers from two and sometimes three generations. Tracking individuals' use of these dialectal features across the generations and within each generation will serve to highlight the extreme degree of variability for PDE among its last generation of speakers. All this contributes to the basic question of what it means in this speech community to "speak Pennsylvania Dutchified English" in the face of dialect shift.

The second unexpected outcome is the emergence of a population of individuals who have not merely shifted from the L1 to the L2 (here, from PDE to SCPE), but who have instead become self-proclaimed bidialectals. By presenting quantitative data on one speaker's use of certain phonological features of PDE, this monograph is able to show the extent of that speaker's bidialectalism—an important contribution given the paucity of literature on bidialectals, but also a vital part of addressing the issue of what it means to "speak PDE" in the current state of the dialect's unraveling. By presenting qualitative data on the attitudes and motivations of that speaker and a supplementary small set of self-proclaimed bidialectals who speak both PDE and SCPE, this work also suggests how bidialectalism can arise in the last phase of a language variety's life cycle.

STUDY INFORMANTS, PROCEDURES, METHODOLOGY

The descriptions and analyses in this work are based on observations of members of the south central Pennsylvania speech community. Data were gathered from informal interviews of PDE speakers in 1993–95 and 2005–9 and of SCPE speakers in 2005–9, all in northern Lebanon County, Pennsylvania. PDE speakers recorded in 1993–95 represented three age groups: the then-oldest generation (over 65, born before 1920), the middle-aged generation (roughly 45–65, born in the 1930s–1940s), and the youngest generation (below 40, those born after 1950). Speakers recorded in 2005–9 included three monodialectal PDE speakers in their 60s (middle-aged, born in the 1940s) and three each of monodialectal PDE and SCPE speakers in the 30–40-year-old age range (born in the 1960s–1970s), this last age range corresponding to the ages of the youngest speakers of PDE found in the speech community. The informants included both males and females; all grew up in rural, working-class, PDE-speaking households in Lebanon County, and all have some tie (either through residence, church networks, or having grown up there) to the mountain hamlets of the northern part of the county. These informants were all recruited from personal acquaintances and relatives of area residents known to the researcher. All but one of the oldest speakers recorded in 1993–95 are/were bilingual in both PDE and Pennsylvania German; all informants recorded from 2005–9 are monolingual in English. Recording was done via cassette tape with a handheld recorder in 1993–95 and via a CD recorder with a condenser microphone in 2005–9. Data collection during these periods was subject to IRB approval, and authorized consent forms were obtained from the informants before they were recorded. Recording sessions consisted of open-ended casual conversation guided by general questions about the history of northern Lebanon County. Unless otherwise indicated (as in the study of acoustic measurements in chapter 4), all data were coded by impressionistic analysis of whether a PDE feature was being used by a speaker or not.

Table 1.1 lists the informants, with their ages at the time of the data collection and the age group they were assigned for the pertinent parts of this study. All the informants recorded in 1993–95 are speakers of PDE; nearly half also speak Pennsylvania German. Note from the initials that some informants (LM, DK, and LK) likewise participated in the 2005–9 data collection, along with three new PDE speakers. Also recorded in 2005–9 were three SCPE speakers who had grown up in PDE-speaking households.

Three self-proclaimed bidialectal speakers also participated to varying degrees in this study. Only one of them (Rachel) was able to finish out the study, and consequently only her recorded data were used for analysis, but the other two shared their views on their use of PDE versus SCPE before they had to withdraw for personal and family reasons, and their input

TABLE 1.1

Study Partcipants

Informant	Bilingual/ Monolingual	Age	Age Group	Sex
PDE Speakers, 1993–95				
BZ	bilingual	over 75	oldest	F
JK	bilingual	over 70	oldest	F
CT	bilingual	over 70	oldest	M
LT	bilingual	upper 60s	oldest	F
EY	monolingual	upper 60s	oldest	F
EK	bilingual	upper 50s	middle-aged	F
LM	monolingual	56	middle-aged	M
WM	monolingual	59	middle-aged	M
BK	monolingual	upper 40s	middle-aged	M
DK	monolingual	27	youngest	M
LK	monolingual	27	youngest	F
PDE Speakers, 2005–9				
LM	monolingual	upper 60s	middle-aged	M
DG	monolingual	upper 60s	middle-aged	M
LG	monolingual	mid-60s	middle-aged	F
DwK	monolingual	30s	youngest	M
DK	monolingual	30s	youngest	M
LK	monolingual	30s	youngest	F
SCPE Speakers, 2005–9				
JL	monolingual	40s	youngest	M
EL	monolingual	30s	youngest	F
RK	monolingual	30s	youngest	F
PDE-SCPE Bidialectals				
Rachel	monolingual	30s	youngest	F
WC	monolingual	30s	youngest	F
SH	bilingual	40s	youngest	F

informs some of the discussion on attitudes and motivations of bidialectal speakers in chapter 7.

This volume presents details about PDE and its unexpected developments in the following manner: chapter 2 sets the stage by discussing the development of Pennsylvania Dutchfied English from its Pennsylvania German roots; it then presents a view of how the study of the development and demise of Pennsylvania Dutchified English fits into the larger body of work on dialect contact. Chapter 3 provides more background on the linguistic climate in south central Pennsylvania by presenting a short description of the South Central Pennsylvania English dialect and discussing its connection to (and distinctions from) the bordering regional dialects of Philadelphia English (spoken in southeastern Pennsylvania) and Pittsburgh/Southwestern Pennsylvania English. Chapter 3 also describes Pennsylvania Dutchified English by providing detailed lists of the phonetic, phonological, morphosyntactic, semantic, and supersegmental features that make up this obsolescing dialect and by discussing areas where PDE and SCPE overlap.

Chapters 4 and 5 specifically address the unraveling of the PDE dialect with regard to certain highlighted phonological features, both consonantal and vocalic. This unraveling is illustrated by frequency data for PDE feature use across generations of speakers and within generations of speakers. These chapters also reveal changes of phonological constraints over the generations in the use of a subset of those features for which such data are available.

Chapter 6 turns to a discussion of bidialectalism in the literature and its relevance in a climate of dialect obsolescence. Chapter 7 presents data from the self-proclaimed bidialectal speakers of PDE and SCPE mentioned above; by delineating how one of those bidialectals compares to her monodialectal peers, the chapter shows how the linguistic situation in south central Pennsylvania could lead to the development of bidialectalism in the last generation of PDE speakers. Chapter 8 finally ties all this together by discussing the processes that have led to the shift from PDE to SCPE in south central Pennsylvania.

Language variety shift and obsolescence is occurring today in many places besides south central Pennsylvania, and it is overly simplistic to assume that it is powered merely by speakers across the generations using dialect features less and less frequently. Through the discussion of the changes in linguistic norms involved in dialect unraveling and the scrutiny of linguistic behavior of a bidialectal, this look at Pennsylvania Dutchified English contributes much-needed insight into the processes that make that shift happen.

2. OUTCOMES OF DIALECT CONTACT AND THE CASE OF PENNSYLVANIA DUTCHIFIED ENGLISH

Tʜᴇ sᴛᴜᴅʏ ᴏꜰ ᴡʜᴀᴛ ʜᴀᴘᴘᴇɴs when speakers of different languages come together has been a fruitful area of linguistics, bringing to light many different kinds of contact phenomena, such as linguistic borrowing, language change, pidgin/creole development, and accommodation. Many studies have concentrated on such outcomes of contact between ʟᴀɴɢᴜᴀɢᴇs, but far fewer have focused on the outcomes of ᴅɪᴀʟᴇᴄᴛ contact (i.e., contact between two mutually intelligible language varieties). Those that have investigated dialect contact have shown that there is an array of attested dialect contact outcomes, ranging from dedialectalization and dialect shift to partial or complete dialect acquisition to new dialect formation (Trudgill 1986). This work intends to add to the array of possible outcomes by documenting the feature changes involved in the unraveling of the Pennsylvania Dutchified English dialect and by presenting a case study of bidialectalism.

Logically, dialect contact can occur in three linguistic contexts:

1. migrations of speakers of a dialect to an area where another dialect is spoken,
2. migratory situations where speakers of two or more dialects of the same language settle together in an area native to neither of them, and
3. areas where more than one dialect has been spoken for multiple generations.

The linguistic situation in south central Pennsylvania most closely matches the third scenario, but this chapter begins with a brief overview of research on all three contexts because of the insight they offer into the language processes involved; these findings are particularly pertinent to the discussion of language shift and the forces undergirding the development of bidialectalism.

2.1. DIALECT CONTACT

ᴍɪɢʀᴀᴛɪᴏɴs ᴏꜰ sᴘᴇᴀᴋᴇʀs ᴏꜰ ᴀ ᴅɪᴀʟᴇᴄᴛ ᴛᴏ ᴀɴ ᴀʀᴇᴀ ᴡʜᴇʀᴇ ᴀɴᴏᴛʜᴇʀ ᴅɪᴀ-ʟᴇᴄᴛ ɪs sᴘᴏᴋᴇɴ. In some dialect contact situations, speakers have migrated from the area where their dialect is spoken natively by the majority to an area where another dialect of the same language is predominantly spoken. Although of course dialect contact in such situations involves issues of accommodation and interdialect development (Trudgill 1986), many studies of this type of contact have focused instead on the acquisition of new features of the dominant dialect by child and adult migrants, assuming that at least a subset of features of the second dialect will be acquired by the migrants. Such studies do not assume that speakers—even children— will ever become native-like in their use of features of the other dialect, but focus instead on restrictions with regard to which features they acquire and, sometimes, the degree of sociolinguistic competence they gain in using those features with native-like patterns (e.g., Payne 1980; Auer, Barden, and Grosskopf 1998).

In an early investigation of dialect acquisition among a population of migrant children, Payne (1980) studied children who had moved into the King of Prussia suburb of Philadelphia from various parts of the United States. Payne found that these migrant children showed remarkable success in acquiring subtleties of certain nonphonemic Philadelphia diphthongal variables (namely, the centralization of the nucleus of [ay] before voiceless obstruents, the fronting and raising of the nucleus of [aw], the raising of the nucleus of [oy] to [u], and extreme fronting and centralization of [uw] and [ow]); each of these variables could, Payne noted, be added to individual children's grammars through the addition of a simple rule. These same children, however, were not nearly as successful in acquiring the so-called Philadelphia short-*a* variable pattern, which involves the following very complex rule set:

> /æ/ is invariably raised and tensed before front nasals or front fricatives followed by another consonant or inflectional boundary, or in the three lexical items *mad*, *bad*, and *glad* (but not *sad*).

> /æ/ is invariably lax in an auxiliary verb or before stops (except in *mad*, *bad*, and *glad*), voiced fricatives, /s/, /r/, and the velar nasal.

> /æ/ is variable before nasal consonants or front voiceless fricatives followed by an optional derivational boundary or a vowel, or before /l/.

> /æ/ is variable in proper nouns and abbreviations. [Payne 1980, 158–59]

Payne found that, although every child in the study acquired the short-*a* pattern at least partially, very few achieved anything close to complete acquisition; those MOST successful were under the age of eight at the time they moved into the King of Prussia neighborhood. Thus, despite the fact that children have a reputation for being able to acquire correctly language variety features to which they are exposed, short-*a* apparently presents unusual difficulties. According to Payne, a child has little chance of acquiring the variant successfully unless born in King of Prussia; even then, a child born in King of Prussia to parents who are not native to that suburb may not acquire short-*a* correctly. Payne's (1980) study clearly shows that even children in a migratory dialect situation may be incapable of complete acquisition of a new dialect, depending on the complexity of rules governing features of that new dialect.

Another study argues, however, that is NOT altogether impossible for a child whose family has migrated to another dialect area to acquire the complexities of a second dialect. In remarkable contrast to the Payne's (1980) study, Evans (2002) found that 29-year-old Noah, born in Morgantown, West Virginia, to Detroit natives who had migrated there, was able to show mastery of both a "Midwestern" vowel system similar to that of his parents and a "Southern" vowel system that more closely matches that of Morgantown natives. Through acoustic analysis, Evans determined that Noah's "Midwestern" system is a rather conservative one, not incorporating many elements of the currently robust Northern Cities Shift, but his "Southern" vowels correspond closely to the current general Southern Shift. These correspondences hold for places where the general "Midwestern" and "Southern" systems overlap, as well as for where they do not. From this analysis Evans demonstrates that Noah's two vowel systems are both acoustically distinct and authentic and thus provides an example of a child who successfully acquired two dialects in a migratory context.

While the families of the informants featured in this monograph did not migrate into south central Pennsylvania like the families of the King of Prussia children and Noah migrated into their respective areas, it is nonetheless true that these informants—all of whom grew up in homes speaking Pennsylvania Dutchified English (PDE)—were not exposed to South Central Pennsylvania English (SCPE) until school age or even older. The implications that this had for acquisition—or lack of acquisition—of SCPE by each generation of informants and by the bidialectals in this study are discussed at length in later sections.

A more extensive longitudinal study that examined adult migrant dialect feature LOSS—in many cases, the logical counterpart of dialect feature acquisition—was undertaken by Auer, Barden, and Grosskopf (1998). In a series of eight interviews conducted over two years with a group of 56 individuals, most of whom were adults up to 52 years old, Auer, Barden, and Grosskopf investigated feature loss for speakers of Upper Saxonian Vernacular (an East German dialect) who had migrated to areas of West Germany for employment. Auer, Barden, and Grosskopf's work built on research by Schirmunski (1930), the first linguist to discuss the role of salience in dialect leveling situations by dividing dialect features into "primary" and "secondary" features; Schirmunski's view was that "primary" (i.e., more salient) features of a dialect were leveled in dialect contact, while "secondary" (i.e., less salient) features were retained. Auer, Barden, and Grosskopf (1998) tested whether Schirmunski's notion of "salience" could explain the dialect feature loss and retention they observed in their Upper Saxonian informants if "salience" is carefully defined both by objective linguistic factors (e.g., articulatory distance of a native dialect feature from its second dialect counterpart, areal distribution of a native dialect feature, etc.) as well as subjective perceptual factors (e.g., use of native dialect features in stereotyping, representation of a native dialect feature in the orthography, etc.) that render a feature "meaningful" for its speakers. In the course of their investigation, all subjects lost certain Upper Saxonian features as they acquired West German ones, but none completely acquired the West German dialect; Auer, Barden, and Grosskopf (1998) determined that salience could account for a certain subset of the outcomes they observed. Their work will be discussed in greater detail in chapters 4 and 5 when their criteria are used to determine whether salience has any effect on the relative rates at which PDE features are being abandoned over the generations by monodialectal PDE speakers.

MIGRATIONS OF SPEAKERS OF VARIOUS DIALECTS TO AREAS WHERE NONE OF THE DIALECTS ARE SPOKEN. A handful of studies have investigated the results of dialect contact when speakers of multiple dialects of the same language migrate together to an area that is native to none of the dialects. For English dialects, this kind of contact has occurred primarily in "new settlement" areas as a result of colonization (in places such as New Zealand, Australia, and North America) or in mass migration to either newly opened areas or "new towns" planned and set up by a government for housing or employment of speakers from a widespread geographical area. Examples of each of these kinds of studies will be discussed below. Each case reveals that, instead of one dominant dialect being acquired by all settlers, a new and unique dialect emerges from the pool of dialects spoken by the settlers. The mechanisms by which that new dialect arises are very revealing in terms of the linguistic strategies speakers develop when confronted with a mixture of dialects. How younger generations of speakers choose which features to adopt—and which to reject—has interesting parallels with the manner in which the children of the youngest speakers of PDE have not been able to acquire PDE successfully.

In their study of the colonial origins of modern New Zealand English, Trudgill et al. (2000, 299) note that "dialect mixture and new-dialect formation are not haphazard processes"; instead, Trudgill et al. (2000) used available data to account for why some phonological variants of old New Zealand English were retained while others were leveled and to determine what mechanisms led to the particular set of features that is today's New Zealand English. Using an archive of recordings of pioneer narratives related by elderly speakers for the National Broadcasting Corporation of New Zealand from 1946 to 1948, as well as census figures from New Zealand's earliest days of English settlement to 1881, Trudgill et al. (2000) developed a picture of the proportion of settlers who came from various Anglophone areas and the consequently varied nature of the linguistic context in which the recorded speakers would have acquired English as children. Dialect acquisition was by no means a straightforward process for children growing up in the early days of New Zealand's colonization:

[F]or non-isolated [Old New Zealand English] speakers [...] there was a kind of supermarket of vocalic and consonantal variants that they could, as children, pick and choose from and put together into new combinations. It is also clear that the inter-individual differences in the way in which these combinations were formed [...] imply a degree of randomness concerning which speakers chose which variants. [Trudgill 2000, 310]

Drawing from this work with New Zealand English, as well as an overview of the results of other studies conducted in similar colonization contexts, Trudgill et al. (2000) proposed the following stages when a new dialect emerges from multiple dialects of the same language that have come into contact:

> Stage 1: Rudimentary leveling of extreme minority, regionally marked, and/or sociolinguistically low status variants.
> Stage 2a: Extreme variability in terms of features used by speakers, including both interspeaker variability and intraspeaker variability.
> Stage 2b: Further leveling of certain variants.
> Stage 3: Focusing of the new dialect into "a stable, crystallized variety."
> [Trudgill et al. 2000, 304–7]

Trudgill et al. (2000) next developed a mathematical model for predicting why certain variants were retained in New Zealand English while others were lost. Based on the probable proportions of various dialectal features that entered into the mix in the first stages of dialect contact in New Zealand as determined from census records, they were able to build a probabilistic model that accounts for the variants New Zealand English has today. In adopting such an approach, they chose to rely on mathematics alone:

Notice that we have quite deliberately eschewed ideology and linguistic attitudes as explanatory factors. What has happened appears to us to be deterministic in the sense that characteristics of the new dialect can be entirely accounted for without them. [...] We believe that we have achieved a probabilistic solution to what was referred to above as the problem of randomness and intergenerational transmission. [Trudgill et al. 2000, 316]

Their analysis found that majority forms appear to have won out in the end for New Zealand English.

While the linguistic situation in south central Pennsylvania over the last 300 years has been different from that of New Zealand, this idea that the outome of dialect contact is based on the proportion of various variants available for children to acquire is one that will enter into an accounting for the unraveling of the PDE dialect later in this work.

Britain (2002) was able to investigate results of dialect contact that involved the mixing of different grammatical systems (rather than phonological variants) in a new settlement situation in the British Fens. The Fens were settled in the seventeenth and eighteenth centuries by English speakers from the Midlands and East Anglia, areas with divergent dialects with regard to their treatment of past-tense *be*. (One dialect leveled all forms to *was* across person, number, and polarity, while the other leveled all forms to *weren't* in clauses with negative polarity.) As farmland in the Fens was drained and became available for settlement, these two dialects came into contact with a third dialect, the quite distinct local traditional variety (with its own low rates of *was* leveling). The result has been the development of a new dialect variety with leveling of both *was* and *were* with two fairly consistent linguistic constraints: (1) a rule favoring *was* in existentials followed by plural nouns and (2) the "Northern Subject Rule," which favors *was* after full noun phrases or when the subject and verb are separated by a clause, and disfavors *was* after pronouns. What Britain found in his comparison of data from three groups of speakers—those born around 1900, those born from 1925 to 1945, and those born between 1960 and 1975—was that the youngest group of speakers, in comparison to the older groups, has focused their use of leveled *was* and *were* on polarity instead of the two rules just mentioned. For this group, *was* is used overwhelmingly in positive polarity contexts and *were* (or, rather, *weren't*) in negative polarity contexts. In fact, among these youngest speakers, over 90% of positive polarity tokens of *be* surface as *was*, and 95% of negative polarity tokens surface as *weren't*. Older speakers make some distinction in their use of *was* and *weren't* along the lines of polarity as well, but the youngest generation has taken it to an extreme, reallocating the two variant traditional *be* forms exclusively according to polarity. This type of reduction/simplification is a process quite similar to what has been enacted by the youngest speakers of PDE in south central Pennsylvania with regard to obstruent devoicing and /aʊ/ monophthongization, albeit not with the reallocation Britain describes; chapters 4 and 5 will show that today's youngest speakers of PDE have, in the last phase of the dialect's life cycle, either simplified the number of linguistic constraints governing the use of obstruent devoicing to a subset of the constraints employed by older speakers or ignored the constraints altogether.

LONG-TERM DIALECT CONTACT SITUATIONS. The studies investigating outcomes of dialect contact contexts that most closely match the linguistic situation in south central Pennsylvania are those which involve two (or at the most, three) dialects that have been in contact for multiple generations. In the United States, many studies in this genre have come out of rural North Carolina (e.g., Mallinson and Wolfram 2002, discussed below, but also Wolfram and Beckett 2000 and Schilling-Estes 1998). In these cases, bi- and triethnic coastal and mountain communities have included African Americans, European Americans, and Americans of Lumbee Indian descent for generations, with the various populations in the community having lived side by side for many decades, yet maintaining English dialects that are distinct from each other in various ways.

Mallinson and Wolfram (2002) sought to gain perspective on the historical use of African American Vernacular English (AAVE) in rural western North Carolina by their study of certain diagnostic AAVE morphosyntactic and phonological variants (namely, verbal -s attachment, third-person singular -s deletion, copula absence, past-tense *be* leveling, consonant cluster reduction, and /aɪ/ ungliding). The sites of their investigation were Beech Bottom, a very small African American enclave community neighboring Roaring Creek, a small European American community. Mallinson and Wolfram discovered that, while some of the diagnostic variants are used today with equal frequency by both African Americans and European Americans, the use of three of them—namely third-person singular -s absence, copula absence, and syllable-coda cluster reduction—differs enough between the two communities to form an "ethnolinguistic divide." Today such traces of distinctiveness between the African Americans and European Americans in this part of North Carolina are eroding in the face of accommodation toward regional norms, but it is evidence that an even greater distinctiveness once existed in this rural area. In south central Pennsylvania, the boundary between SCPE and PDE speakers in south central Pennsylvania is not a racial one as it is in Beech Bottom and Roaring Creek, but in the past this boundary too was an ethnolinguistic one (Pennsylvania Germans versus Pennsylvanians with British or Scotch-Irish origins). As in North Carolina, this boundary is likewise eroding as more and more speakers accommodate to SCPE, the regional norm. The motivations and attitudes responsible for this shift in individuals who grew up in PDE-speaking households will be discussed more fully in chapter 7, some of them mirroring the attitudes at work in the Beech Bottom–Roaring Creek community in North Carolina.

Across the Atlantic, Dyer (2002) explored the use of six phonological variables in the context of intense dialect contact in Corby, a former steel town in the East Midlands area about 100 miles north of London. Corby was a town originally settled by English speakers whose dialect was quite similar to dialects spoken in the villages around Corby. However, when a Scottish company opened a steel mill in Corby in the 1930s, it resulted in waves of immigration from Scotland, particularly from the industrial areas close to Glasgow. The linguistic result is that today one can still hear the original Corby dialect spoken by the oldest inhabitants and Glasgow English spoken by some of the earliest Scottish immigrants; the youngest residents, however, use a sort of mixed Scots English–East Midlands English dialect unique to Corby. This resulting dialect differs significantly from the leveling Dyer (2002) expected to find in such a dialect contact context: instead of leveling prominent dialect features, speakers have developed a mixed dialect that has adopted minority and regionally restricted Scottish features. This dialect is now so distinct as to be recognized by local outsiders as "Corby dialect." Dyer (2002) accounted for this mixed-dialect development through an analysis of how speaker linguistic identity has changed over the generations in Corby: for the oldest generation, self-identity was largely a matter of proclaiming oneself either "Scottish" or "English," and there was animosity, even to the point of physical altercations, between the two ethnic groups; speakers therefore claimed to speak either "Scottish English" or East Midlands English. By the third generation, however, speakers were identifying themselves as "Corby" residents, regardless of their ethnic background, insisting that they "all talk the same round here" (the quotation featured in the title of Dyer's 2002 paper). This collective identity was expressed in interviews in contrast to the identity of those who belong to other local towns. Dyer has interpreted this shift in identity marking as the motivating force behind the outcome of Corby's dialect contact as a mixed dialect, rather than as a leveled dialect (as is the case in the "new settlement" scenarios discussed above).

The linguistic situation in south central Pennsylvania is similarly complex, but a mixed dialect is not emerging—although there is marked influence of PDE on the SCPE spoken in the area, which will be discussed in chapter 3; rather, one dialect (SCPE) is dominating the other and the minority dialect (PDE) is sliding into obsolescence. However, shifts in ideas of self-identity are indeed the major motivation behind PDE's succumbing to pressure from SCPE. This matter will be discussed further in chapters 5 and 7.

2.2. THE DEVELOPMENT OF PENNSYLVANIA DUTCHIFIED ENGLISH

South central Pennsylvania has provided a backdrop for long-term language contact as well as long-term dialect contact, and this has resulted in outcomes not discussed in any of the dialect contact literature mentioned above. Pennsylvania German is itself a variety developed through leveling and convergence processes (like New Zealand English) that took place as speakers of various German dialects immigrated to William Penn's colony in the 1600s and 1700s to take part in what William Penn called his "Holy Experiment." (See Keiser 2012, 12–18, for a more complete description of the German dialects involved in the development of Pennsylvania German, based on immigration patterns.) Eventually these dialects' differences would be leveled, and they would converge to create a New World dialect of German, *Pennsilfaanisch Dietsch*, or "Pennsylvania Dutch" (Pennsylvania German). With large settlements of Pennsylvania Dutch speakers in the area, this dialect of German would be a major language spoken in south central Pennsylvania (alongside English) for over 300 years, remaining a commonly spoken language up until the early decades of the twentieth century, with several hundred thousand speakers of various religious denominations in south central Pennsylvania (Keiser 2012, 14–17). Certainly there were many bilingual English–Pennsylvania German speakers in Pennsylvania in the 1800s and early 1900s; in an 1869 article in the *Atlantic Monthly*, for example, Phebe Earle Gibbons documents the fact that her Pennsylvania neighbors were bilingual in Pennsylvania German and English and spoke "funny English," full of transfer effects from their native German dialect, a "Dutchified" English. Interaction between bilingual Pennsylvania Germans who spoke this "Dutchified" English and English speakers from various parts of Great Britain and Ireland—supplemented by the long contact between English and Pennsylvania German—has also given rise in south central Pennsylvania to yet another English dialect, the regional standard referred to in this monograph as South Central Pennsylvania English (SCPE). The linguistic context in Pennsylvania has always been—and continues to be—complex.

In the last century, Pennsylvania German (in nonsectarian communities) has generally succumbed in the south central Pennsylvania region to the same decline noted among so many immigrant languages in the United States. This was precipitated by the enactment of educational reforms passed by the Pennsylvania legislature in 1895 that mandated that education in the state be provided at the public expense for all children, CONDUCTED IN THE ENGLISH LANGUAGE. (Even today this is a requirement for all instruction in Pennsylvania, including home schooling and charter school operation, as dictated and enforced by the state's Department of Education.) As a result, children from Pennsylvania German–speaking households were compelled to learn English in school. In some rural areas, this mandate was not actively enforced until the 1920s, perhaps due to the lack of qualified English-speaking teachers to supply the many one-room and two-room schoolhouses scattered throughout such areas (see Wilkerson and Salmons 2012 for a similar situation in Wisconsin). When the mandate finally was enforced, the erosion of Pennsylvania German as the language of the home began in earnest: as a rule, nonsectarian (i.e., non-Amish, non-Mennonite) families shifted within a single generation from using Pennsylvania German to speaking English exclusively, to the point where it is now rare (in 2013) to find a nonsectarian speaker of Pennsylvania German under the age of 70.

This enactment of state education laws and subsequent shift in family discourse patterns to the primacy of English as the language of the home for both siblings and parents parallels what took place in other German-speaking communities in the United States in the early twentieth century (Clyne 2003, 43). The same type of verticalization involving the transfer of control of the schools from local boards to the state—and the resulting language shift from German to English—directly parallels what has likewise been documented in other American German speech islands such as Wisconsin German communities (Wilkerson and Salmons 2012, 16–18), Texas German communities (Boas 2009, 244–54), and Texas Alsatian communities (Roesch 2012, 53).

The English spoken by school-aged Pennsylvania Germans in the 1920s was not, however, standard "American English." As these early learners of English struggled to acquire English in school, interference from their native Pennsylvania German came into play, resulting in a unique English variety that they passed down to their offspring—who were often monolingual in English. Today this dialect is popularly referred to in south central Pennsylvania as "Pennsylvania Dutchified English" (PDE) or in academic circles as "Pennsylvania German English" or "Pennsylvania Deutchified English" (in recognition of the dialect's roots in Pennsylvania German). It has been widely spoken now for three or more generations across south central Pennsylvania, alongside the south central Pennsylvania regional standard of English (SCPE) spoken by many non–Pennsylvania Germans. However, just as the south central Pennsylvania speech community experienced a major shift from Pennsylvania German toward English in the 1920s, the speech community began to experience a dialect shift from PDE to SCPE in the 1960s and 1970s. In south central Pennsylvania, this was undoubtedly due in part to the consolidation in the 1960s of small, local one- and two-room schoolhouses into larger schools in school districts across the area; consolidation and bussing of children to school resulted in greater contact between PDE speakers and monodialectal SCPE-speaking teachers and classmates. Children born to PDE-speaking parents in the 1960s and 1970s grew up speaking PDE, as their parents spoke, but once they were exposed to SCPE speakers in school, they lost their linguistic homogeneity: some individuals from the group of PDE speakers born during the 1960s and 1970s (today's 40-somethings) kept speaking PDE, as their parents had; others shifted fully to SCPE. A smaller number consciously chose to become bidialectal in PDE and SCPE—this emerging bidialectalism adds yet another layer to the story of south central Pennsylvania's language varieties. These PDE monodialectals and bidialectals represent a sort of last gasp for PDE, for the next generation (the children of the 40-somethings) is completely SCPE-speaking; even in rural northern Lebanon County, where social and geographical isolation has preserved PDE until now, those under 20 in PDE-speaking households have completed the shift to SCPE, and none are reported to speak the PDE dialect. Because of the overall lack of transmission to those born in the 1980s and beyond, it appears now that PDE—like Pennsylvania German—will be extinct in another 50 years in nonsectarian communities in south central Pennsylvania as its last speakers pass away.

Pennsylvania German itself is following a different trajectory and will remain a viable language in sectarian communities as the Amish population grows within Pennsylvania and across the American Midwest; Keiser (2012, 173) estimates that there will be more than a million sectarian speakers of Pennsylvania German by 2050. Meanwhile, nonsectarian communities are completing the shift to English as the last Pennsylvania German–English bilingual speakers pass away. PDE does not have the same stable speaker base in either sectarian or nonsectarian communities. As mentioned above, children in nonsectarian communities have not acquired PDE, and even bilingual sectarian speakers do not necessarily speak PDE when they speak English. (Kopp [1999] documents that the bilingual Pennsylvania German–English speakers he encountered in his research do not speak PDE;

personal interactions with sectarians in south central Pennsylvania, however, have shown that many sectarian speakers do speak PDE, and that some
actually speak both SCPE and PDE.) In any case, since PDE does not hold
significance for sectarian speakers as a religious or ethnic marker, it is likely
that it will disappear from sectarian communities as well by the end of the
twenty-first century.

This monograph thus has two distinct purposes as it presents the current state of PDE in south central Pennsylvania, and it does so by specifically focusing on the language situation in rural northern Lebanon County.
First, it documents the current state of an unstable and obsolescing dialect
by carefully examining some of the processes that PDE is undergoing as
it obsolesces; it accomplishes this primarily by comparing the use of certain PDE phonological features by multiple generations of PDE monodialectal speakers. This comparison highlights the instability of the dialect
and the consequent simplification (called here "unraveling," because it is
more complex than straightforward simplification) of various phonological
features of PDE as the dialect is dying. Second, this work documents the
emergence of bidialectal speakers in this late phase of PDE's life cycle and
provides insight into the linguistic and extralinguistic forces behind PDE
bidialectalism through the presentation of a case study of one particular
bidialectal individual; from this, this study suggests that the development of
bidialectalism in such intense dialect contact contexts is a legitimate phase
in dialect shift and obsolescence.

3. A WORKING DESCRIPTION OF PENNSYLVANIA DUTCHIFIED ENGLISH AND SOUTH CENTRAL PENNSYLVANIA ENGLISH

To understand the emergence of bidialectalism in the last stages of the obsolescence of Pennsylvania Dutchified English (PDE), it is important to develop a working description of PDE and of its regional standard counterpart in south central Pennsylvania, South Central Pennsylvania English (SCPE), and to understand how these two dialects developed in an environment of intense contact over the last three centuries and more. Both PDE and SCPE have been poorly documented, for reasons that will be explained more fully below in this chapter; thus, a description of the dialects as set out in this chapter is needed before an analysis can be made of how dialectal features are declining. While the description found below of each dialect is by no means exhaustive, this chapter presents an account of each dialect's features that is as complete as is possible at this stage of research.

The first part of this chapter presents research available on South Central Pennsylvania English in comparison with its surrounding regional dialects. As the prestige dialect in the south central Pennsylvania region that is gaining ground as PDE is declining, SCPE is in a unique position in its relationship to PDE. SCPE and PDE have been in contact in many parts of the region for decades or longer, and features of the two dialects inevitably overlap. This section will describe phonetic, morphosyntactic, semantic, and suprasemental features that SCPE shares with Pennsylvania Dutchified English.

The second part of this chapter presents a detailed catalog of PDE features, some of which will be foundational to tracking feature loss in PDE across the generations in the next chapters of this monograph. This description of the obsolescing dialect PDE and its features is drawn from data gathered from the informal interviews of PDE speakers from 1993–95 and 2005–9 described in chapter 1. To be as complete as possible with a list of features for PDE, information is also included in this chapter that represents my knowledge of PDE as a speaker who grew up and lived as an adult in south central Pennsylvania.

3.1. A WORKING DESCRIPTION OF SCPE

South Central Pennsylvania is a part of the Commonwealth of Pennsylvania, to the southeast of the geographical center of the state, generally taken as the area encompassing the counties of Adams, Berks, Cumberland, Dauphin, Franklin, Huntingdon, Juniata, Lancaster, Lebanon, Mifflin, Northumberland, Perry, Schuykill, Snyder, and York. The most populous cities in the region are Lancaster, York, and Harrisburg (the state capital); other notable locations include Hershey (home of the Hershey Company, known for its chocolate) and Gettysburg (the famous Civil War site). Although some of the land of this region lies in the Appalachian foothills, much of it is rolling forests and fields, with the Susquehanna River running through the area's western edge on its way to the Chesapeake Bay. Land in the region was purchased at various times in the first half of the eighteenth century by the colonial Pennsylvania government from the Native American tribes who lived and hunted there, and it was an attractive settlement site during those years for waves of German and Scotch-Irish immigrants who came to the colony, since land was cheaper and more readily available there than in the counties to the east around Philadelphia. Today the area is home to a large number of Amish and Mennonites and is known for Pennsylvania Dutch culture, the Pennsylvania German language, and the Pennsylvania Dutchifed English dialect. A vast proportion of the area is rural, and residents tend to be oriented exclusively toward the region and its issues and events, rather than toward the metropolitan centers of Philadelphia or Pittsburgh; in fact, none of the informants recorded in this study had ever visited Philadelphia or Pittsburgh more than once or twice in his or her lifetime. The data for this particular study were collected in northern Lebanon County, a relatively sparsely populated area on the northeastern edge of the south central Pennsylvania region, with farming and small businesses as the major economic sources of income.

Even though it is the dominant dialect of the region of Pennsylvania under investigation, SCPE has historically received even less attention from linguists than PDE has. Usually the dialect has been subsumed into more general linguistic descriptions of "Mid-Atlantic English" or "Eastern American English," even though it is identifiable as a distinct dialect with unique features, to be described in this section. The one exception to this generalization of SCPE is the TELSUR project, an undertaking of the Linguistics Laboratory of the University of Pennsylvania that resulted in *The Atlas of North American English* (Labov, Ash, and Boberg 2006); TELSUR mapped dialect boundaries according to vowel production across the United States using telephone interviews, with the distribution of phone calls based

FIGURE 3.1
South Central Pennsylvania

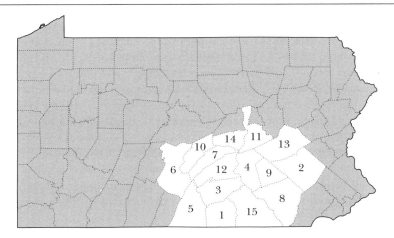

NOTE: Map of south central Pennsylvania showing the counties often considered part of the region: Adams (1), Berks (2), Cumberland (3), Dauphin (4), Franklin (5), Huntingdon (6), Juniata (7), Lancaster (8), Lebanon (9), Mifflin (10), Northumberland (11), Perry (12), Schuylkill (13), Snyder (14), and York (15). Lebanon County, site of data collection for this study, is the second county north from the extreme southeast corner of the shaded area on this map. (Source: http://en .wikipedia.org/wiki/File:SouthCentralPA.PNG)

on population density. TELSUR did indeed attempt to include information about vowel quality in the English of south central Pennsylvania, but unfortunately, due to the comparatively low population of this largely rural region, only two phone interviews were conducted in this area, both with individuals who live in Reading (in Berks County on the eastern edge of the region). With more data analysis, *The Atlas of North American English* (Labov, Ash, and Boberg 2006) has indeed determined that southeastern Pennsylvania, along with southern New Jersey, is a dialect area distinct from surrounding areas; even so, this map does not specify SCPE as a variety distinct from, say, Philadelphia English or southern New Jersey English. Obviously, a fuller description of the SCPE dialect is needed—and fuller description than will be offered here in this study of PDE.

This is not to say that there have not been some "folk linguistic" attempts to describe SCPE. Boeree (2004), psychologist and professor emeritus at Shippensburg University in south central Pennsylvania, had the following to say about the south central Pennsylvania dialect (which he calls the "Susquehanna dialect"):

I live in south-central Pennsylvania, which is a great location for hearing various eastern accents. There are actually five in Pennsylvania: In the northern tier, near upstate New York, the accent is Northern. In Pittsburgh and the surrounding area they say /stil/ and /mil/ instead of steel and meal. In the south, near West Virginia, you hear Appalachian, and people still say you'uns and refer to their grandparents as Mammaw and Pappy!. [*sic*] And, in the center of the state is what is called the Susquehanna accent, which is a variation on the Philadelphia area dialect, with a lot of German and Scots-Irish influences. And we can't forget the Philadelphia accent itself. […] In the Lancaster area (part of the Susquehanna dialect), the Pennsylvania German influence is obvious in some of the words and sentence structure: We red up the room, outen the light, and throw the cow over the fence some hay. We say that the peanut butter is all, the road is slippy, and I read that wunst (once). A slide is a sliding board, sneakers are all Keds, vacuum cleaners are sweepers, little pieces are snibbles, and if you are looking a bit disheveled, you are furhuddled. And at any local restaurant, they will ask you: Can I get you coffee awhile? [Boeree 2004]

While it is too simplistic to think as Boeree does of SCPE as simply a variation of the Philadelphia English dialect, it is true that the two English varieties share certain features. Phonetic features shared by the two dialects include the fronting of /oʊ/ in certain environments to [ɜʊ] (Labov, Ash, and Boberg [2006] show that for the Philadelphia dialect this fronting occurs in any environment where there is not a following liquid, so that the vowel in *goat* is pronounced differently from that in *goal*), tensed [æ] (although it is not entirely clear if this occurs in the same phonological contexts), and the distinction between the vowels /a/ and /ɔ/ (the *cot-caught* distinction). Philadelphia English and SCPE also share certain grammatical features, including positive *anymore* and *youse* as a second-person plural pronoun (pronounced as [jɪz] at least some of the time in Philadelphia English and [juz] in SCPE); the two dialects also share many lexical items, including *hoagie* (a type of sandwich), *jimmies* (also called "sprinkles" in SCPE), and *soda*.

There are many phonetic features of Philadelphia English that are not part of SCPE, however, including the following:

The three-way distinction between the vowels in *merry*, *Mary*, and *marry* (with at least one-third of Philadelphians pronouncing *merry* like *Murray*).

/l/ vocalization intervocalically in word-final position or before consonants (*milk, hollow*).

Raising of /aɪ/ before voiced consonants (*price, like*) and some unvoiced consonants (*tiger, spider*).

Palatalization of /s/ before /tr/ (resulting in [ʃtrits] for *streets*).

Pronunciation of the interdental fricatives /θ/ and /ð/ as the stops [t] and [d].

Laxing of /i/ to [ɪ] before [g], as in [ɪgəlz] 'Eagles'.

[Labov, Ash, and Boberg 2006]

Interestingly, there are two features cited for Philadelphia English that are considered in south central Pennsylvania to be a part of PDE, but not SCPE:

> Reduction of the vowel in final, unstressed, open syllables (hence, [wɪndə] 'window' and [tə'mɑrə] 'tomorrow').
>
> Monophthongization of –*owel* to [æl] in words like *towel* [tæl].

Pennsylvania has one other large metropolitan area, Pittsburgh, and linguists have also identified a Pittsburgh English dialect (e.g., Johnstone, Andrus, and Danielson 2006). SCPE shares some features with Pittsburgh English, as it does with Philadelphia English (although not all the same features), including falling intonation for yes/no questions, *needs* + past participle constructions (as in *The car needs washed*), and various lexical items like *redd up* 'clean up', *jagger* 'thorn', *dippy eggs* 'eggs made sunny side up', and *slippy* 'slippery'. In both dialects, *leave* and *let* are conflated, resulting in a semantic and pragmatic merger. Hence *Leave me alone!* and *Let me alone!* have the same meaning and force, as do *Mom left me go to the store* and *Mom let me go to the store*. This merger has been reported both for Pittsburgh English and more general southwestern Pennsylvania English as well (Johnstone, Andrus, and Danielson 2006).

Like PDE (but not SCPE), Pittsburgh English also has monophthongization of /aʊ/ to [a] (*shower, flour*); it also monophthongizes /aɪ/ before liquids—although Pittsburgh English monophthongizes /aɪ/ to [aː] and PDE to [æ] (*tile* in Pittsburgh English is [taːl], but in PDE is [tæl]) (Johnstone, Andrus, and Danielson 2006).

Various features of Pittsburgh English are distinct from SCPE or PDE, however. Phonetically, Pittsburgh English includes the following Midland dialect features which do not appear in the south central Pennsylvania dialects:

> Merger of the vowels in *caught* and *cot* to [aː].
>
> Epenthetic /r/ in a small number of words (e.g., [warʃ] for *wash*).
>
> Merger of /i/ and /ɪ/ to [ɪ] (homophonous *still* and *steel* as [stɪl]).
>
> Merger of /u/ and /ʊ/ (homophonous *pool, pole,* and *pull* as [pʊl]).
>
> [Johnstone, Andrus, and Danielson 2006]

Finally, Pittsburgh English utilizes *you'uns* as the second-person plural pronoun (nearby southwestern Pennsylvania is said to use *yinz/yunz*) (Johnstone, Andrus, and Danielson 2006), whereas SCPE uses *youse*.

The SCPE area is located geographically between the areas where Philadelphia English and Pittsburgh English are spoken, and settlement patterns brought Germans and Scotch-Irish English immigrants in large numbers to all three areas, originally pushing from Philadelphia westward through north central Pennsylvania to the Pittsburgh region across the Allegheny Mountains. Given the similarities in the source language varieties for today's Philadelphia, Pittsburgh, and SCPE dialects, it is little surprise that SCPE shares some features (but not all) with the other two dialects, but to conclude that SCPE is merely a form of either Philadelphia English or Pittsburgh English is too simplistic: SCPE has also been influenced over the last century or more by PDE, as the next section will discuss.

3.2. OVERLAP BETWEEN PDE AND SCPE

PDE and SCPE have greatly influenced each other for generations in terms of morphosyntax, English lexical items, and intonation patterns, and the two dialects are more similar in these features than in their phonology. Some of this sharing is likely due to the long history of contact between English and Pennsylvania German in the region, but some of the shared features may have originated from the English brought to the area by Scotch-Irish settlers. This section begins by listing morphosyntactic forms common to both dialects in south central Pennsylvania today.

MORPHOSYNTAX OF PDE AND SCPE. *Nonstandard Past Verbal Forms.* Both SCPE and PDE speakers can, like speakers of various other American regional dialects, use bare forms of verbs in informal speech to indicate past tense (see Wolfram 2004 for AAVE; Schilling-Estes 1997 for South Island, Ocracoke, and General Southern English), although in Pennsylvania the verb set with which this can be done is limited to the following items:

1. *run*   *I RUN all the way to Harrisburg to get that part for the lawnmower.*
   eat   *She EAT all the donuts I made for the picnic!*
   come   *He COME around suppertime, so I set out a plate for him too.*
   give   *I GIVE her all the money I had in my wallet.*

The two dialects also make use of the past participle of *see* as a past-tense form; again, this is not unique to south central Pennsylvania:

2. *see*   *I SEEN two deer when I was driving around the lake yesterday.*

Preposition Use. The use of prepositions without objects—preposition "stranding"—is very common in both SCPE and PDE, as it is in other dialects of American English. This is especially common with the preposition *with,* but in south central Pennsylvania, the process involves other prepositions too, as shown in the last example in (3):

3. *Do you want to go WITH?*
   When you leave, take the library books WITH.
   You need to put enough salt IN.

However, in south central Pennsylvania, the juxtaposition of multiple prepositions, often without any object, is also employed by speakers of both dialects:

4. *Could you get me the map FRONT FROM the back seat?*
   You can all come ON DOWN FRONT to get your prizes.

Use of the Present Tense to Indicate Action Begun in the Past but Continuing into the Present.

5. *That's the first time since I'M here that he talked to me.*
   'That's the first time since I have been here that he has talked to me.'

Use of the Preterite and "already" to Correspond to the English Past Perfect.

6. *He went to town ALREADY.* 'He has already gone to town.'

Use of "would" in Irrealis Conditional Sentences Instead of the Subjunctive.

7. *She would tell you the answer if she WOULD be able to.*
   'She would tell you the answer if she were able to.'

Use of "yet" to Indicate Ongoing Action.

8. *Is she crying YET?* 'Is she still crying?'
   Is your grandmother living YET? 'Is your grandmother still alive?'

Use of "needs" + Participle. Like many other dialects in the Northern Midlands area of the United States (Murray and Simon 2002), both PDE and SCPE use the *needs* + participle construction:

9. *Your room NEEDS cleaned up before your friends can come over.*
   'Your room needs to be cleaned up before your friends can come over.'

QUESTION INTONATION PATTERN. Perhaps the most uncommon feature shared by PDE and SCPE that sets them apart from many other varieties of American English is supersegmental: the use of falling intonation both for "information" questions (as in standard American English and many regional dialects) AND for yes/no questions (like Pittsburgh English and unlike standard American English, which uses a rising pitch at the end of such a question [Fries 1964]). This shared intonation pattern, sometimes referred to as "the Pennsylvania Dutch question" (Fasold 1980; cited in

Johnstone, Andrus, and Danielson 2006) was described in detail by Huffines (1980), who noted that the peak pitch occurs on the stressed syllable of the last word of the question. Actually, the peak is at the beginning of the vocalic segment in the stressed syllable of the FOCUS word in the sentence; the vowel of that syllable—whether a short or long vowel—is lengthened slightly, and the peak pitch occurs at the beginning of the vowel. In the examples below in (10), a hyphen is added to indicate this slight lengthening effect, and the focus word of each sentence is highlighted:

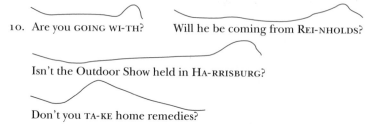

10. Are you GOING WI-TH?   Will he be coming from REI-NHOLDS?

Isn't the Outdoor Show held in HA-RRISBURG?

Don't you TA-KE home remedies?

ENGLISH LEXICAL ITEMS. Finally, certain English lexical items shared by SCPE and PDE also serve, again as a cluster of items (some of which are shared by Southwestern Pennsylvania English and Philadelphia English as well [Johnstone, Andrus, and Danielson 2006]), to set these two dialects apart from many other varieties of American English. Here is a sampling of such words in common use in south central Pennsylvania today:

11. a. *sneaky* 'finicky about food' (*Don't be so* SNEAKY; *you're going to eat that whether you like it or not!*)
 b. *all* 'all gone' (*I need to get to the store soon because the milk is* ALL.)
 c. *awhile* 'while, in the meantime, at the same time' (*I'll run to the store for milk, and you get supper started* AWHILE.)
 d. *back* 'available, reserved in storage' (*Do you want more cake? I have some* BACK.)
 e. *towards* as a comparative (*He's really tall* TOWARDS *his brother* 'He's really tall compared to his brother!')
 f. *against* 'slightly ajar' (*Just put the door* AGAINST *when you leave the room* 'When you leave the room, don't close the door entirely but leave it slightly ajar.')
 g. *'til* 'by the time' (*It will be too late to go to the movie* 'TIL *she gets here!*)
 h. *want* 'predict' (*The weatherman on Channel 21* WANTS *thunderstorms for the rest of the week.*)
 i. *redd up* 'tidy up (not a deep cleaning)' (*You're going to have to at least* REDD UP *your room before you can go to the movies with your friends.*)

In addition, as mentioned earlier, *leave* and *let* have merged semantically and pragmatically for the south central Pennsylvania SCPE or PDE speaker. Hence *Leave me alone!* and *Let me alone!* have the same meaning and force, as do *Mom left me go to the store* and *Mom let me go to the store*. This merger has been reported for Pittsburgh English and more general southwestern Pennsylvania English as well (Johnstone, Andrus, and Danielson 2006).

Like most regions of the United States, south central Pennsylvania also has unique local foods and terms for those local foods, such as *dippy eggs* 'eggs over-easy', *scrapple, (meat) pudding, souse, leb cookies, schnitz und knepp, pot pie* (not the baked pot pie of the rest of the United States, but a dish of broad noodles, potatoes, and meat in broth), *shoofly pie* 'molasses pie', *fasnachts* 'kind of donut', *pepper cabbage, red beet eggs, chicken corn noodle soup, birch beer, chow-chow* 'pickled assortment of vegetables', and *hot lettuce* 'lettuce served with a hot dressing of bacon, egg, sugar, and vinegar'.

This comparison of SCPE to its surrounding dialects (Philadelphia English and Pittsburgh English), as well as the dialect with which it coexists (PDE), is important but does little to point out the unique characteristics of this little-studied dialect. More investigation and research is definitely needed to delineate the properties that make SCPE distinct vis-à-vis its more urban counterparts, and the contributions of this monograph to this endeavor are unfortunately limited. At this point, then, the discussion will turn to a description of the particular characteristics of Pennsylvania Dutchified English that set it apart from SCPE, so as to lay a foundation for the discussion of the unraveling of the dialect and the development of bidialectalism that follow in subsequent chapters.

3.3. A DESCRIPTION OF DISTINGUISHING FEATURES OF PDE

PDE has never received much notice from linguists, apart from a few articles on "oddities" of grammar and lexical items in the dialect (e.g., Struble 1935; Page 1937; Huffines 1980). Nonetheless, the number of features that cluster together to define the dialect is large. This section presents an overview of many of these features; it is not an exhaustive list, but instead represents the documentation of the dialect to date. In the northern Lebanon County speech community (the one from which data were collected for this study), some of these features serve to distinguish a "Dutchified" speaker (a PDE speaker) from a "non-Dutchified" (SCPE) speaker and to indicate a speaker's degree of "Dutchifiedness." (Note that this definition of "Dutchifiedness" differs slightly when the term describes the English of monolinguals versus the incorporation of borrowed English words into Pennsylvania German by Pennsylvania Dutch–speaking bilinguals; Keiser [2012] points out that the term "dutchified" refers in those latter circles to the degree to which English loanwords are pronounced with Pennsylvania German phonology or not, whereas "Dutchified" in English monolingual circles is based on the use of PDE features.) As section 3.2 described, many of these PDE features also overlap with features of SCPE, which is not surprising given that the two dialects have been in such intense contact for so long. The description of features below represents some aspects of a very conservative variety of PDE as it was spoken by the oldest generation interviewed for this study but not necessarily how it is spoken by all speakers today: as the next chapters will demonstrate, the way speakers are using PDE features has changed over the generations and continues to change as PDE approaches extinction. This list is an attempt to capture all the features that have been manifested in the PDE data collected through interviews and through observation.

PHONEMIC AND PHONOLOGICAL FEATURES: CONSONANTS. The consonants of PDE (as it is currently spoken in south central Pennsylvania) are comprised of the following set:

> 12. Consonants of PDE
> Nasals: /m/, /n/, /ŋ/
> Stops: /p/, /b/, /t/, /d/, /k/, /g/
> Affricates: /tʃ/, /dʒ/ (although see the note about this below), /β/ (see note about this below)
> Fricatives: /f/, /v/, /θ/, /ð/, /s/, /z/, /ʃ/, /ʒ/, /h/
> Approximants: /r/, /j/, /w/
> Lateral: /l/

The discussion of PDE consonantal features here centers around the affricate /dʒ/, the bilabial fricative [β], and obstruent devoicing.

The Affricate /dʒ/. For the most part, the phonemic inventory of PDE is identical to that of other Mid-Atlantic varieties of American English, with the same consonants and the same vowel distinctions. However, in the speech of the oldest speakers of PDE, the first Pennsylvania German–English bilinguals, [dʒ] was conspicuously absent, with [tʃ] substituted for /dʒ/ in all environments. If [tʃ] had merely been the devoiced form of [dʒ] in syllable codas and onsets of unstressed syllables—the environment where obstruent devoicing occurs, as will be discussed below—this would not have merited any special attention in a discussion of PDE's phonemic inventory because it would have been an artifact of PDE's rules of phonology. However, [ʧ] surfaces for /ʤ/ in even word- and stressed syllable-initial environments for these oldest speakers of PDE, the very environments where obstruents retain their voicing. Some examples of this include the following:

13. a. *adjust* [ə.ʧʌst]
    b. *jump* [ʧʌmp]

This realization of /ʤ/ as [ʧ] has served as a stereotypical feature of PDE for people in the south central Pennsylvania speech community for over a hundred years (Gibbons 1869), often evoked and joked about when imitating the PDE dialect, and it continues to play that role today. Nevertheless, this realization now has relic status, and even the oldest speakers of PDE—those who are bilingual in Pennsylvania German and English and who may have once also lacked this phoneme—today have [ʤ] as a part of their phonemic inventory. Although there will be no detailed discussion of this later in the monograph, this is yet another example of how, as PDE obsolesces, PDE speakers are abandoning certain of the dialect's most marked features as they accommodate toward SCPE.

Bilabial Fricative [β] *for* /w/ *and* [w] *for* /v/. A much less salient consonantal feature of PDE is the sociolinguistically complex one of the bilabial fricative. This is not a feature for which there is evidence from the data collection done with the oldest speakers of the dialect. Yet, in the speech of today's middle-aged generations of PDE speakers (and in the speech of at least some younger bidialectals [see chapter 7]), [β] is substituted for /w/ in word-initial and stressed syllable-initial contexts, as in (14):

14. a. *away* [əβ'eɪ]
    b. *wag* [βæg]
    c. *why* [βaɪ]

This substitution is a somewhat complex matter, as it dovetails with the substitution of [w] for /v/ in the same word-initial and stressed syllable-initial contexts for the same middle-aged and oldest generations of PDE speakers, as in (15). /v/ in other contexts is devoiced to [f], as will be discussed more fully below in the section on obstruent devoicing.

15. a. *victory* [wɪktri]
     b. *Vicki* [wɪki]
     c. *advice* [æt'wais]
     but
     d. *heavy* ['hɛfi]

Use of this feature is receding, however, as language variety shift progresses, and more detailed discussion will use evidence for the disappearance of this feature as a factor in the unraveling of PDE discussed in chapter 5.

Obstruent Devoicing. The most salient consonantal feature of PDE utilized by all generations of PDE speakers today is obstruent devoicing. As in many German dialects, PDE obstruents are devoiced in syllable codas, but PDE differs from these other German dialects in that obstruents in syllable onsets are also devoiced if that syllable is unstressed.

16. a. *dug* [dʌk] (syllable coda)
     b. *baby* ['beɪpi] (unstressed syllable onset)

In the older generations of PDE speakers, this devoicing has applied to all obstruents, but the data collected for this study reveal that—in the PDE spoken today by the middle-aged and youngest speakers of the dialect—/d/ and /z/ account for almost all tokens of devoicing; unlike "traditional" PDE, /b/ and /g/ are never devoiced. Again it appears that, as PDE progresses along its path of language shift and obsolescence, its speakers are losing consonantal dialect features. A much more complete description of PDE obstruent devoicing, as well as its realization by speakers from different generations of PDE speakers, is provided in chapter 4.

PHONEMIC AND PHONOLOGICAL FEATURES: VOWELS. To date, five vocalic features of PDE have been identified and analyzed. PDE has other features that are not included in the descriptions below, including a lowered and centralized realization of /aɪ/ in closed syllables (as in *right*) and word-final /i/ (as in *very*), but this study will focus solely on the four vocalic features described below.

Monophthongization of /aʊ/ to [a]. The most highly salient vocalic feature of PDE for both PDE and SCPE speakers is the substitution of the monophthong [a] for /aʊ/ in all phonological environments:

17. a. *cloud ~ clod* [klad]
     b. *trout ~ trot* [trat]
     c. *house* [has]
     d. *how* [ha]

Despite this feature's high level of awareness among PDE speakers, its use is also eroding and changing (in terms of its phonological constraints in closed- vs. open-syllable contexts) across the generations of speakers of the dialect, as will be shown in detail in the next chapter.

Centralization of /a/ to [ʌ]. Two other vocalic features that distinguish PDE from other varieties of American English are more complex than mere substitutions since both involve processes that are highly constrained by the phonological environment following the vowels in question. As a result, these two features show up relatively rarely in the data gathered for this study, in comparison with the monophthongization of /aʊ/ to [a] and obstruent devoicing, for example. These are not salient features; neither PDE speakers nor the SCPE speakers who live in south central Pennsylvania indicate any awareness of them, even though they are used by all generations of PDE speakers. One of these processes substitutes [ʌ] for /a/ before nasals in stressed syllables (i.e., /a/ → [ʌ] / __N), as in (6):

18. a. *conference* [kʌnfrənts]
    b. *dominate* [dʌməneɪt]
    c. *Don* [dʌn]

This process is not entirely unique to PDE, since standard American English pronunciation of many high-frequency words already involves a centralized vowel in a stressed syllable before a nasal (e.g., *compass, comfortable, company*). (Due to American English's prevalent reduction of vowels in unstressed syllables, /a/ before a nasal is already pronounced as [ə] in unstressed syllables in most dialects.) PDE is unique, however, in that it can make this substitution for any word in any stressed syllable, including syllables in names. For example, the name of the high-end department store chain Bon-Ton is pronounced with an /a/ in each syllable by SCPE speakers in Pennsylvania and other American English speakers across the country, but with the centralized variant by PDE speakers. The decline in the use of this feature among the youngest generation of speakers—even to the point where some of the youngest speakers do not use the feature at all—will be discussed further in the next chapter.

Monophthongization of /aɪ/ before Liquids. In a similar fashion to the substitution of a centralized vowel for /a/ before nasals, PDE speakers substitute the monophthong [æ] for /aɪ/ before liquids (i.e., /aɪ/ → [æ] / __L):

19. a. *tire* [tær]
    b. *tile* [tæl]
    c. *Palmyra* [palmær]
    d. *pirate ~ parrot* [pærət]

Chapter 5 will discuss in some detail the variability of use of this feature among the various generations of PDE speakers.

Monophthongized /aɪ/ before liquids is also documented as a feature of the Pennsylvania German variety spoken in Lancaster, Pennsylvania, by Louden (1997) and Keiser (2012), so it would appear that this monophthongization as a feature of PDE is a direct transfer effect from Pennsylvania German that has been preserved in the English dialect of even monodialectal English speakers. Interestingly, descriptions of Midwestern varieties of Pennsylvania German noted by Keiser (2012, 96–97) document that Midwestern speakers of Pennsylvania German monophthongize /aɪ/ nearly categorically, across all phonological environments. (Keiser 2012 additionally shows that younger Pennsylvania German speakers in various parts of the Midwest are leading a sound change that produces the monophthong as a fronted and raised vowel with a nucleus of [e], unlike their counterparts in Pennsylvania.) Midwestern Pennsylvania German–English bilinguals also show evidence of /aɪ/ monopthongization in their English, although the rate at which they do depends largely on the Midwestern community in which they live (Keiser 2012, 96–97).

Monophthongization to [æ] in PDE is actually more complex than mere substitution of [æ] for /aɪ/ before liquids. In an exception to the rule that monophthongizes /aʊ/ to [a], mentioned in the last section, /aʊ/ is also unexpectedly monophthongized to [æ] before the liquid /l/ in *-owl/-owel* words and in the oldest-speaker PDE pronunciation of *doll,* as illustrated in (20):

20. a. [skæl] *scowl*
     b. [tæl] (for both *towel* and, as seen in [19], *tile)*
     c. [dæl] (for the homophones *dowel, dial,* and *doll)*

In cases of *-ower* (i.e., /aʊ/ before the liquid /r/), however, /aʊ/ monophthongizes to [a], just as expected:

21. a. *tower* [tar]
     b. *flower ~ flour* [flar]
     c. *shower* [ʃar]

This monopthongization process in (20) is that which yields the distinctive pronunciation of *towel* as [tæl] that has been noted in Philadelphia English (see section 3.1 of this chapter).

Raised [æ]. PDE speakers regularly raise [æ] in various contexts, producing an untensed variant of the vowel that is raised toward [ɛ]. The Mid-Atlantic region of the United States is already known for its tensed [æ] forms, particularly the eastern seaboard cities of New York City and Philadelphia. The tensed [æ] in these cities occurs, for the most part, in highly predictable contexts. Payne (1980) describes the contexts for the occurrence of Phila-delphia-style tensed [æ] as the following (repeated from chapter 2):

1. /æ/ is invariably raised and tensed before front nasals or front fricatives fol-lowed by another consonant or inflectional boundary, or in the three lexical items *mad, bad,* and *glad* (but not *sad*).
2. /æ/ is invariably lax when part of an auxiliary verb or before stops (except in *mad, bad,* and *glad*), voiced fricatives, /s/, /r/, and the velar nasal.
3. /æ/ is variable before nasal consonants or front voiceless fricatives followed by an optional derivational boundary or a vowel, or before /l/.
4. /æ/ is variable in proper nouns and abbreviations. [Payne 1980, 158–59]

Labov, Ash, and Boberg (2006) describe the context for this tensed /æ/ in New York City as the following:

1. Tensed [æ] occurs in closed syllables before /n/, /m/, /f/, /θ/, and /s/, voiced stops, and /ʃ/ (i.e., *man, ma'am, half, bath, stab,* and *mash*).
2. Tensed [æ] occurs in the lexical items *mad, bad,* and *glad.*
3. Lax [æ] occurs in open syllables, function words, and irregular verb forms.

This Mid-Atlantic tensed [æ] has in fact spread west to south central Penn-sylvania and is a feature of current SCPE. The PDE raised [æ], while similar in that it involves the phoneme /æ/, is nonetheless markedly different from the tensed [æ]. Phonetically, raised [æ] does not involve ingliding as the tensed [æ] does; phonologically, it does not have the same distribution as tensed [æ] does. While a complete analysis of raised [æ]'s distribution has not yet been completed, it is clear that, at the very least, raised [æ] occurs in open syllables—the context used for coding raised [æ] in the data col-lected for this study was the extremely common *yeah*; this is a phonological environment where the Mid-Atlantic tensed [æ] does not occur (Labov, Ash, and Boberg 2006). As chapter 5 will show in detail, this feature is a bit unusual among the PDE phonological features explored in this study: it is not declining in use among PDE speakers like the other phonological features mentioned in this chapter are, and, in fact, both the middle-aged and youngest generations of speakers display relatively similar frequencies of use.

PDE MORPHOSYNTACTIC FEATURES. While certain morphosyntactic features, possibly attributable to the influence of Pennsylvania German, are shared by the SCPE and PDE dialects (see section 3.1), certain morphosyntactic features also serve to distinguish PDE from SCPE. This section will focus specifically on such distinguishing features, some of which are quite salient in the speech community, and some which are not. These are all features that have been either attested in the recordings collected for this study or noted in conversations with PDE and SCPE informants in the south central Pennsylvania region.

Placement of Direct and Indirect Objects with Regard to Prepositional Phrases. In English in general, speakers have the option of placing indirect objects before direct objects (e.g., *He told me a story*) instead of in a prepositional phrase with *to* or *for* (e.g., *He told a story to me*). If another adverbial prepositional phrase is involved, that prepositional phrase is usually situated at the end of the phrase, resulting in an IO-DO-PP word order (as in *He told me a story in the car*). In PDE, however, it is also grammatically acceptable to place the prepositional phrase right after the indirect object, resulting in an IO-PP-DO word order (as in *He told me in the car a story*).

Frequent use of such placement of the prepositional phrase—in contexts that may be misparsed if the object immediately following the verb can be interpreted as a direct object even though it is an indirect object—has attained stereotype status in south central Pennsylvania as a means of identifying the "really Dutchified" PDE speaker. The following are examples frequently quoted for humorous effect:

22. *He threw the cow over the fence some hay.*
    'He threw some hay over the fence to the cow.'
    Toss Pop down the stairs his hat.
    'Toss Pop's hat down the stairs to him.'

Although contrived, these sentences are both grammatical in PDE. The humor from the sentences derives, of course, from the idea that the listener will think—at first, at least—that the man is throwing a cow over the fence or that someone has been asked to throw his or her father down the stairs. In reality, PDE sentences are not that common that utilize this word order with verbs that do not usually take that order in more standard varieties of American English, but they do surface in the course of everyday life, especially when indirect object pronouns are involved. The following are two such examples, heard uttered by PDE speakers in south central Pennsylvania:

23. *Reach me down that dish from the top shelf, would you?*
    'Would you get that dish down from the top shelf for me?'
    He tossed me over a dish towel, and I set to work.
    'He tossed a dish towel over to me, and I set to work.'

Because they do not involve a particularly humorous pairing of verb and word order, these everyday examples are not particularly salient for the PDE speaker.

"Once." Speakers of PDE use the adverb *once* in a manner similar to speakers of most American varieties of English to mean 'one time' or 'at one time' (e.g., *I called her once, but then I gave up,* or *I once went to the gym every day, but now I can't find the time*). However, in PDE the particle *once* can also serve as an emphasis marker similar to the German particle *mal*; as such, it unquestionably reflects the influence of Pennsylvania German on the dialect:

> 24. German: *Sag MAL, wenn kommst du?*
> PDE: *Tell me ONCE, when are you coming?*
> Standard American English: *Say (tell me), when are you coming?*

For members of the south central Pennsylvania community of PDE and SCPE speakers, frequent use of this feature is a highly overt stereotype of the "really Dutchified" speaker, and it is often invoked in imitations of PDE, sometimes corrupted to *onst* [wʌnst]. This feature is used by PDE speakers of all ages and both sexes (although not with the frequencies attributed to it by those who utilize it in humorous imitation of PDE). The particle is grammatically acceptable to PDE speakers in all tenses, and at the ends of various phrases that are part of an utterance, as shown in (25). Because particles in any language are notoriously difficult to gloss, and translations into standard English would only approximate the force of the original sentences, this emphasis particle is simply highlighted in these examples in (25):

> 25. a. *Do you want to go with ONCE to the store?* [present tense]
> b. *She really showed up those guys ONCE, when she was the one to come in first!* [past tense]
> c. *We'll just have to get down to your new place to visit you ONCE!* [future tense]

Habitual "still." Like the particle *once*, *still* is utilized by PDE speakers conventionally as an adverbial marker for ongoing states and activities (e.g., *He still likes to ski, even though he broke his leg on the slopes last year*). However, they also use it in a habitual sense in sentence-final position to indicate repeated activity. The example in (26) of this habitual use of *still* in the present tense refers to a person's habit, rather than that person's ongoing activity of attending a certain church:

> 26. *I go to that church STILL.* 'It is my habit to attend that church.'

In the past tense, *still* refers to a habit in the past that is now finished; in (27), it refers specifically to the fact that the person habitually preferred a certain type of pizza:

> 27. *He liked pepperoni pizza STILL.*
> 'He used to like/always did like pepperoni pizza.'

In the future tense, habitual *still* refers to the establishment of a new habit; in (28), the speaker is asking a person to make it a habit to call him or her after the listener moves away, even if that person never called before on any regular basis:

> 28. *When you move away, will you call me STILL?*
> 'Will you make it your habit to call me occasionally, after you move?'

In an interesting contrast to PDE *once*, the habitual marker *still* does not receive overt attention from either PDE or SCPE speakers in the south central Pennsylvania speech community and therefore does not act as a stereotyped indicator of degree of "Dutchifiedness."

PDE Remote Past. Another morphosyntactic feature that is part of the repertoire of PDE speakers is the use of "*had* + past participle of a verb" to indicate a remote past orientation.[1] The most common use of such constructions in standard English varieties is as a past perfect, a method of indicating that two events happened in the past; in standard constructions, the "past perfect" marks the event that happened first, and the "simple past" marks the event that happened second (e.g., *By the time I arrived at the party, all the cake had been eaten*). However, in PDE the "*had* + past participle" construction does not have to co-occur with a simple past tense clause, and it does not have to indicate that an event has any relationship at all to a second event; in such cases it is used with single events to indicate that something happened long ago—or at least long ago from the perspective of the current discourse. The examples in (29), all of which were noted in the context of normal conversations with PDE speakers, illustrate this remote past perspective without any reference to a second event:

> 29. *We HAD LIVED there twelve years when I was a girl.*
> 'A long time ago, when I was a girl, we lived there for twelve years.'
> *Rosemary HAD CALLED this morning. She's sick today.*
> 'Rosemary called me early this morning, long before I saw you to tell you the news. She's sick today.'

In (30), another PDE speaker uses the remote past construction in contrast to simple past to indicate that her father had used a bus as a camper a very long time ago (when she was a child):

30. Conversation about RV camping
    LG (to LM and his daughter R): *Do you have a bus?*
    LM: *Yeah. It was made into a camper.*
    LG: *Oh, is that what you used?*
    R: *That's what we HAD USED.* [with stress on the *had*]
    'That's what we used, but it was a long time ago.'

"What for…?" for "Which…?" or "What kind of." The English phrase *what for* + NP is a relatively direct translation into PDE of the German *was für* + NP construction to indicate a question or introduce a noun phrase about kinds of something, as shown in (31):

31. German: *Was für Bucher hat Johannes gekauft?*
    PDE: *What for books did John buy?*
    Standard American English: *What kind of books did John buy?*

Although data on this feature is limited, it appears from this study that it is used both by Pennsylvania German–English bilinguals (individuals for whom this could be the direct evidence for a transfer effect, since Pennsylvania German was their first language) and by monolingual PDE speakers. Some examples of use of this construction by younger PDE speakers include the following:

32. *WHAT FOR video do you want to rent tonight?*
    'What kind of video do you want to rent tonight?'
    I didn't know WHAT FOR bag of stuff he was going to bring me!
    'I didn't know what kind of bag of stuff he was going to bring me!'

Tag Questions. The final morphosyntactic feature described here, very characteristic of PDE, is the use of *ain't, not,* and *ai-not* as tag questions meaning 'Right?' at the ends of sentences, as in the examples below in (33). These tag questions occur frequently in the speech of all age levels of PDE speakers:

33. a. *He's at work right now, AIN'T?*
    b. *The band will hold their sub sale again next month, NOT?*
    c. *You're coming to the library after school, AI-NOT?*

Furthermore, *ain't* fills a special role on the discourse level, in extension of its tag question function, to act as a sort of back channel agreement device:

> 34. A: *I can't believe the football team made it all the way to the playoffs!*
> B: Yeah, ain't?

PDE LEXICAL ITEMS AND CALQUES. Pennsylvania German lexical items and calques from Pennsylvania German into English have made their way into the PDE dialect and, to some smaller degree, the SCPE dialect in south central Pennsylvania. Despite the occurrence of such forms in both dialects, however, this section is included in the "PDE features" part of this chapter because these lexical items and calques derive directly from Pennsylvania German and are MORE LIKELY to be utilized by PDE speakers than SCPE speakers. In fact, conspicuous use of such items is another salient marker of "Dutchifiedness" in the south central Pennsylvania speech community. At one time, this was because such lexical items and calques were frequently used by Pennsylvania German–speaking individuals who had learned English as an L2 and, hence, were more likely to show evidence of interlanguage transfer effects. Today, however, use of such items in English discourse is no longer as frequent and, due to the sociolinguistic context, is not a conclusive diagnostic of who is a PDE speaker and who is not: many current SCPE speakers grew up in households with PDE-speaking (or even Pennsylvania German-speaking) parents, and such speakers are able to claim certain Pennsylvania German lexical items as part of their English verbal repertoire, even if they do not now speak PDE. In south central Pennsylvania, the SCPE speaker who uses a Pennsylvania German lexical item (probably because it captures just the right intended meaning) is quite likely to be understood by all listeners, at least those over the age of 30. On a commercial level, these lexical items and calques make their way onto tourist items like T-shirts, postcards, and keychains as examples of the English spoken in the Pennsylvania Dutch region; websites on the Pennsylvania Dutch created by tourism bureaus of various south central Pennsylvania counties and Gates's (1987, 1998) humorous dictionaries of Dutchified English provide lists of such words and phrases. Such popular cultural representations of the dialect often focus, of course, on the more unusual examples of lexical items and calques sometimes heard in the region.

It is probable that over the years the Pennsylvania German lexical items often used by PDE speakers and SCPE speakers have taken on shades of meaning in the broader south central Pennsylvania speech community that are not shared with Pennsylvania German speakers; as PDE speakers (and

SCPE speakers who are familiar with Pennsylvania German) have heard and used these lexical items outside of the context of Pennsylvania German sentences, the items have most certainly undergone some slight semantic or pragmatic shifts. Without going into detail about such shifts, the short lists in (35)–(38) contain examples of how some of these Pennsylvania German lexical items are currently used in natural, unelicited discourse by monolingual English speakers in the south central Pennsylvania region:

35. Verbs
    a. *dopple* 'dawdle, take too long to accomplish a task' (*I keep* DOPPLING *around and can't seem to get done with my project.*)
    b. *griesle* 'nauseate someone, usually in a figurative sense' (*The way that new mayor acts like a big shot really* GRIESLES *me!*)
    c. *verhuddle* 'confuse' (*This algebra really* VERHUDDLES *me!*)
    d. *rutch* 'squirm, move around on one's seat' (*The boys made it through the wedding ceremony without misbehaving, but they* RUTCHED *the whole time.*)
    e. *kutz* 'vomit' (exasperated mother walking into her daughters' messy bedroom: *Every time I walk in this room, I could just* KUTZ!)
    f. *fress* 'eat, dig in' (*Let's* FRESS!; note, however, that in German, this is used for animals, and *essen* is used for people, so this is a clear example of a semantic shift in the use of a German word by non–Pennsylvania German speakers)
    g. *soff* 'drink quickly, in large gulps'; used with the English particle *down* (*I only have one bottle of soda, so don't* SOFF *it down, OK?*)
    h. *brutz* 'cry' (*He started* BRUTZING *as soon as the other kid called him a name.*)
    i. *grex* 'complain' (*I know it's hot today, but you needn't* GREX *so much about it!*)
    j. *luder* 'stink, a lot' (*Why didn't you throw your dirty gym clothes in the wash? Now your bag* LUDERS.)
36. Nouns
    a. *dummkupp* 'dummy' (*Don't be such a* DUMMKUPP! *Washington was the first president, not Lincoln!*)
    b. *blutzwagon* 'lit. bounce-wagon', an affectionate name for a vehicle with less-than-wonderful suspension on bumpy roads
    c. *nix noox, snicklefritz*, affectionate terms for a trouble-making child
    d. *wutz* 'someone who eats like a pig' (*I would have had some deer sausage to give you if my husband wouldn't have been such a* WUTZ *and eaten it all!*)
37. Adjectives
    a. *doppich* 'clumsy' (*I am so* DOPPICH *today—I dropped the flour on the floor and broke a glass while I was washing dishes.*)
    b. *scheusslich* 'unsettled, clumsy due to hurrying' (*I can't help feeling* SCHEUSSLICH *when I have twenty things I need to get done in the next hour!*)

   c. *schmutzig* 'dirty' (*Your windshield is so* SCHMUTZIG, *why don't you clean it?*)

   d. *strubly* 'unkempt, untidy'; used to refer specifically to a person's hair (*Do you think I'm too* STRUBLY *to go into the store, or do I need to comb (my hair) first?*)

   e. *rumply* 'wrinkly' (*You'd better iron that* RUMPLY *shirt.*)

38. Phrase
Machts nix! 'No problem!; lit. Makes nothing!'

Calques of Pennsylvania German phrases and relic expressions that are likewise part of the wider speech community include those in (39). Although these expressions were once quite common in the speech of the oldest PDE speakers from the first generation of those who learned English as an L2, the use of these is now considered particularly "Dutchified," and so they are now usually used in a humorous way both by individuals who speak Pennsylvania German and those who do not.

39. a. PDE: *Make out the light!*
Pennsylvania German: *Macht das Licht aus!*
Standard American English: *Turn off the light!*

   b. PDE: *It wonders me…*
Pennsylvania German: *Es wunnert mich…*
Standard American English: *I wonder…*

   c. PDE: *It's making down* or *It's making wet.*
Pennsylvania German: *Es regnet.*
Standard American English: *It's raining.*

This last example does not seem to be a proper calque on the normal Pennsylvania German *Es regnet* 'It's raining'. Nevertheless, it has been attested since the early days of mass Pennsylvania German–English bilingualism (Aurund 1939) as an English expression used by Pennsylvania German speakers. Perhaps it is a calque on a Pennsylvania German idiomatic expression. At any rate, it is considered particularly "Dutchified" and is used when imitating the PDE dialect, and so it is included in this list of relic expressions.

3.4. A SUMMARY OF SHARED AND UNIQUE FEATURES OF PDE AND SCPE

Table 3.1 summarizes features of the SCPE and PDE dialects that have been discussed above in sections 3.1–3.3, thus making it possible to get an idea of the degree of overlap and distinctiveness between the dialects, particularly in morphosyntax and intonation.

TABLE 3.1
Features of PDE and SCPE

	PDE	SCPE
Phonetic Variants		
lack of affricate [ʤ]	✔	
bilabial fricative [β] for /w/	✔	
Phonological Features		
tense [æ] (Philadelphia-style)	✔	✔
raised [æ] (PDE-style)	✔	
/aʊ/ → [a] (*how* [ha])	✔	
/a/ → [ʌ] before nasals (*conference* [kʌnfrənts])	✔	
/aɪ/ → [æ] before liquids (*pirate ~ parrot* [pærət])	✔	
obstruent devoicing (*dug* [dʌk])	✔	
[w] for /v/ in "strong" environments (word-initial and stressed syllable-initial)	✔	
Morphosyntactic Features		
bare verb root as past (*run*)	✔	
past participle as past (*seen*)	✔	
remote past *had* + verb	✔	
preposition "stranding" (*go with*)	✔	✔
preposition "loading" (*front from*)	✔	✔
flexible direct object placement (*Throw Pop down the stairs his hat.*)	✔	
youse as second-person pronoun	✔	✔
once as emphasis particle	✔	
still as habitual marker	✔	
what for 'what kind of'	✔	
tag question *not, ain't, ai-not*	✔	
present tense for present perfect (*I'm studying six years.* 'I've been studying six years.')	✔	✔
conditional for subjunctive in irrealis conditional sentences (*She would be here if she would be able to.*)	✔	✔
yet to indicate ongoing action (*Is it raining yet?* 'Is it still raining')	✔	✔
needs + participle construction (*The dog needs fed.*)	✔	✔
Lexical Features		
use of Pennsylvania German lexical items	✔	(✔)
use of calques on Pennsylvania German phrases	✔	
Intonation		
falling question intonation	✔	✔

To examine more thoroughly the changes occurring in PDE as it slides toward extinction, this study will specifically focus on several of the PDE phonological variants mentioned above, namely:

> obstruent devoicing (the devoicing of obstruents which are neither in the onset of a stressed syllable nor are word-initial) (*bed* [bɛt])
> monophthongization of /aʊ/ to [a] (*house* [has])
> monophthongization of /aɪ/ to [æ] before liquids (*mile* [mæl])
> centralization of /a/ to [ʌ] before nasals (*concert* [kʌnsərt])
> raised [æ]

Phonological variants were chosen over morphosyntactic or lexical variants as the focus of this study because they are most prevalent in the corpus of interview data and thus provided the numbers of tokens necessary for statistical analysis. These particular variants were chosen from the list in table 3.1 because they occur in the data set for PDE monodialectals of all generations (unlike the bilabial fricative, for example, although some analysis of it will also enter the discussions to follow). Some of these still occur rather rarely, due to their inherent phonological constraints. This focus on phonological features allows for a comparison of PDE feature use and variation patterns across the generations, a useful device in discussing the unraveling of the PDE dialect in chapters 4 and 5.

4. PDE PHONOLOGICAL FEATURES AND THEIR USE: UNRAVELING IN ACTION FOR PDE OBSTRUENT DEVOICING

OBSTRUENT DEVOICING—the premiere consonantal feature of Pennsylvania Dutchified English (PDE) as it is spoken today—provides a striking illustration of the complexity of phonological processes that can accompany the unraveling of a dialect as it loses ground to a prestige variety. Not only are today's youngest speakers of PDE using consonantal dialect features less frequently than previous generations, but they are using them with different phonological constraints and in different phonological environments. Sections 4.1 and 4.2 describe PDE obstruent devoicing as it is used by informants recorded in 1993–95 representing three generations: those speakers born before 1930, those born between 1930 and 1960, and those born after 1960. Subsequent sections incorporate data gathered in 2004–9 from middle-aged speakers (born in the 1940s) and the youngest speakers of PDE (born in the 1960s and 1970s). The PDE informant pool includes both males and females; all are working class and grew up in northern Lebanon County in south central Pennsylvania.

4.1. AN OVERVIEW OF OBSTRUENT DEVOICING IN PHONOLOGICAL AND PHONETIC TERMS

Obstruent devoicing is an important and interesting feature of both Pennsylvania German and Pennsylvania Dutchified English. In PDE in particular, not only is it perhaps the most socially salient phonological feature—often joked about and commented upon by PDE and SCPE speakers alike—but it also shows more clearly than any other phonological feature in PDE the consequences of the intense contact between Pennsylvania German and English that has been part of the linguistic landscape of south central Pennsylvania for the last three centuries. Like almost all the phonological features in this study, its rate of use among speakers is declining across the generations: data collected from the oldest participants in this study (in 1993–95) and from the middle-aged and youngest speakers (in 1993–95 and 2004–9) show that the incidence of obstruent devoicing is relatively high among the oldest generation of PDE speakers (those bilingual in Penn-

TABLE 4.1
Overview of Rates of PDE Obstruent Devoicing

Generation	Rate of Devoicing
Oldest	89.8%
Middle-aged	14.7%
Youngest	6.1%

sylvania German and PDE), rather low among middle-aged PDE speakers (most of whom are monolingual in PDE), and very low among the youngest (and last?) speakers of the PDE dialect, as shown in table 4.1.

To speak merely of such decline, however, hides a much more complicated picture of the phonetic and phonological consequences of long-term language contact and dialect contact in south central Pennsylvania. Composite linguistic systems can arise in speech communities that use two (or more) language varieties when aspects of each variety mutually exert linguistic "pressure" on the other variety/varieties; the effects of such bidirectional influence between language varieties results in something quite distinct from simple unidirectional transfer effects. Often in cases like this, speakers reach some kind of linguistic compromise between a linguistic feature's realization in the two varieties, thus creating new norms of realization that are not exactly like those of either language variety (see, e.g., Flege 1987; Sancier and Fowler 1997; Kuha 1998; Bao and Wee 1999; Escobar 2001; Van Rooy 2002). The phonology and phonetics of obstruent devoicing in PDE show evidence for the formation of just such a composite system, with clear bidirectional influences traceable to both Pennsylvania German and American English.

OBSTRUENT DEVOICING AT THE PHONOLOGICAL LEVEL AS A COMPOSITE LINGUISTIC SYSTEM. Much phonological research has been conducted on syllable-final devoiced obstruents in German in the past two centuries, but there is still debate about their inherent phonetic and phonological nature, including whether such segments are neutralized or not (e.g., Dinnsen 1985; Iverson and Salmons 2006). In the view of researchers who hold to the idea of complete neutralization of voicing in contexts where devoicing occurs, devoiced segments are simply segments that were originally [+voice] but become [−voice] due to phonological operations (or, according to Lombardi's [1999] view, segments underlyingly specified for the privative laryngeal feature [voice] become no longer specified for that feature). Other researchers (e.g., Jessen 1998) have suggested that a tripartite (rather than binary) phonological distinction exists between underlyingly voiced obstruents (which are [+voice]), underlyingly voiceless obstruents (which are [−voice]), and these devoiced obstruents. Jessen and Ringen (2002) take this distinction a step further and propose that, at least in German, the distinction between voiced, voiceless, and devoiced obstruents is not a matter of [voice], but of [spread glottis]. The complexity and consequences of the phonological theory of obstruent devoicing are not subjects pursued here, although its relevance to the topic of language variety obsolescence is recognized. Instead, for the purposes of this study, these obstruents will simply be referred to here as VOICED, VOICELESS, or DEVOICED.

Syllable-final devoicing has long been recognized as a feature of standard German (Wiese 1996):

1. a. *Laub* [laʊp] 'foliage'
   b. *Rad* [raːt] 'wheel'
   c. *Zug* [tsuːk] 'train'

PDE extends obstruent devoicing beyond this, however, to include ALL environments except those that involve an obstruent occurring word-initially or—for the most part—in the onset of a stressed syllable (in prosodic terms, at the left edge of a metrical foot). By contrasting voiced obstruents with their voiceless counterparts, the examples in (2) illustrate where obstruents retain their voicing.

2. Environments in which specification for [voice] is preserved
   a. Word-initially
      duck [dʌk] vs. *tuck* [tʌk]
   b. In the onset of a syllable with primary stress
      habitual [həˈbɪtʃuəl] vs. *appendix* [əˈpɛntɪks]
      disease [dɪˈzis] vs. *assume* [əˈsum]
   c. In the onsets of syllables with secondary stress
      holiday [ˈhalɪˌde] vs. *Raritan* [ˈrerɪˌtɪn]
   d. In word-initial clusters
      bleed [blid] vs. *plead* [plid]

Pennsylvania German, a source language for PDE, also preserves voicing specification in these contexts. However, unilke PDE, some varieties of Pennsylvania German extend voicing to at least some voiceless obstruents in word-initial position, as shown in the examples in (3):

3. *Pelschnickel* [bélˌʃnɪ.kl] 'character from Christmastime lore'
   pot pie [bot bai] 'dish of broad noodles, meat, and potatoes'

In PDE, however, all obstruents in such "strong" positions at the left edges of metrical feet preserve their voicing specification, whether they are voiced or voiceless. Voiced obstruents in PDE that occur in any other position (i.e., "weak" positions) in the word are devoiced, as shown in (4):

4. Environments in which voiced obstruents are devoiced
   a. In simple word-final codas
      tug [tʌk]
      leave [lif]
      bed [bɛt]
   b. In simple word-internal codas
      obtuse [ap'tus]
      Agnes ['æknɪs]
      admission [æt'mɪʃən]
   c. In coda clusters
      dogs [daks]
      leaves [lifs]
   d. In unstressed syllable onsets
      habit ['hæpɪt]
      dizzy ['dɪsi]
      lumber ['lʌmpər]
      hungry ['ʌŋkri]
      foggy ['faki]

Because voicing specification is preserved in PDE for obstruents in "strong" positions but not in "weak" positions, some interesting examples of contrasting pairs of English words emerge to illustrate that the voiced obstruents are indeed specified underlyingly for voice:

5. *habitual* [hæ'bɪtʃuəl] ~ *habit* ['hæpɪt]
   disease [dɪ'zis] ~ *dizzy* ['dɪsi]

Thus far, PDE's obstruent devoicing system seems relatively simple: underlyingly voiceless obstruents preserve their voicing specification in all environments, while underlyingly voiced obstruents only preserve their voicing in "strong" environments and are subsequently devoiced in all other environments. However, two complications emerge in this simple account of the pattern of PDE obstruent devoicing, related to two very specific phonological environments: intervocalic /d/ and word-internal onset clusters at the onset of stressed syllables with /b/, /g/, and /d/. With respect to intervocalic /d/, PDE, like many varieties of American English (including SCPE), flaps both the alveolar stops /t/ and /d/ after a stressed vowel and before an unstressed one. (In German, intervocalic /d/ is always realized as [d] when it is not in a position to devoice because flaps are not part of standard German phonology [Wiese 1996].) This flapping aspect of PDE was noted decades ago by Oswald (1943) and is not a modern innovation of the dialect. Some examples of this flapping can be seen below in the minimal pairs in (6), with transcriptions that indicate how these words are pronounced in PDE, SCPE, and standard American English:

6. *riding, writing* ['raɪɾɪŋ]
   waddle, wattle ['waɾəl]
   bidder, bitter ['bɪɾər]

In this intervocalic environment between a stressed and a stressless vowel, then, PDE speakers pronounce both /t/ and /d/ with a voiced flap, despite the fact that other voiced obstruents devoice in this same intervocalic environment (e.g., *habit* [hæ.pit], *dizzy* [dí.si]). Thus, for PDE, flapping takes precedence over devoicing, interfering with the normal devoicing process.

The other phonological environment that complicates this straightforward analysis of the devoicing process is word-internal onset clusters. When such clusters occur at the beginning of stressed syllables, the stops /g/ and /b/ violate the normal devoicing rules for PDE and are devoiced (and aspirated) despite their position in a stressed syllable onset:

7. *agreement* [əˈkʰrimənt]
   Sabrina [səˈpʰrina]

The stops /b/ and /g/ in these clusters behave in a way that is in direct contrast to /b/ and /g/ in the onset of a stressed syllable when they are NOT part of obstruent-liquid clusters, as seen in (8):

8. *about* [əˈbaʊt]
   aghast [əˈgæst]

The voiced stop /d/ does not follow the pattern of the other voiced stops in this case, however; rather, in PDE, it stands out from /b/ and /g/ because it retains its voicing in this same environment (in the onset of a word-internal stressed syllable), whether it is part of an obstruent-liquid cluster or not:

9. a. Simple onsets of word-internal stressed syllables
      indeed [ɪnˈdit]
      reduce [riˈdus]
   b. Obstruent-liquid medial syllable onset clusters (i.e., at the left edge of a foot)
      Madrid [məˈdrɪt]
      address [əˈdrɛs]

However, if /d/ does not occur in a "strong" position (i.e., at the left edge of a metrical foot), it is devoiced just like the other obstruents, even when it is part of an obstruent-liquid cluster:

9. c. /d/ in the simple onset of a stressless syllable
      Audrey ['atri]
      foundry ['fantri]

Why /d/ would behave differently from the other stops in obstruent-liquid onset clusters is a bit of a mystery. It may be that the tendency among PDE speakers to realize this particular phoneme as a flap—as illustrated in (5)—may contribute to the asymmetry between /d/ and the other stops when it comes to voicing. In other words, while /b/ and /g/ are either fully voiced in "strong" positions—with the exception of obstruent-liquid onsets in stressed syllables—or devoiced in "weak" positions, the flap represents some kind of more voiced/less devoiced middle ground for /d/; hence it may seem strange to speakers—due to the frequency with which /d/ is heard by them as something more voiced than voiceless—to devoice /d/ in these onset clusters, even if /b/ and /g/ are devoiced in such onsets.[1] Also, flapped /d/s are never aspirated in English and, unlike devoiced /b/ and /g/ in words such as *Sabrina* and *agreement*, are never in a position in PDE to be aspirated (since it is devoiced only in codas and onsets of unstressed syllables); this inability of /d/ to ever surface in PDE as aspirated may further enhance the asymmetry between it and the other stops.

These exceptions for /d/ aside, it is interesting to note that the "strong" positions where PDE preserves voicing for voiced obstruents are exactly the same positions in which American English aspirates voiceless stops, that is, at the beginning of a word (as the first segment only) and at the beginning of a word-internal stressed syllable (Ladefoged 2001). Set (10) provides examples of this:

10. a. Aspiration in word-initial position (but not in a word-initial syllable onset cluster after /s/)
         pill [pʰɪl], but not *spill* [spɪl]
         tall [tʰal], but not *stall* [stal]
         cull [kʰʌl], but not *skull* [skʌl]
     b. Aspiration at the beginning of a word-internal stressed syllable
         apply [əˈpʰlaɪ]
         attribute (verb form) [əˈtʰrɪbʲut]
         account [əˈkʰaʊnt]

For PDE, then, [voice] can only be preserved in metrical foot-initial position, the same environment where American English aspirates voiceless stops. Thus, PDE has generalized the environment for the marked laryngeal feature [spread glottis] to apply to the other marked laryngeal feature, [voice], as well (Anderson 2001; Davis and Anderson 2003; Davis 2010). In Davis and Anderson (2003) and Anderson and Davis (2013), we argue that what PDE speakers have done is taken a feature of Pennsylvania German grammar (here, obstruent devoicing) and provided an environment for it determined by the structure of American English—that is, the left edges of metrical feet, where both American English and PDE aspirate voiceless stops. That is, just as aspirated stops occur only in foot-initial position in PDE, voiced obstruents can occur only in foot-initial position in PDE; they devoice in all other environments (with the exception of the flapping environment for /d/).

Although it is tempting simply to attribute features of PDE directly to the substrate influence of Pennsylvania German—after all, the first speakers of the PDE dialect learned English as an L2, and their Pennsylvania German had an enormous effect on their English—this PDE obstruent devoicing pattern that preserves the voicing specification of voiced obstruents in the same environments in which American English aspirates voiceless stops actually demonstrates that there has been bidirectional, cross-linguistic influence between Pennsylvania German/PDE and American English. The development of such a composite system does not readily fit a consideration of simpler transfer effects alone. Apparently, in the development of PDE, bilingual Pennsylvania German–English speakers opted for a strategy of phonological compromise between their two languages, creating a new behavior out of laryngeal components of two separate linguistic systems and thereby forming a composite system with regard to the phonology of obstruent voicing/devoicing in their Pennsylvania German and PDE that is distinct from already investigated varieties of German spoken on the European continent today (Davis and Anderson 2003). This system has been retained by their monolingual descendants, and obstruent devoicing has become a salient part of what defines PDE in the minds of the south central Pennsylvania speech community.

4.2. OBSTRUENT DEVOICING AT THE PHONETIC LEVEL AS A COMPOSITE LINGUISTIC SYSTEM

An investigation of the phonology of PDE obstruent devoicing demonstrates clearly how PDE speakers have formed a phonological compromise system between the norms of Pennsylvania German obstruent devoicing and American English aspiration. An acoustic analysis of realizations of PDE obstruents across the generations suggests that PDE speakers have done the same at the phonetic level for obstruent devoicing. While PDE speakers of all generations engage in obstruent devoicing (although to different degrees, as table 4.1 showed), the devoiced obstruents these different groups of speakers produce are not acoustically equivalent, and the youngest PDE speakers (those born after 1960) have reached a sort of a middle ground between the obstruent duration values of their grandparents and their parents. Determining the sociophonetic nature of such differences in obstruent voicing/devoicing within this speech community is important in developing an appropriate and comprehensive characterization of the demise of this feature in the obsolescence of PDE.

To discuss in depth the phonetic nature of obstruent devoicing in PDE, it is first necessary to determine what the phonetic correlates of PDE voicing and devoicing are. Some phoneticians have labeled pairs of voiced-unvoiced segments in German as "tense/lax," "fortis/lenis," and so on (e.g., Goblirsch 1994), but exactly what clusters of phonetic features each of these labels implies is unclear. "Strength" has been evoked as a feature of voicing in some dialects, but the specific attributes of "strength" of German consonants in general varies widely from region to region (Goblirsch 1994, 33–35); in Swiss German, for example, strength is a matter of consonant quantity (Kraehenmann 2001). The triad of voice, aspiration, and duration has also been used to account for voicing/devoicing in the standard Northern variety of German (i.e., the dialects that developed into the prestigious variety of the language between the fifteenth and nineteenth centuries); however, voice and aspiration themselves are not stable enough to provide a constant distinction between tense-lax/fortis-lenis stops on their own even in that variety, and it may be that different German varieties have different complexes of features involved in this distinction (Goblirsch 1994, 33–35). Purnell, Salmons, and Tepeli (2005, 139) found that the "ratio of the duration of glottal pulsing to the duration of the total stop gap" was one factor that proved to be significant in their investigation of obstruents produced by speakers in Watertown, Wisconsin, an area with high rates of German settlement. In light of this, how to characterize devoicing best in PDE (or, for that matter, in Pennsylvania German itself) is consequently rather unclear, but to be consistent with much of the research on German devoicing, obstruent durations will be presumed to be at least one source of acoustic differences between unvoiced and devoiced obstruent pairs in PDE.

As an extension of the use of obstruent durations to characterize voicing/devoicing, another popular correlate of devoicing that has been the focus of phonetic research is the ratio between the duration of the obstruent in question and the duration of the vowel preceding it, a measure of voicing developed by Port and Dalby (1982). Mitleb (1984), for example, used this ratio when he noted that Arabic learners of English (who do not use consonant or preceding vowel durations to distinguish voiced-unvoiced consonant pairs in their native language) similarly did not make duration distinctions in their L2 productions to the extent that native speakers of English would. The consequence of this is that their productions were sometimes interpreted by American listeners as the wrong member of a voiced-unvoiced pair (e.g., the well-known Arabic initial /b/ ~ /p/ problem). Charles-Luce (1985) likewise used consonant and vowel durations and ratios as a measure for devoicing in Catalan, although she reported that some of the effect of either closure duration or vowel duration on the word-final voicing distinction in the Catalan of her informants involved the position of that segment within the phrase. Following their lead, this chapter will also consider vowel and obstruent durations, as well as the ratios between them, as sources of acoustic distinction between voiced and unvoiced obstruents in PDE.[2] As will be shown in the next section, results of an analysis of these durations and ratios indicate that young PDE speakers have used such acoustic means to innovate an obstruent devoicing compromise strategy in the phonetic realm, albeit with a sociolinguistic twist.

For the sake of completeness, it is also important to recognize that the notion of listener perception of voiced/devoiced obstruents is crucial to really understanding the direction of acoustic change in obstruent devoicing uncovered by this study. Much of the work that has been done with voicing neutralization in perceptual studies has focused on vowels (e.g., Clopper and Pisoni 2003; Plichta and Preston 2003; Rakerd and Plichta 2003), but some work on the perception of consonants has also involved neutralization rules. Port, Mitleb, and O'Dell (1981) and O'Dell and Port (1983) investigated the accuracy of German listeners in their perceptual discrimination between voiceless and devoiced word-final obstruents; their findings indicated that subjects were able to distinguish between the two in forced minimal pair choices at a rate significantly better than chance. For English-speaking listeners who took part in the study by Port and Dalby (1982) mentioned above, the perceptual crossover point—the acoustic point at which listeners indicated that they discerned a particular consonant as being either the voiced or unvoiced one in a pair—occurred at vowel duration to consonant duration ratios of 2.74 and 2.33, respectively, for artificially manipulated voiced and devoiced labials and velars (coronals were not investigated). ("Vowel duration" refers to the length in milliseconds of the vowel preceding the obstruent in question; "consonant duration" refers to the length in milliseconds of the obstruent itself. The ratio is the comparison between the two, in other words, length of vowel divided by length of obstruent.) Slowiaczek and Szymanska (1989) found the same ratios to be significant for Polish listeners, although they were also able to determine that listeners discriminated voiceless (rather than devoiced) tokens with greater accuracy. Unfortunately, no perceptual work to determine perceptual crossover points between voiced and unvoiced obstruents has been completed to date in either Pennsylvania German or PDE. Nevertheless, the phonetic analysis presented below will show that vowel-consonant duration ratios serve a significant sociolinguistic function among PDE speakers.

See figure 4.1 for an example of devoicing as evidenced in duration ratio in PDE. These two spectrograms show the pronunciation of the word *bedcovers* elicited from a bidialectal speaker of PDE and SCPE. The top spectrogram shows the SCPE pronunciation of the word with all obstruents preserving their voicing specifications ([bɛdkʌvərz]), while the bottom spectrogram shows the PDE pronunciation of the word with all obstruents devoiced ([bɛtkʌfərs]). Note the longer vowel duration for [ɛ] and shorter consonant duration for [d] in the top spectrogram where the obstruents are voiced; the vowel duration is shorter and consonant duration longer in the bottom example, where the /d/ is devoiced. This is an illustration of the ratio of vowel duration to obstruent duration that is used in this section as a measure of devoicing. Spectrograms were constructed using Praat, sampled at a rate of 44,100 Hz.

ACOUSTIC ANALYSIS OF PDE OBSTRUENT DEVOICING. The first step in performing an acoustic analysis of PDE obstruent devoicing was to choose appropriate phonemes to examine. Whereas all obstruents undergo devoicing in conservative PDE, as they do in Pennsylvania German (Kopp 1999), /d/ and /z/ are by far the most commonly devoiced obstruents in PDE in the data collected, both in terms of numbers of tokens and in terms of proportion of devoiced tokens to voice-preserving tokens. The coronal stop /d/ poses inherent challenges since it holds a special place in PDE's phonology: it is realized as a flap intervocalically. However, for practicality's sake and to be able to run certain statistical analyses, /d/ was nevertheless chosen as the obstruent to investigate in this acoustic analysis. This was simply because it occurs far more frequently in naturalistic conversational data than /z/ or any of the other obstruents, particularly in the syllable-final environment chosen as a focus for the sake of consistency, and because sociolinguistic analyses require as many tokens as possible to ensure accurate analytic outcomes. Even so, as the following section will show, only 213 tokens of voiced and devoiced /d/ in this environment were collected from approximately 12 hours of recorded speech, compared to fewer than 20 tokens each of /b/ and /g/.

METHODOLOGY. The data for the analysis in this section were taken from my taped interviews and casual conversations with PDE speakers, collected in 1993–95 in and near northern Lebanon County in south central Pennsylvania. Because the original study (Anderson 1995) for which these tapes were made focused on the construct of social network (see Milroy 1987) and its influence on the use of PDE by these speakers, all the informants were connected to each other in some way, with all having some tie to the same mountain village in northern Lebanon County. All informants are mem-

FIGURE 4.1
Spectrograms of *bedcovers* in SCPE and PDE

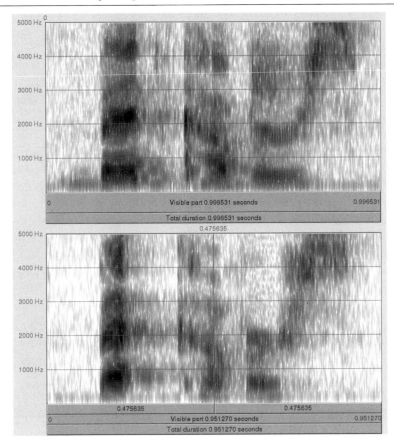

bers of working-class families; all know me personally (also a PDE speaker and member of this speech community) and any others participating in the interviews. Many are monolingual in PDE; some are bilingual in PDE and Pennsylvania German. Informant ages ranged from 27 to about 80 at the time of the recordings. Overall the informant group was comprised of roughly equal numbers of male and female speakers; however, due to constraints on data collection, not every age group or bilingual/monolingual group is composed of equal numbers of both sexes. Classification of the informants according to age group was made according to natural breaks in the series of ages, since one relatively large age gap exists between EY and LT, in their upper 60s, and EK, in her upper 50s, and another gap exists between BK, in his upper 40s, and DK and LK, at 27. Table 4.2 describes the informants in more detail. All interviews were conducted in English.

PROCEDURE. Obviously, it is important in an acoustic analysis such as this to use tokens that occur in a consistent phonological context, so the only tokens of /d/ extracted from the data for further analysis were those preceded by a vowel and occurring in a word-final position (the quintessential environment for obstruent devoicing). Any tokens that occurred at the end of a sentence or phrase were not included in the data set because preliminary analysis revealed significantly longer durations of both consonants and vowels than the norm in such environments. From the available data, using this criterion, 213 tokens were extracted. It is important to note that the choice of tokens for this acoustic analysis was not made on the basis of whether or not tokens sounded devoiced, although an impressionistic analysis of the data indicates that many of the /d/s involved do indeed sound devoiced. Rather, since voicing/devoicing is assumed to be a matter of ratio of an obstruent's duration to its preceding vowel's duration, the values reported below are taken to represent the degree of voicing/devoicing employed by speakers. The 213 extracted tokens of syllable-final /d/ were analyzed and then coded, with special attention paid to the segments surrounding them. Durations for /d/s and for the vowels preceding them were obtained through measuring spectrograms produced by the PC speech analysis program Cool Edit 2000, using speech samples digitized with the Macintosh computer program Soundscope set at a sampling rate of 41.5K. Each token was labeled with the speaker's sex and age and whether the speaker was monolingual or bilingual. Examples of some of these tokens and information about the speakers who uttered them are listed in table 4.3.

As mentioned earlier, many of the tokens of /d/ collected from speakers sounded devoiced in an impressionistic analysis; the oldest speakers'

TABLE 4.2
Informant Characteristics

Informant	Bilingual/ Monolingual	Age	Age Group	Sex
BZ	bilingual	over 75	oldest	F
JK	bilingual	over 70	oldest	F
CT	bilingual	over 70	oldest	M
LT	bilingual	upper 60s	oldest	F
EY	monolingual	upper 60s	oldest	F
EK	bilingual	upper 50s	middle-aged	F
LM	monolingual	56	middle-aged	M
WM	monolingual	59	middle-aged	M
BK	monolingual	upper 40s	middle-aged	M
DK	monolingual	27	youngest	M
LK	monolingual	27	youngest	F

productions sounded mostly devoiced, but it was unclear from simply listening to the speech samples whether that degree of devoicing could be attributed to some quantitative measurement (like durations of /d/) or whether further quantitative differences (like ratios of durations of /d/s to their preceding vowels) existed between the various groups of male versus female speakers, bilingual versus monolingual speakers, and old versus middle-aged versus young speakers. Raw vowel durations were not considered for any of the statistical tests that are applied in the next section of this chapter, except for the purposes of determining ratios of vowel duration to consonant duration. As mentioned earlier, due to the naturalistic (i.e., uncontrolled) character of the data, the vowel durations used in this analysis represent many different vowels, and vowel durations can vary widely from vowel to vowel. Additionally, speakers' rates of speech were not consistent: For example, while speaker LK in table 4.3 produced the vowel [æ] in *had* with a duration of 0.040 ms, the [ʊ] in her pronunciation of *would* had a far longer duration, 0.130 ms. Nevertheless, if the generalizations assumed in this analysis about phonetic correlates of devoicing are correct,

TABLE 4.3
Representative Sample of Tokens with /d/ in Various Contexts

Token in Context	Vowel Duration (ms)	Consonant /d/ Duration (ms)
Speaker BK (bilingual, old, female)		
said where	0.130	0.070
had seven	0.110	0.180
had built	0.120	0.140
kids	0.050	0.030
said that	0.070	0.100
had the	0.040	0.050
did do	0.070	0.130
had a store	0.090	0.040
had a picture	0.080	0.040
Speaker LK (monolingual, young, female)		
would say	0.130	0.100
could be	0.080	0.180
good one	0.130	0.040
dad just	0.110	0.100
dad went	0.100	0.060
had the	0.070	0.040
had that	0.070	0.040
bread or	0.110	0.030
had a	0.040	0.020
said after	0.020	0.020

the ratios of durations of tokens of /d/ to their preceding vowel durations will truly reflect the degree of devoicing.

Table 4.4 shows the mean consonant durations for /d/s for the various groups of PDE speakers represented in the data sample. As the table indicates, the mean consonant duration for females is longer than for males and hence "more devoiced"; the same holds true for bilinguals compared to monolinguals, and for the oldest speakers compared to the other two age groups. Interestingly, the mean value for consonant duration for /d/s uttered by the youngest group of speakers is actually intermediate between the mean values of /d/ for the oldest and the middle-aged speakers, meaning that their productions are presumably devoiced to a degree that falls between the devoicing levels of the other two groups. Overall, the range between the lowest mean and highest mean is actually relatively close, differing by a mere 0.024 ms. Such small differences can be significant, however, and the degree to which these figures differ from each other will be tested statistically in the next section.

Besides duration of /d/, the other phonetic correlate of devoicing used in this acoustic analysis is the ratio of the duration of the vowel preceding the obstruent (/d/) to the duration of the obstruent itself (Port and Dalby 1982; Mitleb 1984). Although the composite duration of a stop and its preceding vowel together stays the same regardless of whether that stop is voiced or voiceless, the relative duration of a vowel is shorter (and the consonant longer) if the consonant is not voiced or DEVOICED; conversely, the duration of the vowel is longer (and the consonant shorter) if the consonant is VOICED. In terms of ratios of relative vowel duration to consonant duration, then, a vowel-obstruent pair with a lower vowel-to-consonant ratio will indicate a voiceless or devoiced obstruent, while a higher vowel-to-consonant ratio indicates a "more voiced" obstruent.[3]

TABLE 4.4
Mean Consonant (/d/) Durations for Groups of PDE Speakers

Group	Mean Durations (ms)
Speaker sex	
male	0.059
female	0.077
Bilingual/monolingual status	
bilingual (PG/PDE)	0.077
monolingual (PDE)	0.060
Speaker age	
oldest	0.083
middle-aged	0.059
youngest	0.069

Table 4.5 shows the mean ratios of vowel-to-obstruent durations for the various groups of PDE speakers included in this chapter. The mean ratio of vowel durations to consonant durations is lower (resulting in "more devoiced" productions) for females than for males. At first glance, this may seem to be indicative of a higher frequency of obstruent devoicing overall for females, but earlier research (Anderson 1995) did not reveal any correlation between devoicing and speaker sex. Hence it seems more accurate to interpret this fact as an overall trend toward "more devoiced" /d/s for females in general. Interestingly, the same higher mean ratio holds true for the monolinguals compared to the bilinguals in the speaker set, underscoring the fact that obstruent devoicing is a feature of PDE in its own right and not solely a transfer effect from Pennsylvania German. If obstruent devoicing were simply a transfer effect, one would expect the BILINGUAL speakers to show the greater degree of devoicing (i.e., lower vowel-to-consonant duration ratios), not the PDE monolinguals. Among the age groups, the oldest speakers show the greatest degree of devoicing and, as in the consonant duration figures in table 4.4, the mean ratio for the youngest speakers is an intermediate value—reflecting an intermediate degree of devoicing—between the mean values of the other two age groups. Testing for statistical significance among these groups is next to determine the effects that intense language variety contact has had on obstruent devoicing in this south central Pennsylvania speech community.

STATISTICAL RESULTS FOR ACOUSTIC MEASURES OF OBSTRUENT DEVOICING. An appropriate model of statistical analysis for this kind of scalar sociophonetic data is one of a group of generalized linear models, a one-way ANOVA

TABLE 4.5
Ratios of Vowel Durations to Consonant (/d/) Durations
for Groups of PDE Speakers

Group	Mean Durations (Vowel:Consonant)
Speaker sex	
male	2.14
female	1.75
Bilingual/monolingual status	
bilingual (PG/PDE)	2.14
monolingual (PDE)	1.73
Speaker age	
oldest	1.75
middle-aged	2.08
youngest	1.96

(i.e., an ANOVA program that compares one continuous dependent variable with one categorical independent variable at a time).[4] This program is designed to perform an analysis of variance "to compare sample means to see if there is sufficient evidence to infer that the means of the corresponding population distributions also differ" (George and Mallery 2000, 132).[5] In these tests, significance is achieved at $p < .05$. Running the ANOVA indicated that consonant duration values differed significantly across the board for each of the three sociolinguistic variables of sex, bilingual/monolingual status, and age, as shown in table 4.6.

As mentioned earlier, the mean durations of /d/ are higher (hence, "more devoiced") for female speakers than for male speakers, and the two groups differ in a way that is statistically significant ($p < .001$). Likewise, the mean durations of /d/ for Pennsylvania German–PDE bilinguals are higher than those for PDE monolinguals to a significance level of $p = .01$, and the oldest speakers have mean durations for /d/ that are longer to a statistically significant degree than the /d/ durations of middle-aged speakers. The comparisons of /d/ durations of youngest speakers to those of the other age groups did not achieve significance.

Not surprisingly, this ANOVA analysis of consonant durations indicates that those speakers with the longest durations of /d/s (the "most devoiced") are the bilinguals and the oldest speakers (recall from table 4.2 that these two groups overlap to some degree, but not completely). The reason females may have longer durations than males here may be simply because the group of female speakers included the two very oldest speakers in the survey and the greatest number of bilinguals of any of the groups, so this study will not speculate any further on the female connection to devoicing. What is more interesting in this assessment of dialect feature use and change, however, is the pattern shown by the different age groups of speakers. Of all the age groups, the middle-aged speakers and oldest speakers evidence durations for /d/ maximally divergent (most significantly different at a level of $p = .002$) from each other; the youngest group of speakers,

TABLE 4.6
ANOVA Results for Consonant Durations

Groups Compared	Mean Durations (ms)	Significance
Male vs. Female	0.059 vs. 0.077	$p < .001$
Bilingual vs. Monolingual	0.077 vs. 0.060	$p = .01$
Oldest vs. Middle-Aged	0.083 vs. 0.059	$p = .002$
Oldest vs. Youngest	0.083 vs. 0.069	not significant
Middle-Aged vs. Youngest	0.059 vs. 0.069	not significant

however, evidences some sort of middle ground between the other two age groups, differing significantly from neither of them.

Matters look just a bit different when conducting an ANOVA analysis with mean vowel-to-obstruent ratios for the speaker groups, as shown in table 4.7. This ANOVA analysis of preceding vowel-to-obstruent ratios only shows results similar to the results from the previous ANOVA analysis of means of obstruent duration with regard to speaker sex: Female speakers had higher mean consonant durations in table 4.6, and female speakers here in table 4.7 have lower ratios (resulting in "more devoiced" productions) than male speakers. This difference in ratios is significant here at a level of $p = .027$. In the analysis of mean obstruent durations in table 4.6, bilingual Pennsylvania German–PDE speakers showed evidence of "more devoiced" /d/s than monolingual PDE speakers, but in this analysis of vowel-to-obstruent ratios, the MONOLINGUALS have the lower mean ratio (hence, "more devoiced" productions) than bilinguals, and the difference between the groups is also statistically significant ($p = .020$). In terms of means of consonant duration in table 4.6, the oldest group of speakers differed significantly from the other two age groups, but here in table 4.7 none of the age groups differs in a statistically significant way from the others for vowel-to-obstruent mean ratios. In the Tukey HSD post-hoc test, $p = .192$ for the comparison of the mean ratio values of the oldest speakers with the middle-aged speakers, $p = .698$ between the oldest speakers and the youngest speakers, and $p = .853$ between the middle-aged speakers and the youngest speakers. None of these values is statistically significant, but, again, ratios for the youngest speakers hold an intermediate place between those of the oldest speakers and the middle-aged speakers, just as their mean consonant durations did in table 4.6.

It is quite interesting that the results obtained by this ANOVA analysis of ratios of vowel durations to consonant durations did not exactly mirror the results from the ANOVA analysis that examined consonant durations alone.

TABLE 4.7
ANOVA Results for the Ratios of Vowel Durations (Vowels Preceding /d/)
to Consonant (/d/) Durations

Groups Compared	Mean Durations (ms)	Significance
Male vs. Female	2.14 vs. 1.75	$p = .027$
Bilingual vs. Monolingual	2.14 vs. 1.73	$p = .020$
Oldest vs. Middle-Aged	1.75 vs. 2.08	$p = .192$
Oldest vs. Youngest	1.75 vs. 1.96	$p = .698$
Middle-Aged vs. Youngest	2.08 vs. 1.96	$p = .853$

Given the research on voicing/devoicing mentioned earlier at the beginning of section 4.3 (e.g., Port and Dalby 1982), it was expected that the two sets of measurements would act in tandem, but such is not the case. Instead, it appears from the levels of significance obtained in the ANOVA analysis that consonant duration alone is the sole indicator of voicing/devoicing differences for these specific PDE-speaking groups rather than mean vowel duration-to-mean consonant duration ratios. (Note the drastically lower levels of p-values—i.e., higher significance—indicated in table 4.6 than in table 4.7.) It may also be that even though Port and Dalby (1982) were able to make a meaningful link between ratio of vowel duration to consonant duration in the obstruent productions of standard German speakers and Slowiaczek and Szymanska (1989) were able to do the same for Polish speakers, this phonetic generalization about ratios and voicing/devoicing just does not hold for PDE, and perhaps not even for Pennsylvania German. Rather, consonant duration alone appears to be the most effective quantitative indicator of devoicing for PDE.

Thus, on the phonetic level, evidence suggests that middle-aged PDE speakers shortened their consonant durations for /d/ in relevant environments for devoicing to make them more like those of the regional standard of English, and then young speakers lengthened their consonant durations back to something more like those of their grandparents; unpredictably, however, no age group altered their vowel-to-consonant duration ratios.[6] This phenomenon is similar to that described by Purnell, Salmons, and Tepeli (2005) in their work on Wisconsin German: the realization of devoicing for the over-65-year-old speakers they interviewed was somewhere between the norms for obstruent devoicing for German and English (146–48).

Although the middle-aged generation of PDE speakers shifted their consonant durations for obstruents toward durations presumably more like the SCPE speakers ("less devoiced," since SCPE retains voicing for obstruents), they show a tendency to keep vowel-to-consonant duration ratios the same. While it is true that this research on the phonetics of PDE obstruent devoicing indicates that a reliance on vowel-to-consonant duration ratio as a cue for devoicing/voicing is not as universal as previously assumed, it is also true that PDE's sociohistorical context sets it somewhat apart from standard language varieties like German and Polish: not only has Pennsylvania German (one of PDE's source languages) been in contact with English (PDE's other source language) in south central Pennsylvania for over 300 years, but PDE itself is spoken today in an environment where it has Pennsylvania German as a substrate influence and constant contact with the regional standard SCPE. This kind of long-term intense contact is bound to have an effect on speakers' linguistic behaviors; it already sets the PDE-speaking community apart from other immigrant language speech communities in the United States, where transfer to English took place much more quickly (Meyers-Scotton 2002).

To restate this all in terms of language variety change, then, the various generations of PDE speakers have behaved differently. Working from a baseline of consonant durations shown by the oldest group of PDE speakers, it appears that the middle-aged group—one of whom is bilingual herself, but all of whom had at least one bilingual parent to model Pennsylvania German obstruent norms for them—shifted their obstruent norms away from their parents' to a statistically significant degree. Although they did shift their vowel duration-to-obstruent duration ratios somewhat from their parents' ratios (a presumably more cognitively complex task than shifting obstruent mean ratios alone), they did not do so to a degree that is statistically significant. The speakers in the youngest group evidence instead mean consonant durations for /d/ that are midway between their grandparents' and their parents' means, not differing in a statistically significant way from either generation. The youngest speakers' vowel-to-consonant ratios, however, are in line with those exhibited by the two older generations. This generation's vowel-to-consonant duration ratios, however, remain in conformity with values demonstrated in the models of PDE presented to them by both their parents and grandparents. In this way, the youngest PDE speakers have created a phonetic norm for obstruent devoicing that is a compromise between and a composite of the norms of the middle-aged and oldest generations of speakers, albeit only in one measure.

Why would different generations of speakers adopt different stances with regard to obstruent devoicing? It is not surprising when the youngest generation of speakers of a minority language variety shift away from their parents' speech patterns and, consequently, even further from their grandparents' speech patterns (see Meyers-Scotton 2002 for immigrant language communities). However, these PDE acoustic data show that the youngest generation of PDE speakers actually devoices /d/s to a slightly greater extent than their parents' generation. This type of situation has emerged in certain other language variety minority situations; Dubois and Horvath (1999), for example, report similar linguistic behavior among Cajun English dialect speakers in Louisiana. In their study, the youngest generation outpaces their parents in production of certain hallmark Cajun English features, such as the stopping of interdental fricatives and strong nasalization. Dubois and Horvath explain that a serious stigma was attached to Cajun English for the middle generation of speakers, who used typical Cajun English features less frequently in a struggle to sound less Cajun (and therefore be less stigmatized). However, Cajun culture has recently received national attention, and there has been a revival of Cajun identity in Louisiana; consequently, younger speakers actually use higher rates of these features to mark the ethnicity they have become proud of. It is not apparent that the youngest PDE speakers have the same motivation: not only is PDE far from "hip," but even the very informants who declare that they are "proud of where they come up from" (one informant's words) sometimes express dismay at how they sound when they hear their own PDE speech. Besides, as was shown in table 4.1, even if consonant durations for /d/ have increased for the youngest generation of speakers, the rate of obstruent devoicing in general has been declining drastically over the generations, and the youngest speakers have the lowest overall rate (6.1%). These figures are sufficient to show that ethnic pride is not a factor that can account for the consonant duration shifts of the youngest PDE speakers. If it were, one would expect rates of devoicing that look similar to Dubois and Horvath's (1999) Cajun English findings, with the youngest generation showing pride in their identity through higher frequencies of use for marked dialect features. Rather, something more subtle than a renewed sense of ethnic identity—at least in the same way as that reported by Dubois and Horvath (1999)—seems to be at work among the youngest generation of PDE speakers in their shifting of consonant durations. While this study does not have a definitive answer, perhaps this devoicing norm has something to do instead with the youngest generation's adoption of behaviors that bring them more into alignment with the oldest generation's perceived expectations, a force that comes into play with the linguistic behaviors exhibited by bidialectals, as will be discussed further in chapter 7.

4.3. THE UNRAVELING OF PDE OBSTRUENT DEVOICING

SALIENCE OF PDE OBSTRUENT DEVOICING. As mentioned earlier, members of the speech community—speakers of PDE and SCPE alike—are well aware of obstruent devoicing, and the high degree of salience of this feature extends beyond a superficial assessment of "salience as speaker awareness." Auer, Barden, and Grosskopf (1998) proposed a set of objective and subjective criteria for salience based on work by Schirmunski (1930) and Trudgill (1986) mentioned earlier; a list of those criteria for salience follows, with a determination of whether obstruent devoicing satisfies each.

Objective (Linguistic) Criteria

Articulatory Distance: NO. PDE devoiced segments are not articulatorily distant from their SCPE counterparts in terms of place of articulation, although they do differ in terms of their laryngeal feature (−voice vs. +voice).

Lack of Areal Distribution: YES. Devoicing of obstruents, particularly /z/, is a feature of various American English dialects, including Midwestern dialects, such as those of northwestern Indiana (José 2010) and Wisconsin (Purnell, Salmons, and Tepeli 2005). However, the particular distribution of devoicing found in PDE and the complexity of phonological environments constraining devoicing (which will be presented in chapter 6) are NOT a feature of other American English dialects in the region surrounding south central Pennsylvania, and so here PDE obstruent devoicing will be deemed to lack areal distribution.

Phonemicity: YES. Devoiced obstruents (or, rather, their unvoiced counterparts) have phonemic status in PDE as in American English.

Dichotomy: YES. Acoustically, there are many degrees of devoicing possible between "fully" voiced and "unvoiced," based on differences in obstruent duration, among other factors. However, listeners perceive obstruents as either voiced or unvoiced, and acoustic experiments have determined that there are perceptual crossover points for individual obstruents (e.g., Port and Dalby 1982) where an obstruent is perceived as one or the other of a pair. Consequently, for this determination of salience, PDE obstruent devoicing is said to be dichotomous.

Lexicalization: NO. PDE devoicing occurs quite prominently in place-names that are pronounced with devoiced obstruents, even by PDE speakers, but it also occurs much more widely than that and is not limited to any particular lexical set.

Subjective (Perceptual) Criteria

Code Alternation: YES. PDE devoicing is used by the bidialectal in chapter 6 to distinguish her PDE speech from her SCPE.

Representation in Lay Writing: YES. PDE devoicing is regularly exhibited in lay representations of PDE with the appropriate unvoiced orthographic counterpart of the obstruent in question. For example, in Gates's (1987, 1998) comedic dictionaries, *garage* is rendered *crotch*, and *Jacob threw a bookie* (boogie) *on the floor* is a description of a child's nose-picking habits; for Gates this is a means of capturing the phonetic quality of the devoiced obstruent while creating a humorous effect. Occasionally, however, letters written by those PDE speakers who are not well-versed in English spelling conventions—especially elderly speakers who may not have gone past the eighth grade in school—also reflect devoicing they would employ in their normal PDE speech; this represents a more naturalistic representation of devoicing in lay writing.

Stereotyping and Mimicking: YES. PDE devoicing is most certainly the first feature referenced when the average south central Pennsylvanian discusses or mimics the PDE dialect or when speakers assess how "Dutchified" another speaker is.

Hindrance to Comprehensibility: YES. Due to the pervasiveness of minimal pairs in English that use voiced/unvoiced pairs (e.g., *dug ~ duck*, *bed ~ bet*, *rabid ~ rapid*, etc.), the opportunities for misunderstanding as a result of the use of this PDE feature are numerous.

PDE obstruent devoicing thus fulfills three of the five objective criteria put forth by Auer, Barden, and Grosskopf (1998), as well as all four of the subjective criteria. By this assessment, obstruent devoicing ranks as "highly salient," with seven of the nine criteria for salience met. Following Auer, Barden, and Grosskopf's reasoning, then, that highly salient dialect features are the most likely to be abandoned by dialect speakers as they are acquiring a second dialect, the use of obstruent devoicing should be declining across the generations. This is indeed the case, as shown in table 4.1. This results in the changes in frequency of use of obstruent devoicing in table 4.8, which also lists the average retention rates for each generation. Note that the oldest generation's values are based here on data obtained from the single monolingual PDE speaker in the oldest generation. The reason for this is to keep the data as consistent as possible across the generations by including measurements for PDE monolinguals only; this eliminates the need to factor in transfer effects from a bilingual speaker's native Pennsylvania German.

Just as Auer, Barden, and Grosskopf's (1998) criteria predicted, obstruent devoicing has eroded from PDE speech across the generations at a remarkable rate. The middle-aged generation has retained this feature at

TABLE 4.8

Changes in Frequency and Relative Retention Rates for PDE Obstruent Devoicing

Generation Compared	Change in Percentage	Retention Rate
Oldest[a] to Middle-Aged	−65.3%	18.4%
Middle-Aged to Youngest	−8.8%	40.0%
Oldest[a] to Youngest	−74.1%	7.3%

a. The oldest generation is represented by data obtained from EY, the only monolingual PDE speakers in that age groups.

only 18.4% of the frequency of use of the oldest-generation bilinguals; the youngest generation of speakers has slowed the erosion down a bit, but they retain the feature at only 40% of the frequency of use of the middle-aged generation. This slowing of the erosion is an added twist to the already complex treatment of obstruent devoicing by the youngest generation of PDE speakers: recall from section 4.3 that the youngest—and last—generation of PDE speakers exhibits both obstruent devoicing and vowel duration–to–obstruent duration ratios that are also more like the oldest generation's than would be expected in an obsolescing dialect. Overall, however, the retention rate of obstruent devoicing by the youngest speakers is still only a paltry 7.3% of that of the oldest-generation monolingual. Despite what acoustic measurements have shown about the youngest generation of speakers, it certainly appears that the decline of PDE obstruent devoicing is further evidence that high salience is an effective predictor of feature abandonment as an outcome of dialect contact.

EVIDENCE OF UNRAVELING IN PDE OBSTRUENT DEVOICING. The erosion of obstruent devoicing in PDE is not merely a matter of speakers using the feature less frequently. Closer investigation reveals that speakers' use of this feature is changing (i.e., the feature is unraveling) in three ways: in the obstruents that are being devoiced, in the frequencies with which individual speakers evidence obstruent devoicing, and in the phonological constraints on when devoicing occurs.

Loss of Obstruents in the Set That Are Devoiced. The data collected in 1993–95 show evidence of devoicing for various obstruents, but in the course of coding and analyzing data collected in 2005–9, it quickly became apparent that no examples of devoiced /b/ or /g/ appeared in the data for the two age groups represented, middle-aged or younger PDE speakers (older speakers were not part of the second data collection), leaving only the apical obstruents as possible candidates for devoicing. Even then, it soon became obvious that /d/ and /z/ dominated the data to a significant degree. This lack of devoiced nonapicals and paucity of devoiced apicals other than /d/ and /z/ is significant in relating the story of the demise of PDE: as chapter 3 explained, historically all obstruents have been devoiced by PDE speakers (Kopp 1999), and data collected in 1993–95 show evidence of devoicing for nonapicals. (Recall the earlier mention in section 4.2 that there were 20 tokens of devoiced /b/ and /g/ noted in about 20 hours of recorded data—not many, yet some tokens.) This devoicing of a variety of obstruents is why a pattern for devoicing of all obstruents was discussed earlier in this chapter, and a formal phonological analysis for all obstruents is presented in this chapter, and in Anderson (2001), Davis and Anderson (2003), and Anderson and Davis (2013). The fact that nonapicals do not appear in the data collected in 2005–9 shows one area in which PDE has unraveled, even for middle-aged speakers, in the course of the last decade and a half: both middle-aged speakers and the youngest speakers of PDE have restricted their obstruent devoicing essentially to only the two obstruents /d/ and /z/, as will be shown in the analysis below.

Extreme Variability of Use of Obstruent Devoicing among Speakers. An investigation of obstruent devoicing by individual speakers reveals that there has also been a shift in individual variation in how frequently speakers use obstruent devoicing. Table 4.9 presents the rates of use of obstruent devoicing for individual speakers of the middle-aged and youngest generations, taken from data collected in 2005–9.

Note that while the middle-aged speakers each show similar rates of obstruent devoicing—the difference between them is not statistically significant, with $p = .43$ (i.e., $p > .05$)—the youngest generation shows a range from a very low 0.5% to a high of 13.6%, a difference that is statistically significant, with $p < .001$. This lack of uniformity among the youngest PDE speakers shows that not only are the youngest speakers using obstruent devoicing less than the middle-aged speakers, but they also do not exhibit consistency within themselves as to how frequently devoicing takes place. This inconsistency is yet another area in which the feature is unraveling.

Loss of Feature Complexity. Probabilistic analysis of the obstruent devoicing data collected for this study brings one more area of unraveling to light using a multivariate regression analysis provided by Goldvarb (Sankoff, Tagliamonte, and Smith 2005), a statistical tool used to describe patterns

TABLE 4.9
Individual Speaker Variation in Use of Obstruent Devoicing

	PDE Tokens	
Middle-Aged Generation		
DG (male)	102/746	(13.7%)
LM (male)	25/144	(17.4%)
LG (female)	70/451	(15.6%)
TOTAL	197/1,341	(14.7%)
Youngest Generation		
DK (male)	3/623	(0.5%)
DwK (male)	17/558	(3.0%)
LK (female)	89/656	(13.6%)
TOTAL	109/1,837	(5.9%)

of structured variation in language. (As one of the most stereotypical of the PDE dialectal variants, obstruent devoicing is also the only diagnostic phonological feature focused on in this study for which enough tokens were collected to make such a multivariate analysis possible.)[7] Given the lack of nonapical devoiced obstruents in the data (as discussed above), only tokens of /d/, /z/, and other obstruents (fricatives, to be more specific) were extracted for a further probabilistic analysis, impressionistically coded as voiced or devoiced, and coded for the following language-internal and language-external factors:

LANGUAGE-INTERNAL FACTORS[8]

Segment Quality (obstruent)
    Morphemic status
        with morphemic status
            /d/ as a past tense marker (e.g., *tagge*D)
            /z/ orthographically realized as "s" to mark possession, pluralization, or the third-person singular present tense (e.g., *brother's*, *dogs*, *hides*)
        without morphemic status
            /d/ (e.g., *bi*D)
            /z/ (e.g., *da*ze)
            other fricatives[9] (e.g., *gara*GE, *leav*E, *ba*THE)
Structure of Syllable Coda (i.e., location of obstruent in coda)
    after vowel (e.g., *ba*D)
    after liquid (e.g., *wel*D)
    before other coda consonant (e.g., *blee*DS)
Following Segment
    none (e.g., *leave* before the end of an utterance)
    vowel (e.g., *bathe* IN)
    voiced obstruent (e.g., *leave* THere, *leave* Days)
    voiceless obstruent (e.g., *leave* THree, *leave* Ten)
    sonorant[10] (e.g., *leave* Many, *leave* Less)

LANGUAGE-EXTERNAL FACTORS
Age of Speaker
    middle-aged
    youngest
Sex of Speaker
Linguistic Status of Speaker
    monodialectal
    bidialectal

When data for all monodialectal PDE speakers involved in this study were subjected to the Goldvarb analysis, the results showed that neither preceding segment (a language-internal factor) nor sex of speaker (a language-external factor) proved significant. The remaining factors patterned as shown in table 4.10, presented in order of significance. Segment quality is the most significant factor when all PDE monodialectal speakers are considered together as a group to determine when the PDE variants of various segments are devoiced. /z/ with morphemic status is most highly favored as an obstruent to devoice; /d/ without morphemic status, /z/ without morphemic status, and /d/ with morphemic status slightly favored for devoicing, or nearly to the same degree. As the table also shows, for all PDE speakers, obstruents besides /z/ and /d/—in other words, all fricatives—are highly disfavored as candidates for devoicing. /b/ and /g/ are completely disfavored, because neither are devoiced at all by any speaker in the 2005–9 data and were therefore not included in this Goldvarb analysis.

The second factor group to favor devoicing in the analysis is speaker age, with middle-aged speakers favoring devoicing over the youngest speakers. This is no surprise, considering the great difference in frequency of obstruent devoicing between the two generations shown above.

Finally, the last factor group to favor devoicing is the segment following the obstruent. For all speakers considered together, an obstruent in a position at the end of an utterance (when there is no following segment, in other words) is a prime candidate for devoicing, a pattern similar to that reported for general American English (José 2010)—although, again,

TABLE 4.10
Obstruent Devoicing: All Monodialectal PDE Speakers
($\chi^2 = 162.2986$; log likelihood = -774.688)

Factors	Tokens		Factor Weight
Segment quality			
/z/ with morphemic status	71/360	(19.7%)	0.708
/d/ without morphemic status	92/934	(9.9%)	0.526
/z/ without morphemic status	70/753	(9.3%)	0.525
/d/ with morphemic status	18/163	(11.0%)	0.524
other fricatives	13/466	(2.8%)	0.252
Age			
middle-aged	177/1,165	(15.2%)	0.657
youngest	87/1,421	(6.1%)	0.377
Following segment			
none	77/378	(20.4%)	0.693
voiced obstruent	45/434	(10.4%)	0.530
sonorant	37/389	(9.5%)	0.493
voiceless obstruent	45/493	(9.1%)	0.484
vowel	60/982	(6.1%)	0.420
TOTAL	264/2,676	(9.9%)	

remember that /b/ and /g/ are never devoiced in this data set. Obstruents in environments where they are followed by a voiced obstruent also favor devoicing; in contrast, obstruents followed by voiceless obstruents disfavor devoicing. One might expect assimilation to play a role in obstruent devoicing and thus result in greater frequency of devoicing before voiceless obstruents, but obstruent devoicing is based on prosody and so, in reality, dissimilation is the process used by PDE speakers. Obstruents followed by sonorants or vowels also disfavor devoicing.

For the remaining Goldvarb results, only language-internal characteristics were considered because each analysis involved only one age group. As mentioned above, sex of speakers was not found to be significant for either the middle-aged or youngest PDE speakers.

Table 4.11 presents the analysis for the middle-aged generation of speakers. The middle-aged PDE speakers show a relatively complicated set of factors influencing their obstruent devoicing patterns. For them, the segment following the obstruent is the most important factor in determining whether that obstruent will be devoiced: obstruents with no following segment (in other words, at the end of a phrasal unit) highly favor devoicing, whereas obstruents followed by voiced obstruents or sonorants only slightly favor devoicing. In contrast, obstruents followed by voiceless obstruents or by vowels disfavor devoicing.

The second most significant factor group for the middle-aged speakers in obstruent devoicing is segment quality. As with all PDE monodialectal speakers considered together (table 4.10), /z/ with morphemic status highly favors devoicing, but the other factors are ranked slightly differently. For this age group, /d/ with and without morphemic status both slightly favor devoicing, but /z/ without morphemic status slightly disfavors it. In agreement with the analysis of all speakers, in table 4.10, other fricatives than /z/ also disfavor devoicing.

Finally, coda structure ranks as the third most important factor in determining where devoicing occurs for middle-aged speakers. In contrast, coda structure was not deemed as significant when considering the analysis of all speakers. For the middle-aged speakers alone, obstruents that are preceded by a coda consonant of some sort (i.e., the obstruent is at a syllable boundary in a coda cluster) most highly favor devoicing; obstruents preceded by vowels or liquids, on the other hand, are either relatively neutral or disfavor devoicing.

The Goldvarb analysis for the youngest speakers reveals quite a different pattern of factors involved in devoicing, however. While the middle-aged speakers have a relatively complex set of factors that determine where obstruent devoicing occurs in their speech—a set made up of segment quality, following segment, and preceding segment—for the young-

TABLE 4.11
Obstruent Devoicing: Middle-Aged PDE Speakers
(χ^2 = 72.0957; log likelihood = −454.096)

Factors	Tokens		Factor Weight
Following segment			
none	54/165	(32.7%)	0.723
voiced obstruent	31/184	(16.8%)	0.545
sonorant	26/158	(16.5%)	0.520
voiceless obstruent	26/214	(12.1%)	0.464
vowel	40/444	(9.0%)	0.404
Segment quality			
/z/ with morphemic status	39/148	(26.4%)	0.643
/d/ without morphemic status	74/388	(19.1%)	0.587
/d/ with morphemic status	16/82	(19.5%)	0.530
/z/ without morphemic status	37/338	(10.9%)	0.453
other fricatives	11/209	(5.3%)	0.307
Coda structure			
with coda consonant	42/148	(28.4%)	0.624
after vowel	120/900	(13.3%)	0.496
after liquid	15/117	(12.8%)	0.374
TOTAL	177/1,165	(15.2%)	

est PDE speakers, only one factor, segment quality, is used to determine their patterns of devoicing. Within that factor group, these speakers match the middle-aged generation in terms of /z/ with morphemic status being the obstruent most favorable to devoicing; however, unlike the middle-aged speakers, for these youngest speakers /z/ without morphemic status also favors devoicing (the middle-aged group disfavored devoicing of that obstruent). The middle-aged generation also at least slightly favored /d/, with or without morphemic status, for devoicing; the youngest generation, however, disfavors devoicing for /d/ with and without morphemic status. Both middle-aged and youngest speakers disfavor devoicing for fricatives.

It has already been shown that the youngest PDE speakers devoice obstruents far less frequently than middle-aged PDE speakers. But the youngest group of PDE speakers has also created a greatly simplified set of factors to govern their language variation patterns for devoicing. Only one factor group, segment quality, significantly influences devoicing for the youngest speakers. Moreover, the youngest speakers have simplified the factors that favor and disfavor devoicing: /z/ (with or without morphemic status) favors obstruent devoicing, while /d/ (with or without morphemic status) and other fricatives disfavor it. This pattern is far simpler than the

TABLE 4.12
Obstruent Devoicing: Youngest PDE Speakers
(χ^2 = 71.5530; log likelihood = −305.363)

Factors	Tokens		Factor Weight
Segment quality			
/z/ with morphemic status	32/212	(15.1%)	0.807
/z/ without morphemic status	33/415	(8.0%)	0.670
/d/ without morphemic status	18/456	(3.3%)	0.445
/d/ with morphemic status	2/81	(2.5%)	0.373
other fricatives	2/257	(0.8%)	0.156
TOTAL	87/1,421	(6.1%)	

middle-aged group's, where both /z/ (with morphemic status) and /d/ (with or without morphemic status) favor devoicing, and /z/ without morphemic status and other fricatives than /z/ disfavor it. In the context of the obsolescence of the PDE dialect, not only is this feature disappearing, but the feature grammars are changing between generations of speakers.

As one last note on factors conditioning PDE obstruent devoicing, it is interesting to note that neither generation of PDE speakers seems to match the devoicing language variation patterns of other dialects of American English, at least not in terms of /z/ devoicing. José (2010) shows that the most influential factors constraining /z/ devoicing in the Midwest are (and have been, since this appears to be a stable feature) the following, in this order:

the segment (or lack of segment) following the /z/
speaker sex
morphological status of the /z/

When an analysis is made for /z/ alone for this study's PDE speakers, the middle-aged speakers show evidence for selection of morphological status first and following segment second; the youngest speakers, in their simplified grammar, do not show evidence for selection of either factor. For them, the only factor group with significance is "segment quality." Also, as mentioned earlier, sex of speaker was not found significant in the present study, perhaps because of the limited speaker pool. While these results are not conclusive in any way—coding for these data differs in many regards from that used in the José (2010) study—it does suggest that even in a context of unraveling, PDE speakers in general have not adopted a grammar for /z/ devoicing that is shared with speakers of some other dialects of American English.

4.4. WHAT DOES THIS ACCOUNT OF OBSTRUENT DEVOICING HAVE TO DO WITH SPEAKING PDE?

The variability of obstruent devoicing between the middle-aged PDE speakers and the youngest PDE speakers, as well as the extreme variation within the youngest group of PDE speakers, raises an important question about how obstruent devoicing fits into what it means to "speak PDE." The speech community considers all six of these speakers "Dutchified" (i.e., they speak PDE), but obviously there is wide variation in the amount of obstruent devoicing the generations produce and the environments in which they produce it. From the speech community's point of view, given the saliency of the feature, a little goes a long way, and in conjunction with other features, even the little bit of devoicing evidenced by DwK (a very minimal 0.5%) and DK (a paltry 3.6%) is evidently enough to "count" when determining whether an individual is "Dutchified."

From the linguist's point of view, this calls into question the issue of threshold of perception: How little devoicing can a speaker produce and still be considered (by members of the speech community) as someone who devoices? How important is devoicing overall in the feature constellation that makes up PDE? In a related vein, how little devoicing can speakers produce and the feature still be available enough for the next generation to acquire that feature? Trudgill (2004) has pointed out, for example, that features used in fewer than 5% of possible contexts are not likely to be noticed by younger speakers acquiring a language variety. Whether this threshold is the same for highly salient features like obstruent devoicing as well as for features with low salience—or if there even is a "magic number" for delineating perception—is a matter worthy of future research. To the extent that these issues can be tackled at this time, they will be addressed more fully at the end of the next chapter in a discussion of what it means to speak PDE when taking into account use of all the PDE features examined in this study.

5. OTHER PDE PHONOLOGICAL FEATURES AND THEIR USE: FURTHER EVIDENCE FOR THE UNRAVELING OF PDE

W HILE PDE OBSTRUENT DEVOICING, the most salient of all the PDE phonological features, provides the most dramatic illustration of the complexity of the phonological processes involved in the unraveling of the PDE dialect, other phonological features also offer a look into the mechanisms at work as PDE slides toward extinction. This chapter highlights the processes involved with a variety of PDE vocalic features, as well as the PDE consonantal features of /v/ and /w/ ~ [β].

5.1. THE PDE VOCALIC FEATURES

This section will focus on the following PDE vocalic features:

the monophthongization of /aʊ/ to [a] (e.g., *house* as [has])
the monophthongization of /aɪ/ to [æ] before liquids (e.g., *mile* as [mæl])
the centralization of /a/ to [ʌ] before nasals (e.g., *John* as [ʤʌn])
raised [æ] (e.g., in *last, band, had*)

These features represent a variety of relationships between the phonological systems of PDE and the regional standard of SCPE; they likewise represent a variety of different approaches in the way that speakers treat them as PDE slides toward extinction. The first feature, /aʊ/ monophthongization, elicits a high level of speaker awareness and is used to gauge a speaker's degree of "Dutchifiedness," while PDE speakers are generally unaware of the others. PDE /aʊ/ monophthongization involves the simple substitution of one vowel for another in a wholesale fashion—and is thus a "simple" rule according to Chambers (1992)—whereas two other features (/aɪ/ monophthongization and /a/ centralization) involve substitutions of vowels only in highly constrained phonological contexts—and thus invoke "complex" rules, according to Chambers (1992). Two of these PDE vocalic features involve monophthongization processes, one involves vowel centralization in certain environments, and one vowel involves a shift (raised [æ]) that differs from its SCPE counterpart. An examination of each feature will illuminate the processes at work in the demise of PDE.

73

"HOW NOW BROWN COW?:" MONOPHTHONGIZATION OF /aʊ/ TO [a]. The first vocalic feature described here is the substitution of [a] for /aʊ/ in all environments. Some examples include the following:

1. /aʊ/ → [a]
   cloud/clout (homonyms as [klat] due to syllable-final obstruent devoicing)
   clown [klan]
   house [has]
   tower [tar]

Monophthongization of /aʊ/ is referred to as a simple rule, because [a] can substitute for the diphthong in all environments, regardless of phonological context. There is no evidence that /aʊ/ monophthongization takes place any more often in high-frequency than in low-frequency words; nor is the substitution of [a] for /aʊ/ limited to any lexical set. This monophthongization occurs in both monosyllabic and polysyllabic words and is particularly striking to the listener when the /aʊ/ is followed by the unstressed syllable *-er* (as in *tower* [tar] and *power* [par]).

After obstruent devoicing, monophthongized /aʊ/ is the most commented-on feature by both PDE speakers and non-PDE speakers alike. Gates's (1987, 1998) humorous "dictionaries" and performances of PDE, for example, devote much space to this particular feature. The title of my master's thesis on PDE (Anderson 1995) included the phrase *How Now Brown Cow?* ([ha na bran ca]) in recognition of the importance speakers accord this feature as an indicator of "Dutchifiedness." As is often true with dialectal features with such a high level of awareness, this feature is also among the most stigmatized, even by the very speakers who use it (see Labov's 1972 discussion of stereotypes). One PDE speaker who took part in this study confessed that he was appalled when he saw a telecast of himself talking with a reporter just after he had won a race at a small local speedway; he regretted how often he substituted [a] for /aʊ/ in the course of his interview, and he recognized how important the feature is in defining PDE cross-generationally: "I sounded awful, just like my mom!" In terms of salience-as-speaker-awareness, monophthongization of /aʊ/ ranks at the top of the list among PDE vocalic features.

The salience of /aʊ/ monophthongization can be delineated in terms that extend beyond this simple definition of "salience as speaker awareness," however. In terms of the objective and subjective criteria put forth by Auer, Barden, and Grosskopf (1998), the monophthongization of /aʊ/ fulfills most of the following:

Objective Criteria

Articulatory Distance: YES. PDE [a] is articulatorily distant from the standard diphthong [aʊ] based on place of articulation, in a strict interpretation of Auer, Barden, and Grosskopf's articulatory distance criterion. In terms of place, [a] is a more centralized vowel than SCPE [aʊ]; in terms of manner, [a] contrasts with the SCPE diphthong [aʊ] in its status as a monophthong.

Lack of Areal Distribution: YES. While it is true that monophthongization of /aʊ/ to [a] appears in many dialects of American English as an alternate pronunciation of the high-frequency possessive pronoun *our* ([ar]) (*The American Heritage Dictionary* 2006), the substitution of [a] for /aʊ/ across the lexicon is a vowel process limited to PDE in the dialects spoken in south central Pennsylvania.

Phonemicity: YES. Since both [a] and [aʊ] are phonemes of PDE in their own right, this vowel monophthonigization process meets this criterion.

Dichotomy: NO. The data collected for this study reveal that this PDE feature involves a small number of possible gradations between SCPE [aʊ] and PDE [a], and thus this feature is deemed continuous, not dichotomous.

Lexicalization: NO. The PDE realization of /aʊ/ as [a] is not exclusive to any particular lexical set, and it applies to both content and function words, as well as to both high-frequency and low-frequency words. This variant, then, is not lexicalized for PDE speakers in any way.

Subjective Criteria

Code Alternation: YES. PDE's monophthongized /aʊ/ is used extensively in code alternation by bidialectals, an observation that will be discussed in detail in chapter 7.

Representation in Lay Writing: YES. Humorous works on the dialect, including *How to Speak Dutchified English* (Gates 1987, 1998), represent the PDE /aʊ/ monophthongization to [a] with an *a* or *ah* (e.g., "hahs" for *house*) or, in the case of words with *-ower*, as *'r* (e.g., "pow'r" for *power*).

Stereotyping and Mimicking: YES. PDE monophthongization of /aʊ/ occurs prominently in attempts to mimic PDE speech, and someone who uses this feature regularly is immediately labeled by members of the speech community as "really Dutchified." As mentioned earlier in this chapter, this is the most stereotypical feature of PDE after obstruent devoicing.

Hindrance to Comprehensibility: YES. At times the PDE /aʊ/ to [a] alternation does indeed interfere with comprehensibility, especially given the large number of minimal pairs based on distinction between the two sounds: *cloud ~ clod, down ~ Don, found ~ fond, tower ~ tar,*[1] etc.

PDE monophthongization of /aʊ/ thus meets only three of the five objective criteria for salience, but all four of the subjective criteria. This high score for perceptual salience is not surprising given the fact that it is used within the speech community as a diagnostic of a person's "Dutchifiedness," but it is interesting to note the extent to which perceptual and linguistic salience are each responsible for the total salience score of this particular feature of PDE. Note that this is exactly the same score—with the same proportions of subjective versus objective criteria met—as obstruent devoicing received in chapter 4.

Trudgill (1986) and Auer, Barden, and Grosskopf (1998) hypothesize that the more salient a feature is in a minority dialect, the more likely it is to be dropped (i.e., the less likely it is to be retained) by speakers who are acquiring features of a second dialect. Does the relatively high salience of this monophthongized /aʊ/ match with its retention rate across generations of PDE speakers? If the hypothesis about the inversely proportional connection between salience of a feature and retention rate is valid, then it is expected that PDE speakers would be abandoning the highly salient feature of /aʊ/ monophthongization across the generations. Table 5.1 shows that this is indeed the case, with available data provided for this feature across three generations of speakers. The data from the oldest generation were collected in 1993–95 and recorded only the percentage of monophthongized tokens used by each speaker; data for the middle-aged and youngest generations of speakers (today's 30–40-year-olds) were collected in 2005–9, as described in the chapter 2, and include token counts. Five of the speakers from the oldest generation—most of whom are now deceased—are/were bilingual in Pennsylvania German and English, with Pennsylvania German as their first language, while all the informants from the middle-aged and youngest generations are monolingual in English. To disaggregate the data to the extent possible with regard to bilingual/monolingual status, the percentage recorded for the single female monolingual PDE speaker in the oldest generation is delineated by parentheses. It is her frequency of monophthongization (100%) that will be referred to in the calculations of retention and loss rates below, since the middle-aged and youngest participants in this study are also English monolinguals. In this way assessment of monophthongization cannot be said to be affected by some kind of possible residual transfer effect in the acquisition of English as a second language for any of the speakers in this sample.

Despite the special considerations inherent in utilizing the data from the oldest PDE speakers, it provides a valuable increase of time depth in an examination of the abandonment of this vocalic feature. Table 5.1 shows frequency of the use of PDE monophthongized /aʊ/ by the three generations of speakers: the 30–40-year-olds, who are the last speakers of PDE; their parents' generation (speakers in their 60s); and the bilinguals and monolingual of their grandparents' generation (who were in their 60s and 70s at the time of recording, but who are or would have been today in their 80s and 90s). Table 5.2 presents an account of how greatly frequencies have changed in each generation, calculated by simply subtracting percentages of use of the feature of one generation from the rate of the generation(s) which preceded them. Table 5.2 also shows the relative rates at which each generation has retained the feature in comparison to the generation(s) preceding them.

The data in table 5.1 indicate clearly that this highly salient monophthonization feature is employed to some degree by every generation of PDE speakers interviewed for this study. EY, the oldest PDE-speaking monolingual, used the PDE variant categorically (at a higher rate than even her Pennsylvania German–PDE bilingual peers), but the rates for the middle generation of speakers show evidence for a high degree of loss of this

TABLE 5.1

Overview of Rates of PDE /aʊ/ Monophthongization

Generation		Rate of Devoicing
Oldest		86.2%
EY (only monolingual)		100.0%
Middle-Aged	137/209	65.6%
Youngest	37/187	19.8%

TABLE 5.2

Changes in Frequency and Relative Retention Rates
for PDE /aʊ/ Monophthongization

Generation Compared	Change in Percentage	Retention Rate
Oldest to Middle-Aged	−34.4%	65.6%
Middle-Aged to Youngest	−45.6%	30.5%
Oldest to Youngest	−81.2%	19.8%

monophthongized feature, since their retention rate for this feature is only 65.6% that of the monolingual English speaker from the oldest generation. The youngest generation shows evidence for an even more accelerated reduction in rates of /aʊ/ monophthongization, with a retention rate of only 30.5% of that of the middle-aged generation (and only 19.8% of that of the oldest monolingual).

Trudgill (1986) and Auer, Barden, and Grosskopf (1998) proposed that a highly salient feature is more likely to be abandoned by speakers acquiring a second dialect than a low-salience feature. Do these PDE frequency and retention rates for this high-salience monophthongization of /aʊ/ support this claim? In this case, the high measure of salience of /aʊ/ monophthongization does indeed correctly predict the abandonment of this feature by PDE speakers as they converge toward SCPE.

Evidence of Unraveling in /aʊ/ Monophthongization. The erosion of /aʊ/ monophthongization in PDE is not merely a matter of speakers using the feature less frequently, however. Use of this feature is changing (i.e., this feature is unraveling) in two ways: in the frequencies with which individual speakers use monophthongization in the middle-aged and youngest generations and in the phonological constraints governing the environments in which /aʊ/ monophthongization occurs. These two areas are discussed in turn below.

Extreme Variability of Use of Obstruent Devoicing among Individual Speakers. While the use of /aʊ/ monophthongization by each generation clearly shows a trend toward reduced incidence of this PDE phonological feature, the individual percentages reveal a more complex picture. Table 5.3 shows that both middle-aged and younger speakers of PDE show evidence for a wide range of variability among themselves for /aʊ/ monophthongization.

Although the two middle-aged males in the sample exhibit high rates of /aʊ/ monophthongization (74.6% and 89.5%) that roughly approximate the overall rate of the oldest bilingual speakers (although they are not quite as high as the rate of the oldest monolingual English speaker), the single middle-aged female speaker used the variant MUCH less frequently (40.6% of the time).[2] This variability between speakers is even more acute among the informants from the youngest generation: DK, the speaker who makes the most use of this monophthong and whose "Dutchifiedness" is predominantly indicated by his use of the PDE monophthong (this will become apparent in the discussion to follow of what it means to speak PDE today), exhibits a frequency rate of 38.5%, only slightly less than that of the lowest-scoring speaker of the middle generation (the female speaker just mentioned). The other two young speakers, DwK and LK, exhibit rates (10.6%

TABLE 5.3
Individual Speaker's Use of /aʊ/ Monophthongization

	PDE Tokens	*Range of Frequencies*
Middle-Aged Generation		
DG (male)	94/126 (74.6%)	
LM (male)	17/19 (89.5%)	
LG (female)	26/64 (40.6%)	
TOTAL	137/209 (65.6%)	26/64 (40.6%) – 17/19 (89.5%)
Youngest Generation (30–40 years old)		
DK (male)	25/65 (38.5%)	
DwK (male)	5/47 (10.6%)	
LK (female)	7/75 (9.3%)	
TOTAL	37/187 (19.8%)	7/75 (9.3%) – 26/65 (38.5%)

and 9.3%, resp.) that are significantly different statistically from DK's rate (p = .013 and .002, resp.). From this data set (with its single monolingual English speaker in the oldest generation), it is impossible to tell if there has long been a large degree of variability in /aʊ/ monophthongization among PDE speakers, but the lack of uniformity among the middle-aged and youngest generations is nonetheless striking. This lack of uniformity among the last two generations of PDE speakers shows that not only are the speakers using obstruent devoicing less frequently with each successive generation, but they also do not exhibit frequencies that are consistent with each other within their generational cohorts.

Loss of Feature Complexity. Further examination of the available data for the last two generations of speakers also reveals that the youngest generation of PDE speakers favors different phonological environments for the variant's use than the middle-aged generation does. (This is also what was revealed for obstruent devoicing in chapter 3.) As it turns out, the two generations differ in how they treat /aʊ/ in open syllables (e.g., *now*) versus closed syllables (e.g., *house*).

Table 5.4 shows that the middle-aged PDE speakers—while they monophthongize /aʊ/ more often than not in both open and closed syllables—actually monophthongize /aʊ/ at a significantly greater rate when the vowel is in a closed syllable compared to when it is in an open syllable (p = .012). Conversely, there is no real difference in how the youngest PDE speakers treat open syllables versus closed syllables when they monophthongize; this group does not favor monophthongization in either context, but when they do, their rates of monophthongization do not differ significantly

TABLE 5.4

Frequency for /aʊ/ Monophthongization for Two Generations of PDE Speakers

Syllable Type	Monophthongized	Not Monophthongized	Significance
Middle-Aged Generation			
open	38/69 (55.1%)	31/69 (44.9%)	$\chi^2 = 6.261; p = .012$
closed	100/138 (72.5%)	38/138 (27.5%)	
Youngest Generation			
open	13/60 (21.7%)	47/60 (78.3%)	$\chi^2 = 0.842; p = .359$
closed	20/124 (16.1%)	104/124 (83.9%)	

in either context ($p = .359$). This split between the generations in the use of phonological context to determine rates of /aʊ/ monophthongization is one way in which this PDE feature is unraveling among its last generations of speakers: as was the case with obstruent devoicing, PDE speakers of the youngest generation appear to have lost the middle-aged generation's complexity of phonological conditioning that governs the rule for use of this particular monophthongization feature.

What Does This Have to Do with Speaking PDE? The speech community considers all six of these informants PDE speakers, but obviously there is wide variation in the amount of /aʊ/ monophthongization they produce and the environments in which they produce it. From the speech community's point of view concerning such a salient feature, LK's 9.3% is enough to count—perhaps along with the production of other features—to mark her as a PDE speaker or to discuss how "Dutchified" she is. In a parallel fashion, DK's high use of this feature compared to his agemates (38.5%) is enough to mark him as a PDE speaker as well, even though his use of other PDE features is minimal. These observations will be revisited in the discussion at the end of this chapter about what it means—in a context of variability for this dying dialect—to be a PDE speaker.

"PARROTS IN SOMALIA": PRELIQUID MONOPHTHONGIZATION OF /aɪ/ TO [æ]. The second vocalic feature that involves monophthongization in PDE substitutes /aɪ/ with [æ] before liquids. Whereas the monophthongization of /aʊ/ takes place in all phonological contexts in PDE, the environment for the monophthongization of /aɪ/ is constrained solely to preliquid environments. Below are some examples in which this feature occurs, both word-internally and word-initially:

2. /aɪ/ → [æ]/__L
   tire [tær]

tile [tæl]

aisle [æl]

island [ˈælənd]

iron [ærn] (pronounced as a single syllable)

pilot, pallet [ˈpælət]

pirate, parrot [ˈpærət]

This monophthongization takes place regardless of the place of the liquid in the syllable structure of the word; note that the [æ] variant occurs both in one-syllable words when the liquid is the coda of the syllable (e.g., *tire, tile*) and in multisyllabic words when the liquid is in the onset of the next syllable (e.g., *island, iron*).[3] Even though this particular monophthongization process changes the quality of the vowel just as drastically as the monophthongization of /aʊ/ to [a], it does not attract the overt notice of PDE or SCPE speakers, perhaps because this monophthongization occurs in such a constrained phonological environment. English words with /aɪ/ + liquid are relatively rare—far rarer than words with /aʊ/ in any phonological context, at any rate, as evidenced by the low numbers of tokens in the data (see table 5.5). This monophthongization of /aɪ/ in PDE is a complex rule according to Chambers's (1992) criteria, based on the restriction of environments in which it can occur.

In terms of a generic definition of salience as "speaker-awareness," this feature ranks very low for the PDE speech community. In terms of Auer, Barden, and Grosskopf's (1998) specific criteria for salience, however, it ends up garnering a mid-range score, as shown here:

Objective (Linguistic) Criteria

Articulatory Distance: YES. PDE [æ] is articulatorily distant from [ai] in these preliquid contexts in terms of place of articulation ([æ] is a mid-vowel while [ai] is a diphthong that ends on a high vowel); it also differs in manner of articulation (the transformation of an underlying diphthong into a monophthong).

Lack of Areal Distribution: YES. Non-PDE speakers in the south central Pennsylvania area do not monophthongize /aɪ/ to [æ] before liquids for any lexical items, nor has this feature made its way in any form into general American English speech. Southern American English speakers also monophthongize /aɪ/, but they typically monophthongize it to [aː], either in all phonological environments or at the ends of words and before voiced (but not voiceless) consonants, depending on the particular dialect of Southern American English they speak.

Phonemicity: YES. The PDE monophthong neutralizes the contrast between /aɪ/ and /æ/ in the context of a liquid by mapping both onto [æ], a vowel with phonemic status, but /aɪ/ also has phonemic status in PDE.

Dichotomy: NO. A number of gradations between [aɪ] and [æ] are possible for PDE speakers, and so this feature is considered to be continuous.

Lexicalization: NO. There is no particular set of words to which this PDE monophthongization of /aɪ/ applies; nor does frequency seem to have any effect on the rates at which PDE speakers monophthongize /aɪ/.

Subjective (Perceptual) Criteria

Code Alternation: YES. The PDE-SCPE bidialectal whose data is related in chapter 7 uses PDE monophthongized /aɪ/ some of the time when she is speaking PDE, but not SCPE.

Representation in Lay Writing: NO. There is no evidence available of PDE monophthongized /aɪ/ appearing in any form in writing of the PDE dialect.

Stereotyping/Mimicking: NO. The PDE preliquid monophthongized /aɪ/ is not commented upon or used in stereotyping or mimicking by either PDE or non-PDE speakers in the south central Pennsylvania area.

Hindrance to Comprehensibility: YES. The PDE monophthongization of /aɪ/ does indeed hinder comprehensibility,[4] but PDE speakers are still not aware of it.

This PDE feature classifies as having a medium amount of salience according to these criteria, since it meets three of the five objective (linguistic) criteria and two of the four subjective (perceptual) criteria. This is somewhat lower than the number of criteria met by the PDE monophthongization of /aʊ/, although the number of objective criteria met by both features is equivalent. The key subjective criteria of "use in stereotyping/mimicking" is not met, however, and that seems to encapsulate the large difference in speaker awareness between the two types of monophthongization. The mid-level degree of salience according to objective and subjective criteria together for /aɪ/ monophthongization would imply, according to Auer, Barden, and Grosskopf's (1998) assertion that more salient features are more likely to be abandoned, that the PDE preliquid monophthongization of /aɪ/ MAY or MAY NOT be eroding across the generations of speakers (i.e., here level of salience would not be expected to have predictive power). However, as the data in table 5.5 show, the feature is indeed being abandoned as the youngest generation uses it with much lower frequency than the middle-aged generation, the two generations for whom data are available from interviews conducted in 2005–9. (Data for the oldest generation of speakers collected from 1993–95 were not analyzed for this dialect feature, and so results for that age group are not available.) Table 5.6 shows the overall loss of this feature as a calculation of the difference between the rates of use of the middle and the youngest generations, as well as the retention rate for the feature by the youngest speakers, calculated according to the same formula used in table 5.2 in the section on /aʊ/ monophthongization.

The data for this PDE feature, such as it is with such low token counts, show that /aɪ/ monophthongization is in fact being abandoned at a prodigious rate, since there has been such a huge change (−56.9%) in the rate with which the youngest generation of speakers uses it compared to the middle-aged speakers. It is possible that the low number of tokens is hiding some of the vigor of this dialectal feature among either middle-aged or younger PDE speakers, but it is more likely that this PDE feature is truly being abandoned by speakers, and the stated retention rate of 10.5% (calculated according to the overall rates for each group of speakers, whether token counts were low or not for any individual) will serve this study's purposes for comparison of retention rates across phonological features. Regarding the connection between level of salience and feature retention/loss, it would appear that having a mid-level of salience does not render a dialect feature immune from erosion nor is its erosion rate mitigated by the fact that its salience level is somewhere above "low."

TABLE 5.5
Overview of Rates of PDE /aɪ/ Monophthongization

Generation	Rate of Devoicing	
Middle-Aged	7/11	63.6%
Youngest	1/15	6.7%

TABLE 5.6
Changes in Frequency and Relative Retention Rates
of PDE /aɪ/ Monophthongization

Generation Compared	Change in Percentage
Middle-Aged to Youngest	
Change in Percentage	−56.9%
Overall Retention Rate	10.5%

Extreme Variability of Use of Obstruent Devoicing among Individual Speakers.
While the overall frequencies of /aɪ/ monophthongization for the two generations clearly show a severe reduction in this PDE phonological feature,
the detailed picture is more complex. Individual speakers' use of the feature is listed in table 5.7.

As discussed earlier, token counts are quite low for this particular feature; in this unelicited data set taken from natural conversation, two of the
three middle-aged speakers (LG and LM) only have two instances each
in which the PDE monophthongized variant could occur, and one of the
youngest speakers (DK) has only one. Of these speakers, one (middle-aged
LM) uses the PDE variant categorically in his few tokens, while middle-aged
LG and young DwK do not use the variant at all, at least in the interview setting (although at least LG has been observed using it in informal contexts
away from a recorder).[5] It is noteworthy that the speakers in the youngest
generation in this study, with seven possible instances to use the feature,
either do not use the feature at all (like both DK and DwK) or use it at a
fraction of the rate exhibited by the middle-aged speakers (as does LK).

What Does This Have to Do with Speaking PDE? As with the other features, the
speech community considers that each of these six speakers speaks PDE,
but obviously there is wide variation in the amount of /aɪ/ monophthongization they produce. Assuming the oldest generation of speakers (recorded
in 1993–95, but from whom data were not collected for this particular feature) did indeed monopthongize /aɪ/, the fact that middle-aged LG and
youngest speakers DwK and DK do not use the feature at all suggests that
the feature has become unstable and as such is now categorized as "nones-
sential" in terms of what makes a speaker "Dutchified."

TABLE 5.7
Individual Speaker's Use of /aɪ/ Monophthongization

	PDE Tokens	Range of Frequencies
Middle-Aged Generation		
DG (male)	5/7 (71.4%)	
LM (male)	2/2 (100.0%)	
LG (female)	0/2 (0.0%)	
TOTAL	7/11 (63.6%)	0/2 (0.0%) – 2/2 (100.0%)
Youngest Generation (30–40 years old)		
DK (male)	0/1 (0.0%)	
DwK (male)	0/7 (0.0%)	
LK (female)	1/7 (14.3%)	
TOTAL	1/15 (6.7%)	0/1 (0.0%) – 1/7 (14.3%)

"I WONDER AS I WANDER": PRENASAL /a/ CENTRALIZATION. Another vocalic feature of PDE is the centralization of /a/ to [ʌ] before nasals. This centralization occurs whether the nasal in question is in the coda of the syllable with the /a/ or is in the onset of the following syllable, as in the examples below:

3. /a/ → [ʌ] / __ N
   conference ['kʌnfrəns]
   Bon Ton [bʌn tʌn] (name of a high-end department store)
   continental [ˌkʌntɪ'nɛntəl]
   honor ['ʌnɚ]
   bomb, bum [bʌm]
   wander ~ wonder ['wʌntɚ]

Like the preliquid monophthongization of /aɪ/ to [æ], discussed in the last section, this PDE centralized variant of the low vowel /a/ before a nasal is noted by neither PDE nor SCPE speakers, despite the fact that this feature is used categorically by the middle-aged PDE speakers in this study. This centralization is a complex rule according to Chamber's (1992) criteria, involving substitution in a constrained phonological environment. This centralization rule applies in syllables with both primary and secondary stress (e.g., in both *cónference* and *còntinéntal*) and both in cases where the /a/ is preceded by a consonant (*bomb*) and where it is not (*honor*). In PDE, as in general American English, unstressed syllables with the same phonological context are pronounced with [ə] (e.g., *concíse, consólidate*). Although the context in which /a/ centralization occurs is more prevalent in naturalistic data than the preliquid context for /aɪ/ monophthongization, tokens are not particularly abundant for this variant either, as the data below will demonstrate.

In terms of salience-as-speaker awareness, this feature ranks quite low for PDE, but how salient is it according to the objective and subjective criteria from Auer, Barden, and Grosskopf (1998) outlined earlier?

Objective Criteria

Articulatory Distance: YES. While both [a] and [ʌ] are centralized vowels, [a] is a low, front, centralized vowel, while the PDE variant [ʌ] is a mid, back, centralized vowel. Although the same in terms of manner of articulation (the two variants are monophthongs), the two are articulatorily distant from each other based on place of articulation.

Lack of Areal Distribution: NO. Prenasal [ʌ] is a feature that is exhibited in even the stressed syllables of certain words by some speakers of SCPE and other regional dialects in the area as an alternative pronunciation for certain lexical items, such as *compass* (['kam.pəs] or ['kʌmpəs]) and *concrete* (['kankrit] or ['kʌnkrit]). Hence, there is a certain amount of areal distribution of this feature in south central Pennsylvania.

Phonemicity: YES. While not very distant from either /a/ (which has phonemic status in American English varieties) or [ə] (which does not), PDE [ʌ] does indeed have phonemic status.

Dichotomy: YES. There is at least one intermediate step possible between the PDE prenasal [ʌ] and SCPE [a], namely [ɐ], although it was not observed in the data collected from either PDE or SCPE speakers. Thus, for the purposes of this study, the PDE dialectal variant [ʌ] is considered dichotomous.

Lexicalization: NO. The data do not indicate that the PDE [ʌ] variant is restricted to any lexical set, although terms of address like *Mom* and names like *John* and *Donna* make up a large proportion of tokens in which the centralized variant appears.

Subjective (Perceptual) Criteria

Code Alternation: YES. The PDE prenasal [ʌ] for /a/ is used by the bidialectal presented in chapter 6 when she is speaking PDE but not when she is speaking SCPE.

Representation in Lay Writing: NO. This [ʌ] prenasal variant of /a/, a feature not noted by most PDE speakers, has no representation in lay writing of the dialect.

Stereotyping/Mimicking: NO. Non-PDE speakers do not exhibit awareness of PDE prenasal [ʌ] and do not utilize it in stereotyping or mimicking PDE speakers.

Hindrance to Comprehensibility: YES. In a very few instances, the use of the [ʌ] prenasal variant of /a/ by PDE speakers does affect comprehensibility, as in minimal pairs *wander ~ wonder*, *Tommy ~ tummy*, and *bomb~bum*.

The PDE prenasal [ʌ] variant meets approximately half the criteria for salience set out by Auer, Barden, and Grosskopf (1998) and thus rates as mid-level on the salience scale, as did the preliquid monopthongization of /aɪ/; like its counterpart, it meets three of the five objective criteria and two of the four subjective criteria. Like its counterpart, it also fails to meet the criterion of "used in stereotyping/mimicking" that is so important in encapsulating speaker awareness of a feature. Since /a/ centralization's salience lies somewhere between "low" and "high," it is unclear whether this feature is likely to erode. The data, however, show that this feature, like every feature discussed thus far, is declining at a rapid pace. Table 5.8 shows average rates of this feature from the two generations for which data were available (the middle-aged and youngest generations), and table 5.9 relates the change in rate of use by the youngest speakers in comparison with the middle-aged speakers, as well as the retention rate of the feature by the youngest generation (compared to the middle-aged generation).

As with /aɪ/ monophthongization, it would appear that the mid-level of salience for prenasal /a/ centralization does not render it immune to erosion, nor does the fact that the middle-aged speakers of PDE used this variant categorically in the recorded data. This feature, like so many others in PDE, has lost ground dramatically among the youngest speakers.

Extreme Variability of /a/ Centralization among Individual Speakers and What This Has to Do with Speaking PDE. While the overall group rates of /a/ centralization clearly show a reduction in use of this PDE phonological feature, the individual percentages paint a more complex picture. Table 5.10 shows that while middle-aged speakers use the feature categorically, the younger speakers of PDE show evidence for a wide range of variability among themselves.

As mentioned earlier, there are not abundant tokens of this feature in the data set; in fact, two of the middle-aged speakers had only one or two lexical items in which /a/ could be centralized to [ʌ]. It is nonetheless interesting that the middle-aged speakers used the centralized variant cat-

TABLE 5.8
Overview of Rates of PDE /a/ Centralization

Generation	Rate of Devoicing	
Middle-Aged	20/20	100.0%
Youngest	3/35	8.6%

TABLE 5.9
Changes in Frequency and Relative Retention Rates of PDE /a/ Centralization

Generation Compared	Change in Percentage
Middle-Aged to Youngest	
Change in Percentage	–91.4%
Overall Retention Rate	8.6%

TABLE 5.10
Individual Speaker's Use of /a/ Centralization

	PDE Tokens	*Range of Frequencies*
Middle-Aged Generation		
DG (male)	17/17 (100.0%)	
LM (male)	2/2 (100.0%)	
LG (female)	1/1 (100.0%)	
TOTAL	20/20 (100.0%)	20/20 (100.0%)
Youngest Generation (30–40 years old)		
DK (male)	2/10 (20.0%)	
DwK (male)	0/12 (0.0%)	
LK (female)	1/13 (8.0%)	
TOTAL	3/35 (8.6%)	0/12 (0.0%) – 2/10 (20.0%)

egorically, not just the low-token speakers LM and LG, but also the speaker with 17 tokens, DG. But even if the low numbers of tokens for LM and LG do not accurately represent their use of the PDE centralization of /a/, it still shows that the [ʌ] variant is definitely part of their linguistic repertoire. The youngest speakers seem to exhibit very different behavior from the middle-aged generation: none of the three used the variant more than 20% of the time (DK had the highest percentage with 20.0%), and DwK did not use the variant at all; the combined use for the three youngest speakers is a mere 8.6% of the overall use for the middle-aged generation (based on the data available). Of all the PDE features that will be discussed in this chapter, the erosion of centralized /a/ is the most dramatic, and, the wide range of frequencies evidenced by the youngest speakers show that this feature is also unraveling as an indicator of the PDE dialect.

VOWEL QUALITY: PDE RAISED [æ]. PDE's raised [æ] is unique in this study's list of phonological features because it involves a difference in vowel quality rather than some other vowel-transforming process. In the data collected for this study in natural conversational contexts, speakers who use this feature raise the low front vowel [æ] to a more mid vowel position, almost to the level of the front mid vowel [ɛ], in both open and closed syllables. This variant of [æ] is slightly lengthened compared to SCPE [æ], but it is not diphthongized like the well-known Mid-Atlantic tensed [æ]—which has a more pronounced inglide, [eːə]—documented in New York and Philadelphia (Labov, Ash, and Boberg 2006).

As with the PDE variants of monophthongized /aɪ/ and centralized /a/, the PDE raised [æ] is a feature of which speakers have no overt awareness. Nevertheless, this variant is relatively pervasive among PDE speakers and serves in the south central Pennsylvania speech community as one means to distinguish PDE speakers from SCPE speakers, even in the absence of other features of PDE in a person's speech. Such is the case with young speaker DwK, presented below as part of the discussion of what it means to speak PDE.

Raised [æ] occurs frequently in the data collected, so for the purposes of maintaining consistency in phonological environment in this analysis, the word *yeah* (a lexical item with [æ] in an open syllable) was the item specifically coded for. PDE raised [æ] occurs in closed syllables and other open-syllable words as well, but *yeah* was by far the most common single lexical item containing either SCPE (nonraised) [æ] or PDE (raised) [æ] used by speakers in this data set; speakers who used raised [æ] in *yeah* used the variant in other lexical items as well, even though they were not coded for. In this set, no distinction was made between *yeah* as an indicator of agreement and *yeah* as a back channel mechanism.

In terms of salience as speaker awareness, this feature again rates very low in the south central Pennsylvania speech community, just as the last two vocalic features did. So how salient is this feature according to the criteria developed by Auer, Barden, and Grosskopf (1998)?

Objective (Linguistic) Criteria

Articulatory Distance: NO. PDE raised [æ] exhibits very little articulatory distance from its nonraised version, especially since it is not quite as high as [ɛ].

Lack of Areal Distribution: YES. The PDE raised [æ] is not observed in the speech of the SCPE monodialectals in this study, and there is no evidence that it has undergone any areal distribution, although there are various realizations of tensed and raised [æ] in other American English dialects (see Labov, Ash, and Boberg 2006).

Phonemicity: NO. The PDE tensed [æ] definitely varies in a subphonemic fashion from its SCPE counterpart.

Dichotomy: NO. It is likely that there are indeed intermediate stages between the PDE raised [æ] and the SCPE [æ], and it is probable that there is some kind of identifiable threshold beyond which the south central Pennsylvania listener would label a speaker's [æ] as sounding like it was spoken by a PDE speaker rather than an SCPE speaker. Further acoustic analysis would identify this point. For now, this variant is considered to be continuous.

Lexicalization: NO. Although this study coded for raised [æ] only in the word *yeah* for the sake of consistency, PDE raised [æ] is not limited to any particular lexical set.

Subjective (Perceptual) Criteria

Code Alternation: YES. The bidialectal featured in this study in chapter 7 uses this PDE feature when she is speaking PDE, but not when she is speaking SCPE.

Representation in Lay Writing: NO. PDE raised [æ] has no representation in lay writing and does not appear in any form in Gates's (1987, 1998) dictionaries.

Use in Stereotyping/Mimicking: NO. PDE raised [æ] is not used in either of these capacities.

Hindrance to Comprehensibility: NO. There is no evidence that PDE raised [æ] is a hindrance to comprehensibility, even though it is raised toward the vowel [ɛ] and there are numerous minimal pairs that would involve a distinction between these vowels (i.e., [æ] and [ɛ]), such as *bad ~ bed* and *sad ~ said*. It does not appear that listeners in south central Pennsylvania mistake the raised [æ] for [ɛ] in any of these contexts.

PDE raised [æ] thus scores quite low on the salience scale, fulfilling only one of the five objective criteria and one of the four subjective criteria. According to the assertion that the features speakers most readily abandon in second dialect acquisition are those which are highly salient, this extremely low salience score for PDE raised [æ] would imply that it is a variant which is not eroding across the generations of PDE speakers. Is this supported by the data compiled for this study?

Table 5.11 shows the rate of use of this feature for the two generations of speakers for whom data are available; table 5.12 presents the change in percentage of use of PDE tokens of the youngest generation compared to the middle-aged generation, as well as the rate of retention of the feature between the middle-aged and youngest generations of speakers:

Trudgill (1986) and Auer et al. (1998) made the assertion that highly salient features are more likely to be abandoned by speakers in a dialect contact situation; the converse implication is that features with low salience are less likely to be abandoned by speakers. The comparison of rates of use of PDE raised [æ] appear to support this latter implication: overall, PDE raised [æ] is holding its ground from the middle to the youngest generation of PDE speakers.[6]

TABLE 5.11
Overview of Rates of PDE [æ] Raising

Generation	Rate of Devoicing	
Middle-Aged	25/158	15.8%
Youngest	21/128	16.4%

TABLE 5.12
Changes in Frequency and Relative Retention Rates of PDE [æ] Raising

Generation Compared	Change in Percentage
Middle-Aged to Youngest	
Change in Percentage	+0.6%
Overall Retention Rate	103.8%

Extreme Variability in Use of PDE Raised [æ]. Despite the fact that this feature is not eroding in PDE, it is nonetheless unstable. As in the cases of the other phonological variants presented, frequencies for individual speakers vary widely, even though neither generation uses it more frequently than the other to a statistically significant degree ($\chi^2 = .013$; $p < .05$), as shown in table 5.13.

The two speakers with the lowest rates of use are middle-aged speaker DG (1.9%), and youngest-generation speaker DK (2.6%). The speaker with the highest occurrence of this variant is DwK (34.7%) from the youngest generation; interestingly, in his case, the bulk of his "Dutchifiedness" (his use of PDE features) rests in his relatively prevalent use of this PDE raised [æ]—he exhibits a low rates of use for the other PDE features, as will be shown later. Why this might be the case will be discussed in greater detail in

TABLE 5.13
Individual Speaker's Use of [æ] Raising

	PDE Tokens		Range of Frequencies
Middle-Aged Generation			
DG (male)	1/52	(1.9%)	
LM (male)	6/22	(27.3%)	
LG (female)	18/74	(24.3%)	
TOTAL	25/148	(16.9%)	1/52 (1.9%) – 6/22 (27.3%)
Youngest Generation (30–40 years old)			
DK (male)	1/39	(2.6%)	
DwK (male)	17/49	(34.7%)	
LK (female)	3/40	(7.5%)	
TOTAL	21/128	(16.4%)	1/39 (2.6%) – 17/49 (34.7%)

the last section of this chapter as part of an overall discussion of the unraveling of PDE. However, the retention of this unstable feature by PDE speakers seems to support the assertion that a low-salience feature is less likely to be abandoned by speakers who are in contact with a second dialect.

How is this particular feature contributing to the unraveling of the PDE dialect? The robustness of raised [æ] across the generations of PDE speakers means that it is not declining in frequency of use. There is also no indication that these data (focused on the single word *yeah*) point out any differences between the generations in terms of constraints on when the raised [æ] variant is or is not used. Nevertheless, it must be kept in mind that these 30–40-year-old PDE speakers are from the last generation of speakers of PDE, and despite the frequencies seen here, this feature too will disappear when PDE is extinct: PDE raised [æ] has not been observed in the speech of the 30–40-year-olds' (non-PDE-speaking) children.

5.2. PDE CONSONANTAL FEATURES: [w] FOR /v/ AND [β] FOR /w/

This study concludes its presentation of PDE phonological variants and their part in the unraveling of the dialect by turning to two consonantal features and showing how their use has changed over the decades for the middle-aged and youngest generations of PDE speakers.

[w] FOR /v/. Recall from the description of the PDE dialect given in chapter 2 that /v/ in strong positions in words (i.e., word-initial position or in the onset of stressed syllables) has historically been pronounced as [w] by speakers of PDE. This was not a feature coded for in this study, but I observed while living among PDE speakers that this feature too is eroding at a tremendous rate, both between generations and within the middle-aged generation. This feature is highly salient and is part of the repertoire of features commented on by PDE and SCPE speakers alike when talking about individuals who are quite "Dutchified." According to the salience criteria laid out by Auer, Barden, and Grosskopf (1998), it also rates highly, even more highly than obstruent devoicing and /aʊ/ monophthongization:

Objective (Linguistic) Criteria

Articulatory Distance: YES. The use of [w] for /v/, while retaining a bilabial place of articulation, involves a change in manner of articulation with the necessary lip rounding.

Lack of Areal Distribution: YES. This feature is not observed in the speech of the SCPE monodialectals in this study, and there is no evidence that it has undergone any areal distribution.

Phonemicity: YES. /v/ and /w/ are indeed separate phonemes in PDE; in fact, in "weak" contexts (i.e., contexts that are not word-initial or in the onsets of stressed syllables), /v/ is a candidate for devoicing to [f].

Dichotomy: YES. [v] and [w] are not continuous.

Lexicalization: NO. The realization of /v/ as [w] is not limited to any particular lexical set, and includes a wide range of content and function words, such as proper nouns (*Vicki*), common nouns (*victory*), adverbs (*very*), etc.

Subjective (Perceptual) Criteria

Code Alternation: NO. Although the bidialectal speaker featured in this study in chapter 7 uses many other PDE features when she is speaking PDE, this feature is not one of them.

Representation in Lay Writing: YES. This variant is realized as "w" in lay writing and in Gates's (1987, 1998) dictionaries.

Use in Stereotyping/Mimicking: YES. This variant is commonly evoked by those mimicking the dialect, by PDE and SCPE speakers alike.

Hindrance to Comprehensibility: YES. On occasion this variant does lead to obstacles to comprehension, especially with proper names unfamiliar to the listener and in a few minimal pairs, such as *vine ~ wine*.

Thus, the PDE realization of /v/ as [w] fulfills four of Auer, Barden, and Grosskopf's objective criteria and three of their four subjective criteria. With such a high measure of salience—and its use in stereotyping/mimicry in particular—it is a prime candidate for abandonment by the youngest generation of speakers.

This is indeed the situation in south central Pennsylvania. Substitution of [w] for /v/ is noticeable in the speech of both the oldest speakers and middle-aged speakers of both sexes, but not younger speakers (including the bidialectal in chapter 7). This is not in itself that surprising, given the abandonment of almost every other PDE phonological feature by the youngest participants in this study in comparison to the middle-aged generation. What is more surprising is that even among middle-aged speakers, its use is receding among certain groups. For example, data collected from

1993–95 show that two males, both PDE speakers, usually—if not always—pronounce my first name as [wɪki]. In the data collected in 2005–9, however, they pronounce it with a full [v]. One of these informants, a pastor, shared with me that he has worked hard to eradicate the PDE feature from his speech, since he feels that it does not befit sermon delivery style. In contrast, two females from the same age cohort and social set as these men retain a strong [w] for /v/, even in relatively formal contexts (i.e., speaking in front of a congregation at church). Because this feature was not one that was coded for in the collected data, there are no token counts of frequency data available, but it appears that this PDE feature is disappearing, just as the use of [tʃ] for the affricate /dʒ/ has, and that men might be at the forefront of the change.

While this highly salient feature is often evoked in mimicking the dialect, its total absence among the youngest speakers shows that it is not a core feature in determining who is and who is not a speaker of PDE. The complete abandonment of this feature by the youngest generation of speakers, as well as the conscious abandonment of the feature by middle-aged PDE speakers, shows that this feature is eroding both across generations and within at least one generation who uses it.

THE BILABIAL FRICATIVE FOR /w/. The description in chapter 3 of the PDE dialect stated that one of the consonantal features of the dialect is the substitution of the bilabial fricative [β] for /w/ in "strong" environments (i.e., in word-initial positions or in the onset of a stressed syllables). Sociolinguistically, this substitution is somewhat complex in terms of its relationships with age, sex, and language attitudes: the oldest speakers and youngest monodialectal speakers of PDE do not utilize [β] at all in the collected data, but the middle-aged speakers of both sexes and the bidialectal speaker in chapter 7 do. Table 5.14 indicates the frequencies with which the middle-aged informants in this study used this variant.

This variant is low with regard to "salience as speaker awareness"; no generation of speakers makes any reference to this particular variant, even

TABLE 5.14
Frequency of Use of [β] for /w/ by Middle-Aged PDE Speakers

Middle-Aged Generation		
DG (male)	125/452	(27.7%)
LM (male)	20/80	(25.0%)
LG (female)	12/222	(5.4%)
TOTAL	157/754	(20.8%)

though it is as robust among the middle-aged generation of speakers as other phonological variants discussed thus far. In terms of Auer, Barden, and Grosskopf's (1998) criteria, this variant also ranks rather low, as seen below.

Objective (Linguistic) Criteria

Articulatory Distance: YES. The use of [β] for /w/, while retaining a bilabial place of articulation, involves a change in manner of articulation with regard to lip rounding.

Lack of Areal Distribution: YES. This feature is not observed in the speech of the SCPE monodialectals in this study, and there is no evidence that it has undergone any areal distribution.

Phonemicity: NO. [β] is not phonemic in PDE.

Dichotomy: YES. [β] and [w] are not continuous.

Lexicalization: NO. The realization of /w/ as [β] is not limited to any particular lexical set and appears in a wide range of content and function words, such as proper nouns (*Wilson*), common nouns (*wheel*), and discourse particles (*well*).

Subjective (Perceptual) Criteria

Code Alternation: YES. The bidialectal speaker featured in this study in chapter 7 uses this feature when she is speaking PDE, but not when speaking SCPE.

Representation in Lay Writing: NO. There is no representation of this variant in lay writing or in Gates's (1987, 1998) dictionaries.

Use in Stereotyping/Mimicking: NO. This variant is not used by either PDE or SCPE speakers when mimicking the dialect.

Hindrance to Comprehensibility: NO. The use of the bilabial fricative for [w] does not result in hindrance to comprehensibility.

Thus, the PDE realization of /w/ as [β] fulfills three of Auer, Barden, and Grosskopf's five objective criteria and one of their four subjective criteria and is therefore classified as "low salience," in a similar fashion to the feature of PDE [æ] raising. However, while the latter feature has held its ground between generations of PDE speakers (although it is not used at all by the children of the youngest speakers of PDE), the bilabial fricative has not. Its low salience does not render it immune from erosion, and it is not utilized at all by the monodialectals in the youngest generation of speakers.

Like so many of the phonological features discussed in this chapter, there is great variation among the speakers who use this feature: the middle-aged males informants DG and LM use the feature in 27.7% and 25.0% of appropriate contexts, respectively, but the female middle-aged informant LG uses it only 5.4% of the time. Such a significant difference ($p < .001$ in both cases) shows the degree of instability of this feature even within the generation of middle-aged speakers.

5.3. THE PREDICTIVE POWER OF SALIENCE?

Various researchers of dialect shift have pointed out that SALIENCE is a problematic concept because of the concept's inherent circularity. Kerswill and Williams (2002) have compellingly argued that it is circular to claim that greater awareness attaches to salient forms; in fact, of the components of salience set out by Trudgill (1986), only those of phonological contrast and phonetic distance ("phonemicity" and "articulatory distance," in Auer, Barden, and Grosskopf's [1998] terms) stand outside the circularity to provide truly testable criteria for salience. Even those two criteria, Kerswill and Williams (2002) caution, are not sufficient to determine the true salience of a feature: extralinguistic, cognitive, social, psychological, and pragmatic factors must also be taken into account. For example, in their study of speaker awareness of dialectal features in the English cities of Reading, Milton Keynes, and Hull, Kerswill and Williams (2002, 86) found that each variant must be viewed carefully in terms of its social embedding and the level of language to which the feature belongs (e.g., phonetic, phonological, syntactic, lexical). Kerswill and Williams found that speaker awareness of those features varied widely, differing between features and between various socioeconomic groups. While salience is an attractive concept to use in predicting the outcomes of dialect contact, it is necessary to tease out its fundamental components by considering the context of the speech community itself and the awareness of features shown by a community's speakers.

Much work obviously remains to be done to understand the components of salience well enough to use it as an effective predictor of the outcomes of dialect contact. Even if the components are understood, "[i]n the end, it may not be possible, even in principle, to predict levels of salience.

It may also be impossible to determine whether a given level of salience, once established, leads to the adoption or the non-adoption of features in d[ialect] c[onvergence] or d[ialect] d[ivergence]" (Hinskens, Auer, and Kerswill 2005, 45).

Nevertheless, salience remains an attractive predictive factor in dialect shift and has been cited in various studies of dialect contact as a prime motivator—sometimes acting in conjunction with other factors—behind certain kinds of language change since Trudgill's (1986, 11) definition of SALIENCE as based on speaker awareness, phonetic difference, and pho-nemicity. A striking example of this is a case study of a migrant from East Germany (Auer, Barden, and Grosskopf 2000) who was originally included in the wider study of long-term dialect accommodation mentioned earlier in this chapter (Auer, Barden, and Grosskopf 1998). In the course of sev-eral interviews conducted after his arrival in West Germany, this particular speaker showed rapid abandonment of his Upper Saxon dialectal features in favor of features of his new dialect area. The features he abandoned were highly salient according to the formulation of "salience" promoted by Auer, Barden, and Grosskopf (1998); in other words, they met the same objective and subjective criteria for salience used to assess PDE features in this chapter. Thus, originally this speaker's behavior strongly supported the notion that salience can act as a predictor of feature abandonment. Subsequent to that first set of interviews by Auer, Barden, and Grosskopf, however, this speaker was unfortunately involved in an industrial accident that made it impossible for him to work. As he lost his employment-related contacts with West Germans and rebuilt his social ties with fellow migrants from East Germany, he began to revert to his Upper Saxon variants, also at a rapid rate, and the features he was "reacquiring" were again those that were highly salient. In both phases of the informant's feature inventory "development," criteria for salience—considered in conjunction with social network ties—were able to account well for his linguistic behavior (Auer, Barden, and Grosskopf 2000).

Bethin (2010) also successfully applied salience in her study of the dis-semination of /a/ through various dialects of Eastern Slavic in pre-tonic, stressed syllables (a phenomenon dubbed *ahken'e*). Departing from lists like those developed by Trudgill (1986) and Auer, Barden, and Grosskopf (1998), Bethin (2010) based her criteria for salience instead on more auditory cues, such as duration, vowel timbre, and intonation pitch peaks. Undoubtedly these acoustic features tie in with the criteria for objective (linguistic) salience used in this chapter posited by Auer, Barden, and Grosskopf (1998). Through her analysis Bethin (2010) determined that the notion of salience—at least in terms of her particular conceptualization—is indeed useful in explaining the regular path which this dissemination of /a/ has taken.

Van Bree (1992) likewise demonstrated the ability of SALIENCE to explain results of his study of the stability of language elements in the Dutch village of Twente, a dialect contact area where eastern Standard Dutch and eastern Dutch meet. Van Bree determined that "consciousness" (salience) of various language elements is a primary factor affecting the "stability" (retention) of dialect features at certain linguistic levels for the speakers involved; in other words, elements of lexical phonology, morphology, and content words from the nonstandard dialect were likely to be abandoned, while elements from levels of language of which speakers are less conscious (e.g., "accent," dialectal constructions, and word order) were more likely to be retained. He additionally noted that various "secondary" factors affect consciousness of a dialectal feature, including degree of deviation from the second dialect (Auer, Barden, and Grosskopf's [1998] criteria of "articulatory distance," "phonemicity," and so on), comprehensibility (one of their subjective criterion), and degree of regional and social spread (their "areal distribution" criterion).

Not all dialect contact studies, however, have been able to establish a correlation between salience and feature loss. As mentioned earlier in this chapter, Auer, Barden, and Grosskopf (1998) attempted to apply the salience criteria they had used with the unemployed Upper Saxon speaker to the data they collected as part of their accommodation study from the rest of the 56 Upper Saxon Vernacular speakers who had migrated to West Germany. Overall, only some of their criteria for salience—mostly subjective (perceptual) criteria—correlated regularly with the abandonment of Upper Saxon phonological forms in favor of forms from the new dialects the speakers encountered, and even then only in the case of what Auer, Barden, and Grosskopf describe as "intermediate (weak)" forms (i.e., variants which are neither strongly like the first dialect or the second dialect). For strong Upper Saxon dialectal variants (those that differed significantly from the second dialect's variants), high degree of salience exhibited absolutely no predictive power with regard to the overall change in informants' feature use.

Similarly, in a study of the speech of teens in three U.K. cities (Reading, Hull, and the "new town" Milton Keynes), Kerswill and Williams (2002) found that salience could be used only in a qualified sense to explain some of the dialect feature leveling processes they investigated. Contrary to Auer, Barden, and Grosskopf's (1998) study of Upper Saxon speakers migrating to West Germany—which found the most consistently effective criteria to be subjective (perceptual) criteria—Kerswill and Williams (2002) found that the most predictive facets of salience among the U.K. teens were the objective (linguistic) ones of phonological contrast and phonetic difference. Even so, the linguistic criteria applied unequally to consonants, vowels, and morphological variants and showed limitations because of that. For example, the salience criteria did not seem to explain the loss of consonantal features (e.g., [ʔ] for intervocalic /t/, [v] for syllable-initial /ð/, and [f] for syllable-initial /θ/), and only phonetic difference seemed to trigger a feature switch for vowels (like variants of /aɪ/ and /aʊ/, for example). Moreover, even though salience corresponded closely with the pattern of loss of morphological variants (e.g., the use of *them* as a demonstrative, and zero definite article), it was clear that not all speakers in the community considered those features equally salient.

Another study that could not successfully correlate salience with accommodation in a dialect contact situation was conducted by Llamas, Watt, and Johnson (2009) on the use of three Scots English dialectal variants by speakers in Berwick-upon-Tweed, a city located near the Scottish-English border. Adopting Trudgill's (1986) salience criteria of phonemicity, phonetic difference, and speaker awareness, Llamas, Watt, and Johnson (2009) assigned salience scores to three dialectal variants. One variant, rhoticity, was deemed salient. (Scots English is rhotic, whereas the more standard dialect of British English spoken near Berwick-on-Tweed is not.) Two variants were deemed nonsalient, namely "Scottish vowel length" (the environmental conditioning of the length of certain vowels through following segment or morpheme boundary) and a retracted form of the vowel in [-ər] unstressed syllables. In complete contradiction of salience as a predictor of the abandonment of dialectal features, speakers did NOT show evidence of accommodation toward the standard dialect for rhoticity, the single salient feature in their list. For Berwick-on-Tweed speakers, accommodation instead took place with the two nonsalient vocalic features, "Scottish vowel length" and retracted [-ər]. Llamas, Watt, and Johnson (2009, 401) conclude, "Overall, it appears that Trudgill's assertion that in dialect contact situations speakers modify features of their own varieties of which they are most aware is not borne out by the data." Salience is extremely attractive as an explanation for the outcomes of dialect contact, but it is clear that it alone is not a sufficient predictor in every dialect contact situation.

SALIENCE AND THE PDE DATA. Before entering into a discussion of how well the criteria for salience proposed by Auer, Barden, and Grosskopf (1998) predict whether dialectal features are retained or dropped across generations of PDE speakers, it is helpful here to summarize the various PDE features examined in this chapter. Table 5.15 presents their respective salience

TABLE 5.15

Salience Criteria Scores for PDE Features

PDE Feature	Objective		Subjective	
	Score	Criteria Met	Score	Criteria Met
Obstruent devoicing				
	3/5	lack of areal distribution	4/4	code alteration
		phonemicty		represented in lay writing
		dichotomy		stereotyping/mimicking
				hinders conprehension
		OVERALL SCORE: 7/9 (high)		
Monophthongization of /aʊ/ to [a]				
	3/5	articulatory distance	4/4	code alteration
		lack of areal distribution		represented in lay writing
		phonemicty		stereotyping/mimicking
				hinders conprehension
		OVERALL SCORE: 7/9 (high)		
[w] for /v/				
	4/5	articulatory distance	3/4	represented in lay writing
		lack of areal distribution		stereotyping/mimicking
		phonemicty		hinders conprehension
		dichotomy		
		OVERALL SCORE: 7/9 (high)		
Monophthongization of /aɪ/ to [æ] before liquids				
	3/5	articulatory distance	2/4	code alteration
		lack of areal distribution		hinders conprehension
		phonemicty		
		OVERALL SCORE: 5/9 (mid)		
Centralization of /a/ to [ʌ] before nasals				
	3/5	articulatory distance	2/4	code alteration
		phonemicty		hinders conprehension
		dichotomy		
		OVERALL SCORE: 5/9 (mid)		
[β] for /w/				
	3/5	articulatory distance	1/4	code alteration
		lack of areal distribution		
		dichotomy		
		OVERALL SCORE: 4/9 (mid)		
Raised [æ]				
	1/5	lack of areal distribution	1/4	code alteration
		OVERALL SCORE: 2/9 (low)		

scores and criteria met, with the PDE features ordered from the highest scores to the lowest.

Table 5.16 summarizes the rest of the information that was presented about each feature in other parts of this chapter and in chapter 4, namely, the simple or complex status of the rule according to Chambers's (1992) criteria, the overall salience scores of each feature, each feature's rate of retention or loss between the middle-aged generation and the youngest generation of PDE speakers, and whether speakers are aware of the feature. A more detailed breakdown of information about change in rate of use and retention rates between the oldest, middle-aged, and youngest generations of speakers—at least for those features for which such data were available in Anderson (1995)—is stated in notes below table 5.16.

In light of the information contained in these tables, can salience be said to be an effective predictor of retention or abandonment of the PDE phonological features investigated in this study? For the two PDE features of which speakers are aware, obstruent devoicing and monophthongization of /aʊ/ to [a], the high salience scores as determined using Auer, Barden, and Grosskopf's (1998) criteria do indeed seem to correspond to feature loss:

TABLE 5.16
Summary of Information for PDE Features

PDE Feature	*Simple/ Complex*	*Salience Score*	*Change in Rates*[a]	*Retention Rates*[a]	*Speaker Awareness*
Obstruent devoicing	complex	7/9 (high)	–8.8%	40.0%[b]	yes
Monophthong. of /aʊ/	simple	7/9 (high)	–45.6%	30.5%[c]	yes
Monophthong. of /aɪ/L	complex	5/9 (mid)	–56.9%	10.5%	no
Centralization of /a/N	complex	5/9 (mid)	–91.4%	8.6%	no
Raised [æ]	complex	2/9 (low)	+0.6%	103.8%	no
[β] for /w/	complex	4/9 (mid)	–20.8%	0.0%	no
[w] for /v/	complex	7/9 (high)	—	—	yes

a. Unless otherwise noted, all rates are a result of comparing the middle-aged generation with the youngest generation.

b. Between the oldest and the middle-aged generations, the change was –65.3%, and the retention rate was 18.4%; between the oldest and the youngest generations (the overall change), the change was –74.1%, and the retention rate was 7.3%.

c. Between the oldest and the middle-aged generations, the change was –34.4%, and the retention rate was 65.6%; between the oldest and the youngest generations (the overall change), the change was –81.2%, and the retention rate was 19.8%.

the youngest PDE speakers together devoice obstruents at a relative rate of only 40.0% of the frequency that the middle-aged generation does, and only 7.3% of the frequency of the oldest-generation monolingual speaker. As for /aʊ/ monophthongization, that same youngest generation only uses the PDE variant with a relative rate of 44% of the frequency of the middle-aged generation of speakers, and only 20% of the frequency of the oldest-generation monolingual speaker. For the substitution of [w] for /v/, the loss of the feature is complete in the youngest generation. For these features, high salience and high erosion rates go hand in hand.

The effectiveness of the predictive power of Auer, Barden, and Grosskopf's (1998) salience criteria becomes less clear-cut in an examination of PDE's other phonological features, however. Both monophthongization of /aɪ/ to [æ] before liquids and centralization of /a/ before nasals rank in the mid-range in overall salience, as does the bilabial fricative, so it is unclear whether their salience-as-predictor model would forecast the abandonment or retention of these two PDE features. Neither vowel has a high proportion of tokens in any given naturalistic data set; speakers are not aware of either feature, and they consequently both rank low in terms of subjective (perceptual) salience. Yet all three features are undergoing extreme erosion: the retention rate for all three features among the youngest speakers is a small percentage (10.5%, 8.6%, and 0.0%, resp.) that of the middle-aged generation, the lowest retention rates for any PDE features examined in this dissertation. Thus, a mid-range salience level evidently does not ensure that a dialect feature is protected from abandonment, at least for PDE. But, does DEGREE of salience correlate with degree of feature abandonment? Auer, Barden, and Grosskopf (1998) may have conceptualized salience scores as belonging to a binary set of categories—that is, either a feature has high salience or low salience—but obviously, with the list of criteria given, a feature can fall somewhere along a scale of salience as well. If high degree of abandonment is considered to correlate with high degree of salience—in other words, if the MORE HIGHLY salient a feature is, the MORE LIKELY it is to be abandoned—then /aɪ/ monophthongization, /a/ centralization, and the bilabial fricative for /w/ are problematic for the specific-criteria model: Though they have lower, mid-range salience scores than obstruent devoicing and /aʊ/ monophthongization, monophthongized /aɪ/ and centralized /a/ have a much lower relative retention rate (10.5% and 8.6%, resp.) than either /aʊ/ monophthongization (30.5%) or obstruent devoicing (40.0%). The use of the bilabial fricative for /w/ has been completely abandoned by the youngest generation of speakers. Could this partly be due to the type of salience criteria these respective features meet? Monophthongized /aɪ/ and centralized /a/ are both higher in objective salience than subjective salience, for example, while the two highly salient features are higher in subjective salience as opposed to objective salience (they actually have the same objective salience rating as the other features; see table 5.15). Perhaps features with higher objective (linguistic) salience—as opposed to subjective (perceptual) salience—are more likely to undergo radical erosion. However, in their data on the 56 Upper Saxon Vernacular speakers in West Germany, Auer, Barden, and Grosskopf (1998, 184) found exactly the opposite to be true, since the Upper Saxon features that underwent the greatest degree of erosion in their study were those with high subjective salience. Moreover, as Llamas, Watt, and Johnson (2009) found in their investigation of Scots English variants in Berwick-on-Tweed, this PDE example also clearly illustrates that, in dialect contact situations, even nonsalient (or lower salience) features can be abandoned at drastic rates. It is not yet clear whether subjective or objective salience plays a more prominent role in determining the degree of abandonment of a feature in a dialect contact situation.

The converse of the assertion that highly salient features are more likely to be abandoned—in other words, the claim that nonsalient features are LEAST likely to be abandoned—does, in fact, make accurate predictions for PDE raised [æ]. Of all the phonological PDE features investigated in this study, it alone is not being abandoned by the 30–40-year-old cohort of PDE speakers; in fact, its use among these youngest PDE speakers is actually slightly higher than their parents' use, although not at a statistically significant level. This feature, at least, is holding its own with the youngest speakers of PDE, but it is not being transferred to the children of these youngest speakers and will presumably disappear with the death of the last of the PDE speakers. The same claim that nonsalient features are LEAST likely to be abandoned does not hold true either for the use of the bilabial fricative, since the youngest generation of monodialectal speakers does not use the feature at all.

In short, then, salience has mixed effectiveness as a predictor of abandonment or retention of features for these PDE phonological variants:

> High salience does indeed effectively predict that the youngest speakers have been abandoning certain PDE features (namely, obstruent devoicing and /aʊ/ monophthongization).

> It is unclear how one should interpret a mid-level of salience. Does mid-level salience logically imply that a feature may or may not be in the process of abandonment? For the PDE features of /aɪ/ monophthongization, /a/ centralization, and the bilabial fricative, a mid-level of salience correlates with feature abandonment.

Degree of salience does not appear to be an accurate predictor of the EXTENT TO WHICH features are being abandoned in PDE. For the youngest generation compared to the middle-aged generation, the relative retention rates is 30.5% for high-salience /aʊ/ monophthongization but a mere 8.6% for mid-salience /a/ centralization. If degree of salience accurately predicted the extent to which features are abandoned, the retention rate would be lower for the features with the highest salience.

Low salience can, indeed, effectively predict that a feature will show immunity to erosion, as with PDE raised [æ], a feature holding its own among the youngest speakers of PDE. Low salience can also be a poor predictor of immunity to erosion, since the low-salience bilabial fricative has been completely abandoned by the youngest monodialectal speakers of PDE.

These data from PDE show that, at least in the case of an obsolescing dialect, salience—whether defined carefully as Auer, Barden, and Grosskopf (1998) did or defined simply as "speaker awareness"—clearly has serious limitations as a predictor of what features will be abandoned and at what rate they will be abandoned. Whether features have low salience or high salience, each one (except raised [æ]) has been or is being abandoned by the youngest PDE speakers, and all these features will be ultimately abandoned by speakers in south central Pennsylvania, since the children of the youngest generation of PDE speakers are not acquiring them.

Is the distinction then between "simple" and "complex" rules a better predictor of feature retention or loss than salience? Chambers (1992) posited that simple rules are more quickly ACQUIRED than complex rules by learners of a second dialect; since acquiring features of another dialect often means swapping one set of features for another, it seemed that complex rules in the native dialect would be jettisoned first by speakers. The data in table 5.16, however, do not support this hypothesis: the only PDE feature involving a simple rule, the monophthongization of /aʊ/, is declining in the same manner as the other PDE features, each of which involves a complex rule. Moreover, the sole PDE feature not being abandoned by the youngest speakers, raised [æ], involves a complex rule of some sort: although a complete analysis is not available at this time, its use may be conditioned, at least in closed syllables, by the type of segment following it. (Of course the variant also occurs with great frequency in open syllables, and *yeah* was the chosen lexical item for coding in this study.) Clearly a categorization of rules as "simple" versus "complex" is, like salience, not enough to predict whether a dialectal variant will be abandoned or retained across generations of speakers.

Does relative frequency of a particular feature better predict whether features will be lost or retained? At the least, does relative frequency need to be considered in an assessment of salience? Recall that for the PDE data, the two least frequently occurring dialectal variants—in other words, the ones which had the most constrained phonological environments and, therefore, had the lowest number of tokens counted in this naturalistic data set—were those with the lowest relative retention rates of all: the youngest PDE speakers used both monophthongization of /aɪ/ and centralization of /a/ with a mere 10.5% and 8.6% relative retention rate of the frequency of those features in the speech of the middle-aged generation, whereas the more frequently occurring variants showed 40.0% and 30.5% relative retention rates. There may be an undeveloped principle here, although it will require more investigation. Auer, Barden, and Grosskopf (1998) found in their study of Upper Saxon Vernacular speakers in West Germany that features with low frequency remained low frequency (but were not entirely abandoned by speakers): "Changes usually failed to reach the 5% level of significance for those variables for which values were very low from the start, i.e., in those features which were hardly present in the first interview" (179). In contrast, from the viewpoint of the acquisition end of the process, Bardovi-Harlig (1987) pointed to frequency (in her terms, "availability of input") as a measure of "saliency" that was responsible for the fact that the ESL learners in her study unexpectedly learned a marked grammatical form (preposition stranding, e.g., *Who do you need to give this to?*) before an unmarked form (preposition pied piping, e.g., *To whom do you need to give this?*). Perhaps "availability of input" does indeed need to be included in the consideration of what is meant by "salience" when one attempts to use it to predict the ultimate outcome for a feature in a dialect contact situation. For the low-frequency PDE features of /aɪ/ monophthongization and /a/ centralization, the outcome undeniably is radical erosion—but not complete abandonment—among the last generation of speakers; the question is whether low frequency actually has anything to do with this fact.

SALIENCE AND SPEAKER AWARENESS. A last issue inextricably linked with salience is that of speaker awareness. Auer, Barden, and Grosskopf (1998) provided, with their objective criteria, testable characteristics for dialectal variants that are independent of speaker awareness, while their subjective criteria list the ways speaker awareness of dialect features is manifested. Speakers are aware of only three of the PDE phonological features discussed in this study—obstruent devoicing, /aʊ/ monophthongization, and [w] for /v/; for the first two of these features, the greater proportion of salience criteria fulfilled are, by a slim margin, subjective (perceptual), and they fulfill far more subjective criteria than any other feature. ([w] for /v/ fulfills slightly more objective criteria.) Both of the first two features have

a combined relative retention rate among the youngest speakers of 30.5–
44.0%—not a very large retention rate, but huge when compared to the
paltry 10.5% and 8.6% relative retention rate of /aɪ/ monophthongization
and /a/ centralization, respectively. ([w] for /v/ has not been retained by any
of the last generation of PDE speakers.) It is possible that the two features
that enjoy high speaker awareness have such high relative retention rates
because of a factor Trudgill (1986, 11, 37) called EXTRA-STRONG SALIENCE.
According to this concept, some dialectal forms with abundant perceptual
salience (i.e., forms used in stereotyping and/or overt stigmatization) carry
such a high degree of salience that the speaker awareness itself actually
hinders accommodation to the prestige dialect variant (and, hence, complete abandonment of the dialect feature) "in the absence of any other
factor promoting it" (as explained in Llamas, Watt, and Johnson 2009,
401). This notion is not without difficulties: Kerswill and Williams (2002,
89), for example, note that such a definition for extra-strong salience is
completely unsatisfactory for developing criteria for what salience really
is, because how can the very factors that lead speakers to notice features
be precisely those that lead to a feature being retained? (This contradicts
the basic premise that the high-salience features are those which are most
likely to be abandoned by speakers, simply because certain features have
extraordinarily high salience.) Nevertheless, it is true that, for PDE, two of
the features with higher salience are eroding at a lesser rate.

5.4. DEVELOPING A PROFILE OF PDE

This chapter concludes with a profile of the complicated state of contemporary PDE, developed from the data presented above. In particular, what
does it mean to be a speaker of PDE today? While this study lists variants
that are phonological features of PDE, not every speaker uses every feature
with the same frequency. As previous sections in this chapter and chapter
4 demonstrated, the youngest speakers of PDE use almost all PDE features
less frequently—sometimes FAR less frequently—than the middle-aged
informants, as one would expect in a case of dialect obsolescence. But the
data also make apparent the great variation between speakers within the
youngest generation and (sometimes) within the middle-aged generation.
The variation for the youngest generation even extends to which features
are used at all: while the middle-aged speakers are relatively homogeneous
in terms of what PDE features they exhibit (exceptions will be noted below),
the youngest generation of speakers are not; for example, one young male
(DK) monophthongizes /aʊ/ and centralizes /a/, but he exhibits little or

no evidence of obstruent devoicing, raised [æ], or monophthongization of /aɪ/, while another young male (DwK) evidences a high rate of raised [æ], as well as some monophthongization of /aʊ/, but little obstruent devoicing and little or no monophthongization of /aɪ/ or centralization of /a/. Only the female speaker in the youngest group shows evidence for a wide range of features (and, even then, she does not utilize the bilabial fricative or the [w] for /v/ of the middle-aged generation). PDE is not only declining in terms of the lower frequencies of feature use or abandonment of features among the youngest generation of speakers, but it is also unraveling as the last two generations of speakers are not using the features in a mutually consistent manner. Table 5.17 compiles some of this information on feature use to facilitate a discussion of this disintegration of the dialect. Trudgill (2004) points out that features used in fewer than 10% of possible contexts are not likely to be noticed by younger speakers acquiring a language variety, so table 5.17 highlights those features with rates higher than 10%, counting them as "core features" of the dialect. ([w] for /v/ is not included here because frequencies and token counts are not available.)

What does this summary reveal as the "core" features of PDE for the middle-aged generation? Three PDE features are used by every middle-aged speaker with a sufficient enough frequency (>10%) to count as "core": /a/ centralization (the categorical variant in prenasal contexts for these speakers), /aʊ/ monophthongization, and obstruent devoicing. Raised [æ] and /aɪ/ monophthongization are more variable for this age group, since LG does not monophthongize /aɪ/[7] and DG has a very low incidence of raised [æ]. In the creation of a profile of the PDE dialect, these latter features can be considered "optional" when it comes to being classified as a speaker of PDE. Thus, speaking PDE means—at least for the middle-aged generation—that an individual uses the core PDE features of /a/ centralization, /aʊ/ monophthongization, and obstruent devoicing with sufficient frequency and that individual also optionally uses /aɪ/ monophthongization, raised [æ], and the bilabial fricative.

How do these "core" features of PDE compare for the youngest generation? Table 5.17 shows that, for the youngest generation, there is only a single feature used by every speaker with sufficient frequency (>10%) to count as "core": /aʊ/ monophthongization. Features like [w] for /v/ and the bilabial fricative are not part of any young monodialectal's PDE. Every other feature, even highly salient obstruent devoicing, is either not part of some individual's repertoire or is used too rarely to classify as "core." Thus, speaking PDE means, for the youngest generation, using /aʊ/ monophthongization; all other PDE features are "optional." Only one speaker, LK, displays a range of PDE phonological features at all, and only two of those

TABLE 5.17
PDE Feature Use by Speaker

Middle-Aged Generation
    DG (male)

obstruent devoicing	102/746	(13.7%)
monophthongization of /aʊ/	94/126	(74.6%)
monophthongization of /aɪ/	5/7	(71.4%)
centralization of /a/	17/17	(100.0%)
raised [æ]	1/52	(1.9%)
bilabial fricative	125/452	(27.7%)

    LM (male)

obstruent devoicing	25/144	(17.4%)
monophthongization of /aʊ/	17/19	(89.5%)
monophthongization of /aɪ/	2/2	(100.0%)
centralization of /a/	2/2	(100.0%)
raised [æ]	6/22	(27.3%)
bilabial fricative	20/80	(25.0%)

    LG (female)

obstruent devoicing	70/451	(15.5%)
monophthongization of /aʊ/	26/64	(40.6%)
monophthongization of /aɪ/	0/2	(0.0%)
centralization of /a/	1/1	(100.0%)
raised [æ]	18/74	(24.3%)
bilabial fricative	12/222	(5.4%)

Youngest Generation
    DK (male)

obstruent devoicing	3/623	(0.5%)
monophthongization of /aʊ/	25/65	(38.5%)
monophthongization of /aɪ/	0/1	(0.0%)
centralization of /a/	2/10	(20.0%)
raised [æ]	1/39	(2.6%)

    DwK (male)

obstruent devoicing	17/558	(3.0%)
monophthongization of /aʊ/	5/47	(10.6%)
monophthongization of /aɪ/	0/7	(0.0%)
centralization of /a/	0/12	(0.0%)
raised [æ]	17/49	(34.7%)

    LK (female)

obstruent devoicing	89/656	(13.6%)
monophthongization of /aʊ/	7/75	(9.3%)
monophthongization of /aɪ/	1/7	(14.3%)
centralization of /a/	1/13	(8.0%)
raised [æ]	3/40	(7.5%)

with greater than 10% frequency. Of the three speakers presented here, she would be considered the "most Dutchified" by others in the speech community, although it is not clear if this is directly related to the range of features that she employs. As Sturtevant (1917, 146–47) pointed out long ago, "The unity of a dialect is a unity, not of sounds produced, but of sounds perceived; it is subjective rather than objective." This is particularly clear in the case of PDE, since each of the individuals in this study is a speaker of the dialect in the minds of members of the south central Pennsylvania speech community.

The PDE dialect is unraveling, and as it is, the youngest speakers contrast with their parents' generation (the middle-aged speakers) in the following ways:

1. They do not use the full range of features that the middle-aged generation uses.
2. They do not use the features that they do use with frequencies close to those exhibited by the middle-aged generation of speakers.
3. They treat features that were "core" for the middle-aged generation as optional.
4. They are inconsistent with each other in terms of frequencies with which they use features.
5. They have simplified the phonological conditioning for highly salient features, such as obstruent devoicing and /aʊ/ monophthongization.

The route of PDE's obsolescence is thus not only one of reduced frequencies of feature use, but also of different treatment of even the most "core" dialect features across the generations.

It is not difficult to postulate reasons why the youngest PDE speakers are converging toward SCPE and showing such dramatic abandonment of features. In a scenario characteristic of many minority dialects, the low prestige of PDE and a long history of stigma on PDE imposed by SCPE speakers (especially within the school system) would in themselves have been motivators for a speaker to abandon PDE features, especially ones with high levels of speaker awareness. Strikingly, however, this abandonment is currently occurring for speakers who have become adults who speak PDE. The reason this is striking—as chapter 7 will discuss in greater detail—is that many peers of this same youngest generation spoke PDE as young children but abandoned it in favor of SCPE as they entered school and faced pressure there from teachers and SCPE-speaking peers to shift to SCPE. For some set of reasons, which (again) will be discussed in chapter 7, the youngest monodialectal speakers in this study retained their PDE dialect through all that pressure, into adulthood. Now that they are adults, however, changes in what identities PDE speakers wish to portray and shifting notions of what linguistic features portray those identities in south central Pennsylvania may be hastening the abandonment of PDE features by these same 30–40-year-old speakers. As Brown (2003, 20) so poignantly concluded in her study of English borrowing in Louisiana French, "When language contact is ubiquitous and unremitting, this persistent linguistic pressure erodes code boundaries." This constant influence from SCPE on PDE has been an increasingly powerful force in the linguistic landscape of south central Pennsylvania for the last three to four decades and has inevitably affected which features speakers use and how frequently they use them. The reduction has been dramatic, however: it appears from the above comparison of "core" and "optional" features that the linguistic marking of a PDE speaker today has essentially collapsed to use of a single feature, /aʊ/ monophthongization. This feature has thus taken on an unexpected level of indexicality for the south central Pennsylvania speech community: Wassink and Dyer (2004) have demonstrated how such changes in feature indexicality can take place for a robust language variety, and perhaps the changes can be even more drastic for a dying dialect like PDE.

A much more difficult issue to grapple with concerning PDE is WHY this obsolescing dialect is unraveling in this manner as it approaches extinction.[8] What could lead a minority language variety to such a compromised state in one generation such that only one core feature is left? One real motivator behind this kind of dialect unraveling may lie in the lack of consistent norms provided for children acquiring mastery of the PDE language variety, at least with some features; recall how the middle-aged generation of speakers already shows wide variability in the use all the features investigated here, except for /a/ centralization and obstruent devoicing. When Dorian (1994) encountered a high degree of linguistic variability in a relatively homogeneous group of East Sutherland Gaelic speakers that could not be explained by the usual sociolinguistic factors (age, sex, socioeconomic status, social network, language proficiency, etc.), she dubbed the phenomenon "personal pattern variation" and noted that such extreme linguistic behavior is a hallmark of an obsolescing language variety. The extreme variation among her speakers, she concluded, could be accounted for, at least in part, by the "absence of any locally workable prestige norm" (631). A similar lack of prestige norm may be responsible for the observed behavior of the youngest PDE speakers in south central Pennsylvania today.

Another possibily powerful motivator behind the unraveling of PDE may come from the mixed target models of English that the youngest PDE speakers encountered as they grew up. As target models became diversified in this Pennsylvanian dialect contact situation—or as "available input" (to use Bardovi-Harlig's [1987] term again) of PDE came into competeition with input from SCPE—the consequence was perhaps the widely varying linguistic behavior evident today among the youngest PDE speakers. From a historical perspective, the scenario probably proceeded like this: For PDE speakers of the middle-aged generation, PDE input was comparably consistent as they grew up. Almost all their parents spoke PDE (some as an L2 with considerable influence from their native Pennsylvania German, in fact), and their teachers and classmates would also have been almost exclusively PDE speakers. In other words, in their formative years, the middle-aged generation of PDE speakers would have been exposed primarily to input from PDE sources. For today's youngest PDE speakers, however, the linguistic environment looked quite different: although they all grew up in households with PDE-speaking parents, by the time these young PDE speakers reached school age in the 1970s, they were exposed in school to SCPE-speaking teachers and classmates, and PDE began its decline. Some individuals who grew up in PDE-speaking households chose to shift to SCPE; others chose to maintain PDE. But even this latter group—in contrast to speakers from the middle-aged generation—would have been exposed to input from a mixture of PDE and SCPE sources in their formative years. A purely deterministic input model (see Trudgill et. al 2000)—even without considering language attitudes and issues of identity—would predict that the direct result of such SCPE-rich input for the youngest generation of PDE speakers would be an instability in the way features are realized in PDE. To reiterate, then, the evidence from this study shows that the negative consequences to the PDE dialect are actually fourfold:

1. decline of the PDE dialect in terms of reduced frequencies of feature use,
2. the reduction of the PDE "core" of features for individuals labeled as "PDE speakers,"
3. simplification of the phonological constraints governing the use of certain features, and
4. inconsistency between speakers with regard to which features mark their PDE.

All these factors together make up the unraveling so evident in today's PDE.

The other unexpected development in the decline of PDE is the emergence of bidialectal PDE-SCPE speakers among the last generation of those who speak PDE. Chapter 6 provides an overview of what bidialectalism is (and isn't), and chapter 7 provides an in-depth look at the linguistic behaviors and attitudes/motivations of one bidialectal speaker.

6. ON THE TRAIL
OF THE BIDIALECTAL

THE PREVIOUS CHAPTERS have demonstrated the processes involved in the unraveling of Pennsylvania Dutchified English (PDE) as the south central Pennsylvania speech community undergoes language variety shift toward SCPE. Yet another development during this last stage of the PDE life cycle, however, is the emergence of speakers who use both PDE and the regional standard, South Central Pennsylvania English (SCPE). This development is noteworthy (as well as unexpected) for two reasons: First, extraordinarily few bidialectals (i.e., speakers with native proficiency in two separate dialects of one language) have been overtly mentioned in the literature on dialect contact and so it is not a given that bidialectals would arise in the south central Pennsylvania context of dialect shift. Second, some linguists have even gone so far as to argue that true bidialectals cannot exist; such claims will be examined later in this chapter, with a particular emphasis on those made by Hazen (2001). As unlikely as it may be, however, some south central Pennsylvanians profess to speak both PDE and SCPE, using the two dialects strategically (in a sociolinguistic sense) with different interlocutors and in different settings. Chapter 7 focuses on one particular bidialectal speaker, "Rachel," and presents her use of the diagnostic PDE phonological features discussed in chapters 4 and 5. An analysis of her linguistic behavior will determine whether she meets Hazen's (2001) criteria for a "true" bidialectal and, if so, how well.

Before discussing bidialectal behavior in south central Pennsylvania, this chapter takes on the task of discussing what bidialectalism is and what it is not. Section 6.1 presents criteria gleaned from the literature on what constitutes true dialectal differences between a bidialectal's two modes of speaking, categorizing them according to whether they involve an intra-speaker comparison (i.e., the distinction between the linguistic forms of an individual's two modes of speaking) or an inter-speaker comparison (i.e., the comparison between each of an individual's two modes of speaking and the speech patterns of monodialectals whose dialects correspond to them). Section 6.2 discusses what bidialectalism is not, giving examples of linguistic behaviors documented in the dialect contact literature that are NOT the same as bidialectalism (even though they may appear to be so on the surface). Section 6.3 lists individuals mentioned in the literature who are either described as bidialectals or who might qualify as true bidialectals if their linguistic behaviors were more closely analyzed. For almost all these cases, the focus of the research was some speech phenomenon other than bidialectalism, so reference to the potentially bidialectal speaker is often incidental, albeit—for this study's purposes in exploring bidialectalism—important. In conjunction with the data presented in chapter 7 on bidialectals in south central Pennsylvania, these cases will provide a context from which to draw conclusions about bidialectalism and about bidialectal behaviors and motivations in intense dialect contact situations.

6.1. THE BIDIALECTALISM CONTROVERSY

As described in the review of the dialect contact literature in chapter 2, most dialect contact takes place in one of three contexts:

1. Situations in which native speakers of one dialect have moved to another dialect area (often for employment, as did the East Germans who migrated to West Germany in Auer, Barden, and Grosskopf [1998], for example)
2. Situations in which speakers of various dialects have migrated to an area where the native dialect of none of them is spoken (e.g., New Zealand [Trudgill et al. 2000] or the British Fens [Britain 2002])
3. Long-term dialect contact situations in which speakers of two or three dialects have lived side by side for multiple generations (like the bi- and tri-ethnic enclave communities of North Carolina (e.g., Beech Bottom and Roaring Creek [Mallinson and Wolfram 2002])

Literature reporting dialect outcomes in these situations has not specifically made mention of bidialectals among the informants. This is not to say that bidialectalism has not been a result in those contexts; it simply means that the researchers did not note it or label it as such. Certain sociolinguists, however, have purposely sought bidialectalism in the populations they were investigating and have not found evidence for the phenomenon. For example, a phone study conducted by Sharon Ash, reported in Labov (1994), asked randomly selected white speakers of English to imitate AAVE; invariably subjects failed miserably at the task, with even the best imitators modifying only voice quality, tempo, and intonation, but not any segmental dialect features. Similarly, Preston (1992, 337) found that white imitators of AAVE—as well as African American imitators of white speakers—altered only some voice characteristics, making only "limited use of low-level linguistic features." Based on these poor performances, Labov (1994) restated his earlier opinion that bidialectal individuals cannot really exist:

He (the individual with two modes of speaking) may succeed in convincing his listeners that he is speaking the vernacular, but this impression seems to depend upon a number of unsystematic and heavily marked signals. [Labov 1972, 215]

In research with the West Virginia Dialect Project, Hazen (2001) was also unable to find bidialectal speakers. Of the group of self-professed bidialectal informants interviewed—all college students who had moved from various dialect areas of West Virginia to attend university in Morgantown— none were able to show systematic use of two distinct dialect systems. In fact, these speakers only showed evidence of skill in PASSIVE BIDIALECTALISM (i.e., the ability of speakers to understand and even pick out features of a dialect other than the one they normally speak); none showed evidence of skill in PRODUCTIVE BIDIALECTALISM (defined by Hazen [2001] as the ability to match dialectal feature use of monodialectal speakers both qualitatively and quantitatively). Of all linguistic researchers of dialect contact, Hazen (2001) has most directly addressed the question of whether anyone can be bidialectal in the same way that many speakers are bilingual (i.e., in such a way that speakers can switch between their language varieties as coherent sets of language patterns). He and the researchers of the West Virginia Dialect Project have made it a goal to find and analyze the speech patterns of child and young adult speakers who live in the dialect contact situation in Morgantown, West Virginia. Speakers who took part in one phase of these studies were children who—like the suspected bidialectal Noah (Evans 2002) discussed in chapter 7—grew up in different areas than those in which their parents were raised (Hazen and Hall 1999). Another phase studied college students who had left their home area to attend West Virginia University in Morgantown; this group included self-proclaimed bidialectals who insisted that they "spoke differently" at home than they did at school (Hazen 2001, 94–95). Close analysis of the subjects' speech patterns, however, revealed that none of the college students interviewed were able to switch consistently between discretely different language variation patterns as they demonstrated their "abilities" in two dialects. Even the children in the initial 1999 study—who would have been exposed to a second dialect at a more reasonable age for more successful acquisition—showed evidence of a mixed set of dialect features in their speech, rather than two distinct dialects (Hazen 2001, 95).

These results led Hazen (2001, 86) to speculate that there may be no real bidialectals and that there is, in fact, no inherent motivation for productive bidialectalism, since humans are capable of receptive bidialectalism (i.e., they can understand, to some degree, other speakers of their own language, even if those speakers speak a variety other than their own). Therefore, in an effort to ground bidialectalism (if it exists) in a more concrete theoretical linguistic framework and to distinguish between true bidialectals and those who are simply imitating two dialects, Hazen (2001) has proposed the following criteria for bidialectalism:

1. In a qualitative view, for a person to be bidialectal, and not simply party to two styles drawn from different social or regional dialects, that person [...] would need to produce the features of both [dialects] A and B in a mutually exclusive manner. [2001, 92]

2. With quantitative constraints, the bidialectal speaker should be able to match the language variation patterns of native dialect speakers. [2001, 93]

3. If bidialectalism is possible, it is the social factors which motivate it, and precisely determining the social factors involved is critical to the study of bidialectalism. [2001, 94]

In other words—according to Hazen (2001)—for a person to be considered a genuine bidialectal, that speaker must...

1. produce the same sets of features as monodialectal speakers of both dialects, without overlap,

2. produce those features in the same "language variation patterns" that monodialectals do, and

3. possess a social motivation for acquiring the second dialect while retaining the first one.

Particulars of Hazen's (2001) studies will be more fully discussed in section 6.3.

Does this lack of research evidence to date really make bidialectalism a linguistic impossibility? Given the type of informants recruited for the studies just mentioned—speakers who can imitate another dialect but do not really control it and speakers who only received significant exposure to a second dialect as young adults when they went off to college—it is not surprising that interested researchers have concluded that true bidialectals do not exist. Other factors have further complicated the matter: there are issues in determining what constitutes a separate dialect for any individual speaker, for example, and sociolinguistics has faced inherent challenges in pinning down a conclusive, linguistically sound definition for "dialect" (Hazen 2001, 85–86); as a result, proving that an individual uses two separate dialects has proven challenging. Bidialectal speakers are also difficult to find, given the sociolinguistic strategies they employ for using one dialect or the other in their linguistic milieu; anyone who uses two dialects could likely go unrecognized by a researcher, since researchers do not often see speakers in settings varied enough to prompt the use of a separate dialect. These difficulties make it evident that the lack of verifiable bidialectalism in the body of linguistic research is just as likely due to challenges in research design and informant recruitment as it is to the supposed impossibility of bidialectalism arising as a result of dialect contact.

6.2. TESTS FOR BIDIALECTALISM: WHAT BIDIALECTALISM IS

No single test exists that can adequately determine whether a person with two modes of speaking is bidialectal, although various researchers have suggested criteria for bidialectalism that they feel are critical to such an assessment. These criteria fall into two general categories: those that involve an intraspeaker comparison of an individual's two ways of speaking, and those that involve an interspeaker comparison of an individual's speech patterns with those of the rest of the speech community.

INTRASPEAKER COMPARISON: TESTS FOR DISTINCTIVENESS BETWEEN TWO MODES OF SPEAKING. Logically speaking, for a person to be considered bidialectal, he or she needs to be able to produce two authentic modes of speaking that are sufficiently distinctive from each other that they warrant the label "dialect" instead of "imitation," "style," or the tag of some other linguistic behavior. In other words, the two modes of speaking of the true bidialectal must consist of sets of mutually exclusive features and rules of use, and/or the two modes of speaking must exhibit features or processes that occur at different rates or in language-internal environments that are sufficiently different from each other (Hazen 2001, 91–93).

The literature on dialect contact presents several interrelated methods for determining the internal consistency of a speaker's modes of speaking and the distinctiveness between those modes. Almost all these methods focus on phonological processes.

Dialect Differences Are Low-Level. Noting the dependence on rather surface-level features by speakers asked to imitate a dialect they do not normally speak, Labov (1972) has stated that real "differences between dialects depend on low-level rules which appear as minor adjustments and extensions of contextual conditions" (1972, 215). Trudgill (1996), in his development of a dialect typology, zeros in specifically on fast-speech rules as indicators of true mastery of a dialect in a context of dialect contact:

Why do skilled non-native speakers not use as many fast speech phenomena as native speakers? The answer is obviously that they do not use them because they are unable to. [Trudgill 1996, 7]

Other areas indicative of native-like dialect mastery, according to Trudgill (1996, 13–17), are the low-level domains of syllable lengths and phonemic inventories.

From these notions comes the criterion, then, that for a speaker to be considered genuinely bidialectal, his or her two modes of speaking must systematically differ from each other at the LOW levels of language (areas that an imitator or nonnative learner of the dialect would not be able to master).

Dialect Differences Involve Differences in Constraint Rankings. Taking the idea of low-levelness one step further, Hazen (2001) and Guy and Lim (2005) have suggested that one diagnostic of dialect distinctiveness is that they involve differences in constraint rankings. CONSTRAINT RANKINGS refer here to the quantitative patterning of feature use across phonological environments. As an early example of this principle in the sociolinguistic literature, Guy and Lim (2005) cite Labov's (1966) famed study of the use of /r/ in two different New York City department stores. Labov found that Saks 5th Avenue customers used /r/ (a socially marked feature) 30% of the time before a consonant and 63% of the time before a word boundary when using their non-emphatic style; this use of /r/ increased to 40% and 64%, respectively, when using their emphatic style. Although the relative quantity of /r/ usage varied between speakers' two styles, the comparative weight of the phonological environments in which /r/ was used did not change (Guy and Lim 2005). Because the comparative weights of the phonological environments did not change, Guy and Lim (2005) concluded that the different usage rates represented differences in style alone, not dialectal differences. Thinking conversely then, if it can be shown that the two different codes used by a single speaker differ from each other in terms of their constraint rankings for the same segment, then it can be said that the speaker is authentically using two different dialects (not styles) and that he or she is indeed bidialectal.

Dialects Differences Involve Complex Phonological Processes. In his work on dialect acquisition, Chambers (1992, 682–87) asserts that genuine differences between dialects on the phonological level are more than simple wholesale substitutions of segments for one another; true differences manifest themselves in complex ways (as in substitutions that take place only in a certain phonological environment) and in very complex ways (as in substitutions that involve more abstract kinds of structural considerations in determining the correct environments for substitution or involve other abstract generalizations governing substitutions). This complexity criterion was also used by Payne (1980) in her classic study on second dialect acquisition by Philadelphia children, in which she determined that the children who had not been born in King of Prussia were unable to master the "lexicalized" rules for /æ/-raising in the Philadelphia dialect and, hence, never became authentic users of that dialect. If it can be proven that a speaker's two ways of speaking involve not just simple phonological substitutions, but complex and very complex rules of substitution, then it can be said that the speaker genuinely controls two dialects and is a true bidialectal.

Dialect Differences Involve Features That Are Salient as Well as Those That Are Not. Trudgill's (1986) treatise on dialect contact and Auer, Barden, and Grosskopf's (1998) work on long-term accommodation have pointed out the role of salience in determining how speakers behave with regard to native dialect features when they are put in long-term contact with a second, more prestigious dialect. This work has assumed that a speaker's treatment of dialectal features is largely unidirectional in favor of the second dialect: salient features of the speaker's native dialect are lost, while salient features of the second dialect are acquired, or there is some assimilation of the two dialects (Auer, Barden, and Grosskopf 1998, 163). Conversely, non-salient features of the two dialects are less likely to be either lost or gained (163–64). This research predicts that dialect contact will result in salient features always accommodating to the second dialect (163–64).

As an extension of this idea, then, if a speaker can be shown to use non-salient features of a second dialect, then he or she can be said to have truly acquired that dialect. In the same vein, if a speaker uses salient features of both dialects (in a mutually exclusive manner, of course), then that person can also be said to have maintained his or her first dialect while acquiring the second. Such a speaker thus can be proven to fulfill the requirement of having mastery of two distinct dialectal systems and can be rightly labeled bidialectal.

Dialect Differences Involve, Well, Just Differences (The Levenshtein Principle). In their work on Bulgarian dialects, Heeringa and Norbonne (2001) have developed a method to distinguish between dialects that does not rely on designations of rules as "complex" or "noncomplex" or as "high-level" versus "low-level." Their quantitative tool to measure phonological differences between dialects—the Levenshtein Principle—recognizes only substitutions, insertions, and deletions, calculating "the cost of (the least costly set of) operations mapping one string to another. The basic costs are those of (single-phone) insertions, deletions, and substitutions. Insertions and deletions are half as costly as substitutions" (380). Values are assigned accordingly to differences in phonological realization between the two dialects for any given lexical item; the distance between them can then be calculated. By this measure, differences between dialects can be quantified. If a certain feature in an individual's two modes of speaking has a score large enough to constitute a difference between dialects, the speaker can be said to have mastery of two dialectal systems and can be rightly termed a bidialectal.

INTERSPEAKER COMPARISON: TESTS FOR MATCHING MONODIALECTALS. The other primary criterion for determining bidialectalism is proposed by Hazen (2001) and involves interspeaker comparison. In meeting this requirement, the authentic bidialectal will match monodialectal speakers' use of dialect features both qualitatively and quantitatively. In other words, the true bidialectal will use all the features of a dialect that monodialectal speakers of each dialect do—in a mutually exclusive manner, of course, for features that are not shared by the two dialects—and will, moreover, use those features with the same frequency and in the same environmental conditioning as monodialectals do. Chapter 7 will apply this criterion to the representative bidialectal speaker and show how well she matches monodialectal PDE and SCPE speakers' speech patterns, thus showing that she truly merits the label "bidialectal."

6.3. BIDIALECTALISM COMPARED TO OTHER DIALECT CONTACT PHENOMENA: WHAT BIDIALECTALISM IS NOT

In their investigation of dialect contact, researchers have noted several interesting types of individual speaker linguistic behaviors in response to contact with another dialect, including imitation/performance speech (Schilling-Estes 1998; Evans 2002), language crossing (Rampton 1995), accommodation (Auer, Barden, and Grosskopf 1998) and extreme personal pattern variation (Dorian 1994). On the surface, it may appear that the south central Pennsylvanians with two modes of speaking are engaging in one of these linguistic behaviors, but, as the data in chapter 7 will demonstrate, these PDE-SCPE speakers are indeed bidialectal. Nevertheless, to understand more fully the role that bidialectalism plays in south central Pennsylvania for the individual and for the speech community in the context of a dying dialect, it is necessary to distinguish clearly between bidialectalism and these other language variety contact phenomena. Below is a description of each language behavior as discussed in the literature, as well as an explanation of how the behavior of this study's bidialectals differs from each.

BIDIALECTALISM IS NOT...

... *Imitation/Performance Speech.* As mentioned earlier in this chapter, some sociolinguists (e.g., Preston 1992, 1996; Labov 1972, 1994) have examined speakers' on-demand performance of dialects—dialects subjects do not natively control—and have noted that these dialect imitations are notoriously inaccurate and incomplete. Typical imitation/performance strategies are limited to surface-level changes in speech tempo, voice quality, and intonation; imitators who only use such strategies do not show mastery or any real understanding of the nuances of morphosyntax or the low-level phonological processes that are the hallmark of the authentic dialect speaker (Labov 1994). Research by Evans (2002), however, provides a counterexample to such findings. Her informant Noah—son of parents from Michigan, raised in West Virginia—was referred to briefly in chapter 2 and will be referred to again in chapter 7 as an example of a probable bidialectal from the literature; he reports that he uses a Northern Midwestern–style dialect as his "normal" speech and a West Virginia–style dialect as his "imitation" code. By comparing measurements for formants of vowel nuclei, Evans (2002) was able to demonstrate that the vowel systems of Noah's two modes of speaking correspond closely to a conservative Northern Midwestern variety that does not include elements of the Northern Cities shift and to a general "Southern" variety that does include elements of the ongoing Southern Vowel Shift. Although Evans (2002) labels Noah's West Virginia-style speech as "imitation" (because that is the dialect he claims he does not normally use), such skill in matching native speaker vowel patterns arises out of true mastery of a dialect by a genuine native speaker. Noah is not simply an imitator.

Acoustic analysis will not be included in the discussion of the PDE-SCPE bidialectal in chapter 7, but she demonstrates, like Noah, enough skill in using the low-level features of both her dialects to prove that "imitation" is inadequate to describe either of her two ways of speaking. The same holds for the term "performance speech," defined by Schilling-Estes (1998, 63) as "that register associated with speakers' attempting to display for others a certain language or language variety, whether their own or that of another speech community." The key characteristics of this particular register that distinguish it from other uses of a dialect are that it is put on for display and that it is, by definition, self-conscious. Performance speech segments are often uttered either because they have been solicited or are providing out-of-context humor, with no relevance to the propositional content of the conversation. The Pennsylvanian bidialectals under consideration do not, however, normally "perform" either of their ways of speaking, nor do they normally rely on stock phrases to show off particular features. Instead, they make use of their two ways of speaking as part of daily life, not as a self-conscious or humorous display of either dialect.

Schilling-Estes makes it clear that speakers who perform dialects are only able to use the features they perceive in that performance (1998, 63); hence, if a speaker uses features that he or she cannot perceive, it can be inferred that the individual is not performing, but is engaging in true native use of a dialect that he or she controls. As chapter 7 will discuss in more detail, Pennsylvania bidialectal speakers are typically aware of only a few of the phonological variants discussed for PDE, yet they utilize variants of which they are unaware as well. These speakers are clearly not simple dialect imitators using perceptible features, but masters of both PDE and SCPE

...*Language Crossing*. In his pioneer work on language crossing behavior into Creole, Punjabi, and Asian English by adolescents in a South Midlands multiracial neighborhood in the United Kingdom, Rampton (1995) observed several characteristics that set this linguistic behavior apart from other inexpert uses of target language varieties:

1. Ethnic group differences: The language crosser has a different ethnic background than the individuals who use the language variety he or she is crossing into and, moreover, he/she did not grow up in a household or community where the language variety could be acquired natively.
2. Lack of competence: The language crosser is not able to use the target language variety accurately or completely.
3. Frequent insertions of lexicalisms or expressions: Because of the speaker's lack of competence in the target language variety, language crossers can attain only a very surface-level degree of "nativeness" in that variety.
4. "Flagging" of such lexicalisms and expressions by pauses, hesitations, and other means of advertently or inadvertently bringing attention to the language crosser's attempt at using the target variety.
5. Liminality of the social interactions space of the language crosser: Language crossers are not considered full members of the groups whose language they are attempting to use.

Because the linguistic behavior of PDE-SCPE speakers is not marked by the criteria mentioned above, the use of the term "language crossing" to describe their speech patterns is also inaccurate. There is no ethnic difference between these speakers and their monodialectal (in either SCPE or PDE) peers; in fact, all the speakers in this study come from the same Pennsylvania German background, the same communities, and (sometimes) the same families. Moreover, these SCPE-PDE speakers do not show a lack of competence in using either dialect; rather, as chapter 7 will show, the sample bidialectal exhibits mastery of even complex, low-level PDE features that go far beyond the lexicalisms and expressions that are the stock strategies of the language crosser, all without any kind of flagging behavior. Finally, liminality is not an issue for these PDE-SCPE speakers; they are full participants in the social networks in which they use their two dialects, not just fringe members who are not fully accepted as part of the group (as is the case with language crossers).

…Interpersonal Accommodation. Interpersonal accommodation involves the momentary convergence of the speech of an individual speaker toward the speech patterns of his or her interlocutor (see Giles, Taylor, and Bourhis 1973). This convergence is not complete—speakers do not exhibit all the interlocutors' speech patterns. Instead, it is a linguistic move in the GEN-ERAL DIRECTION of those speech patterns, using features that the speaker can perceive to sound "more like" the interlocutor. It is true that the use of PDE or SCPE by bidialectal speakers in a given situation is typically based on the dialect used by the interlocutor and hence is a sort of accommoda-tion in a very basic sense. However, in contrast to simple accommodation like that described by Giles, Taylor, and Bourhis (1973), this choice involves much more than a mere "movement" toward the interlocutor's dialect or an imperfect kind of convergence toward a few perceived features. For SPCE-PDE speakers, rather, it is a full-fledged use of each dialect as a medium of conversation, exhibiting both features the speakers perceive as well as those they do not.

…Extreme Personal Pattern Variation. Extreme personal pattern variation has been documented by Dorian (1994), who noted that the variation she encountered in her study of East Sutherland Gaelic-speaking communities could not be accounted for by differences between speakers in terms of area of residence, fluency in East Sutherland Gaelic, or any of the usual social variables invoked in sociolinguistic analysis, yet it was not merely "an unusual distortion of a dying language" (Dorian 1994, 631). Extreme intra-speaker variation was also found to striking degrees (even approaching free variation) by Connell (2002) in his work on Cambap, a "contracting" Mambiloid language spoken in Cameroon by only about 30 people. Like Dorian (1994), Connell (2002) asserted that this extreme variation is not the result of the obsolescent status of the language, since closer investiga-tion reveals that the differences between speakers can be attributed neither to the impact of the dominant language on speakers' productions (i.e., the replacement of Cambap features by features of one of the more domi-nant languages spoken in the area) nor to the lack of speaker practice with speaking Cambap, since speakers in his sample used Cambap on a daily basis in communication with each other. Extreme interpersonal variation

in East Sutherland Gaelic and Cambap therefore exists, but it is not a function of obsolescence.

PDE is an obsolescing dialect, and chapters 4 and 5 illustrated the degree of variation between monodialectals, particularly in the youngest generation of speakers. Bidialectal speakers are rare even in south central Pennsylvania, so it might be tempting to dismiss the linguistic behaviors of PDE-SCPE speakers simply as extreme interpersonal variation. However, what sets these bidialectal speakers apart from those who show evidence of personal pattern variation is that they use two separate, consistent feature SYSTEMS which align with the two dialects spoken in south central Pennsylvania today. This is unlike the Cambap and East Sutherland scenarios, where speakers demonstrated variation within a single language system. Viewing bidialectals merely as speakers who are exhibiting abnormal degrees of inter- or intraspeaker variation misses the opportunity to study their linguistic behavior and the social motivations behind their bidialectalism in the sociolinguistic context of a dying language variety.

... Style-Shifting. The classic taxonomies of style-shifting presented in sociolinguistic research by Labov (2001) and Baugh (2001) involve the separation of categories of speech into "casual" and "careful" or "informal" and "formal," with the distinguishing characteristic of different styles being how much attention speakers are paying to their speech when using that particular style. Style-shifting in general relates to the use of features of which community members are socially aware; by extension, this awareness is, generally, directly related to how abstract a feature is, with awareness being greater for the less abstract feature alternations. Even within a single conversation, the driving motivation behind style-shifting is topic shifts, and Labov (2001) and Baugh (2001) have developed instruments for classifying such data collected in the course of sociolinguistic interviews.

So do PDE-SCPE speakers actually switch between styles—and not between dialects—with PDE serving as the "informal" code choice and SCPE as the "formal" code choice? No, because they do not display undue attention to their speech or shift from PDE to SCPE only when the topic shifts; rather, according to information collected in interviews, code choice is usually made based on the presumed dialect (PDE or SCPE) of the interlocutor. Moreover, these speakers use both SCPE and PDE in situations where they pay great attention to their speech as well as in situations in which they do not, in both formal and informal contexts. The bidialectal speaker featured in chapter 7, for example, reports how careful she is to use SCPE when she teaches, but also how careful she is in her use of PDE when she is talking with elderly people who are PDE speakers. Although it is tempting to assume that speakers like this would simply use PDE for their "casual" style and SCPE for their "careful" style, their actual use of the two dialects is typically based on the dialect of their interlocutor and cuts across the grain of what style-shifting represents.

This section has focused on what bidialectalism is not, but, of course, this "process of elimination" of dialect contact phenomena can only describe what a group of speakers is NOT doing, not what they ARE doing. For "bidialectalism" to be a valid description of the Pennsylvanian PDE-SCPE speakers, it must exhibit characteristics that set it apart from other forms of dialect contact. Acceptance of bidialectalism as a possible outcome of dialect contact may marshal new approaches to dialect contact research.

6.4. BIDIALECTALS FROM THE LITERATURE

South central Pennsylvania speakers of PDE and SCPE are, of course, not the only bidialectal speakers in the world. As mentioned earlier, research on bidialectals is almost nonexistent, but a close examination of the literature does unearth at least a few individuals who seem to meet criteria for bidialectalism. While these speakers are labeled "bidialectal" in the works in which they are described, only some are the actual focus of the research; most are mentioned only in passing because the researcher is focused on some other linguistic issue. The discussion below separates such speakers into two categories: those who were specifically investigated for their bidialectal tendencies, and those whose behavior—reported in passing—seems to indicate that they may indeed be bidialectal.

FOCUS ON RESEARCH SUBJECTS AS "BIDIALECTALS." A few researchers have purposely investigated the differences between the "ways of speaking" used by individuals whom they believed to be bidialectal. These include Linnes (1998) and Johnstone (1999).

Linnes (1998). In an investigation of the speech patterns of individual speakers who use both Standard American English and African American Vernacular English (AAVE), Linnes (1998) compared their use of a range of widely accepted phonological and morphosyntactic features distinctive of AAVE. To her surprise, Linnes discovered that younger speakers did not actually use many—or in some cases, any—AAVE morphosyntactic variables, but relied instead on phonology to distinguish between their AAVE and their SAE modes. The notable exception to this was their use of AAVE zero past-tense marking, which younger speakers used at a much higher rate than older speakers. The motivation for speakers, both older and younger, behind switching between dialects did not vary with either the interlocutor's race or dialect, but instead centered on topic. Topics that had more to do with AAVE and an Afro-American identity sparked a switch to AAVE; topics that did not tended to encourage SAE instead.

Johnstone (1999). Johnstone (1999) specifically studied the dual use of "Texan" and "Southern English" by four women to provide ethnographic support for a certain type of bidialectal behavior. Their "Southern English" is a variety they have used since youth and are fluent in to the extent that "their uses of it sound native, as well as in the sense that they are members of or at least at the margins of the groups whose use defines fluency" (509). Their "Southern" way of speaking is interesting because it is not linked to a specific geographical area but rather to a whole region of the United States and is, hence, a collection of super-regional features; no one learns it as a first dialect. It is characterized (in Johnstone's study) by indirectness in interaction, overt displays of politeness, honorific address and reference forms, and diphthongization or "multiphthongization" of vowels—thus resulting in perceived slower speech, the famed "Southern drawl." Johnstone's evidence that these women do indeed maintain two distinct modes of speaking is based on their own reports and the manner in which they were able to display their abilities for the researcher. In other words, even though each woman makes use of a variety that for them is "part self, part other" (506) and even though they reported being very strategic about their switch from vernacular "Texan" into "Southern," these speakers switch between the varieties unselfconsciously, in firm belief that both varieties offer them a means of expressing different aspects of their identities, or, at the least, two identities they believe they possess (510–14).

INCIDENTAL REFERENCES TO BIDIALECTALS. In addition to the bidialectals purposely examined in the literature, there are also passing references to bidialectals by linguists investigating other contact phenomenon. In each case, the researcher either stated that bidialectals were present in their sample or that they assumed that bidialectals were present in the larger population of the speakers they were studying. Some examples of this include Mæhlum (1996) and Sjöström (2008):

Mæhlum (1996). In his critique of Blom and Gumperz's (1972) conclusions regarding code-shifting Norwegian speakers in Hemnesberget, Mæhlum urged caution in interpreting their findings as applying to most Norwegians: while bidialectal speakers abound in Norway, those who switch most clearly between standard and local dialects are those who lived outside their native villages or towns for a period of time (similar to the group of "dialect shifting" college students Blom and Gumperz described in 1972). The "bidialectalism" Mæhlum (1996, 751–52) attests to in Hemnesberget is actually a productive use of the local dialect coupled with a relatively passive knowledge of Bokmal, the standard dialect. Individuals with this level of control of the two dialects would fall in the "receptive" rather than "productive" category of bidialectals outlined by Hazen (2001, 3). However, while investigating bidialectal subjects in Oslo who had moved to the city from other places in Norway, Mæhlum did find speakers who alternated between codes, although it is not clear from his article to what degree they do this or at what levels of language this occurs (752–53).

Sjöström et al. (2008). A male speaker who took part in a voice identification experiment conducted by Sjöström et al. (2008) was described as a bidialectal speaker of Stockholm Swedish and the Scanian Swedish variety. This subject had moved from Stockholm to Scania as a 5-year-old child but continued to use Stockholm Swedish until middle school; at that age he worked to acquire Scanian Swedish to fit in with his peers. At the time of the experiment, the speaker reported that he spoke Stockholm Swedish with his relatives and children (despite the fact that they used Scanian) and Scanian Swedish with his wife and most of his colleagues. The voice identification experiment Sjöström et al. (2008) designed required him to be recorded speaking each dialect; his production of each dialect was masterful enough that no listening subject in the experiment identified him as the same speaker (Sjöström et al. 2008, 156–58).

This handful of case studies certainly opens up the inquiry into bidialectalism, but significantly more empirical evidence is needed before methodical analysis of bidialectal behavior is possible. That is how the next chapter makes an important contribution. In presenting an ethnographic account of the sociolinguistic strategies of three bidialectal PDE-SCPE speakers, as well as an in-depth examination of the linguistic behavior of one particular bidialectal PDE-SCPE speaker, chapter 7 goes beyond the scope of the case studies just mentioned: it will present a broader range of detailed linguistic information than these other studies do and will situate the single bidialectal into the context of a community of speakers with the same motivations and (presumably) similar behaviors. By looking at clusters of speakers who exhibit bidialectal tendencies, bidialectalism can be studied as a group behavior governed by basic sociolinguistic principles, and not just as a set of idiosyncratic behaviors exhibited by isolated individuals.

7. THE EMERGENCE
OF BIDIALECTALISM AT THE END
OF THE LIFE CYCLE OF PDE:
A CASE STUDY

Part of the last stage of PDE's life cycle, as the south central Pennsylvania speech community shifts to SCPE, is the development of PDE/SCPE-speaking bidialectals: individuals who have developed two distinct modes of speaking that correspond to PDE and to SCPE to cope with the demands of being part of two overlapping worlds dominated by monodialectal speakers of PDE and SCPE. This chapter investigates the linguistic and extralinguistic characteristics of one such bidialectal's speech patterns and the motivations behind the bidialectal behavior of two other informants. By examining the various processes at work when individuals choose bidialectalism to meet their linguistic needs, this chapter will help to inform the study of bidialectalism in other contexts of intense dialect contact.

Section 7.1 begins this chapter's description of the ephemeral phenomenon of PDE-SCPE bidialectalism in south central Pennsylvania by presenting a detailed linguistic account and sketch of the social context of a single self-reported bidialectal, comparing that individual's use of PDE features with use by monodialectal speakers to test the authenticity of her bidialectalism according to Hazen's (2001, 92–94) criteria delineated in chapter 6. This information, paired with data concerning the social milieu in which she and other self-proclaimed bidialectal speakers from south central Pennsylvania live, will provide the necessary background to develop a general profile of a bidialectal speaker in section 7.2. In particular, this section will propose general principles about the kinds of linguistic environments in which such speakers arise, the ways in which a bidialectal speaker moves between two sets of language features and language variation patterns, and the motivations that lead a speaker to become bidialectal in the first place. Finally, section 7.3 concludes by critiquing Hazen's bidialectalism criteria and making recommendations for more informed ways of isolating and studying bidialectal behavior.

7.1. A BIDIALECTAL IN PENNSYLVANIA

This chapter focuses on a single bidialectal speaker, "Rachel," who was born in Lebanon County, Pennsylvania, and grew up in Green Point, a tiny rural community of homes spread through the forested mountains of the extreme northern part of the county. Demographically, she is a good match for the other PDE- and SCPE-speaking monodialectal informants in this study, because, like them, she is from a working-class, nonsectarian, PDE-speaking family. Like them, she grew up in close proximity to extended family—in fact, the mobile-home-turned-house she grew up in is situated on the edge of her grandparents' farm—and she spent much of her time as a child and teen with grandparents, aunts, uncles, and cousins. Also, like every PDE and SPCE speaker in her age cohort that took part in this study (the 30–40-year-olds), she learned PDE as her first dialect from two PDE-speaking parents and did not encounter SCPE until she started elementary school. Besides school, Rachel's other source of social interaction with people outside the family was church (although all but a handful of people at the Green Point church she attended are distantly related to her), and there she also spent a significant amount of time with both older people and peers (especially her second cousin, who became her best friend). Like her home, church was a PDE-dominant environment, since nearly everyone in this country church, including the pastor, spoke PDE.

When children from PDE-speaking families started elementary school when Rachel did, in the early 1970s, it did not take long for them to realize that there existed a very real tension between the language variety that they spoke (and that they heard their families speak) and the variety teachers expected them to use in the classroom; in fact, some teachers were quite vocal in their attempts to stamp out "Dutchifiedness." Perhaps following the lead of these teachers, SCPE-speaking children also began to look down on their PDE-speaking peers, saying that they sounded "hick" and "dumb." In response, by their late preteens and early teens, most PDE speakers either abandoned PDE if possible[1] (to fit in with SCPE speakers, sound intelligent, and please the teachers) or kept speaking PDE (to continue to fit in with PDE-speaking peers and family).

Family dialect was not the only factor involved in the decision about which dialect to speak. For many young PDE speakers of Rachel's generation, the choice of which dialect to embrace was also influenced by the composition of one's peer network: if a young PDE speaker had almost all PDE-speaking friends, it made sense just to keep speaking PDE, but if a young speaker had many SCPE-speaking friends, it was advisable (because of the stigma against PDE) to adopt SCPE instead. Perhaps the deciding factor in a PDE speaker's ultimate choice of dialect, however, went beyond social network to the speaker's career aspirations,[2] a factor reflected in the "track" students chose when they entered junior high school. PDE speakers enrolled in the business or college-bound tracks were greatly encouraged by teachers to adopt SCPE so they would—in the words of the informants— "sound intelligent," "be taken seriously," and "get ahead." Vocational-track students did not have the same pressures put on them. Informants' peer networks were typically drawn primarily from students in the same track— the students with whom one spent the most time in class—and the peer network's language attitudes inevitably had an effect on the language choices of individual speakers. Most young people who grew up speaking PDE thus chose either to retain the dialect if they aspired to vocational positions (carpenter, farmer, mechanic, etc.) and had PDE-speaking peer networks or to abandon PDE entirely in favor of SCPE if they aspired to professional positions (secretarial posts, or professions requiring college training) and had SCPE-speaking peer networks (Anderson 1995).

This dilemma was further complicated by the fact that older PDE speakers were themselves sensitive to the way that SCPE-speaking outsiders viewed PDE. From the 1960s onward, increased mobility (due to affordable cars) and the creation of jobs away from the farms of northern Lebanon County fostered more contact than before with SCPE speakers, often in the context of employment with larger firms like Bethlehem Steel or Hershey Company. Many SCPE speakers showed disdain for the "dumb Dutchmen" who spoke PDE, and some sensitive older PDE speakers reacted to this by viewing the youngsters in their own families as somehow "disloyal to their roots," "uppity," and "thinking they're better than us" if they began to speak the more prestigious regional dialect. This covert prestige for the PDE dialect is, in part, an offshoot of the cultural mindset of many Pennsylvania Germans that values a certain kind of humility (*demut* in Pennsylvania German [Keiser 2012]) that discourages one from putting oneself forward and encourages one to remain simple and down-to-earth; for older speakers of PDE, speaking the dialect was seen as an important part of that. In an intergenerational society in which many of one's social interactions outside school involved such older relatives, negative labels implying disloyalty to family and the accompanying disapproval could have serious emotional consequences.

Instead of choosing one dialect over the other, however, some young PDE speakers like Rachel acquired SCPE while simultaneously maintaining PDE. For Rachel, this was a direct result of feeling the need to belong to two separate worlds. For example, she was proud of her Pennsylvania Dutch heritage and even wished she could speak Pennsylvania Dutch with her bilingual (in Pennsylvania German and PDE) grandmother, with whom she spent a significant amount of time as a caregiver;[3] Rachel took four years of German in high school (since that was the language offered that was closest to Pennsylvania Dutch), and she and her grandmother loved to compare German words with Pennsylvania Dutch words. Rachel also spent a lot of time with her father and with other extended family members, and she vividly remembers feeling the need to speak PDE to please the older generation. But she was also a good student, on a college-bound track in school (which encouraged speaking SCPE), and graduated high school third in her class. She loved reading and abstract thought and in general had an appreciation for arts and learning that were far removed from her PDE-speaking world. Given her desire to go off to college, it would have been easier for Rachel to abandon PDE altogether, but she was socially sensitive enough to feel that, if she wanted to fit into both her "different worlds," she was going to have to learn to speak both PDE and SCPE.

What motivates a speaker to retain PDE while also learning to speak SCPE is an interesting question, especially given how far the PDE dialect has unraveled, even for those whom the speech community considers to be monodialectal PDE speakers. Chapter 5 dealt in detail with what it means to be a speaker of PDE at a time when the dialect shows such a high degree of variability between individuals' speech patterns in the last generation of PDE speakers: it seems an individual is considered to be a PDE speaker simply by noticeably using one or more of the "core" features of the dialect and, optionally, some more "peripheral" features. For a bidialectal to be seen as a PDE speaker when interacting with PDE speakers, it is imperative to utilize PDE features in much the same manner as the monodialectals, but what exactly that means in such a context of instability is unclear. At the very least, a bidialectal should produce "core" features of the dialect when speaking PDE, although it is not certain what percentage is necessary to "match" the monodialectals.

Before going further it should be noted here that Rachel is far from the only self-proclaimed bidialectal speaker of PDE and SCPE in south central Pennsylvania, and the description of her social situation is quite common to individuals from her generation; however, she is the only bidialectal who completed this study. When I was a teenager in south central Pennsylvania, I had many acquaintances and friends who described themselves as bidialectal, but when this study was completed over 20 years later, there were few who still claimed such status, and almost all those who had formerly claimed to be bidialectal had gravitated toward SCPE. Even so, in 2005 there were four individuals who called themselves bidialectals who initially participated in this study; however, for a variety of family and personal reasons, three of them had to drop out, and only Rachel was able to see the study to its conclusion. (One of these bidialectals, Rachel's second cousin and best friend through much of high school, also grew up in a nonsectarian PDE-speaking home and attended the same church Rachel did. The other two bidialectals, a brother and sister from a Mennonite household, grew up speaking both Pennsylvania Dutch and English and developed their bidialectalism in PDE and SCPE in a slightly different linguistic and social environment than did Rachel and her second cousin.)

The qualitative and quantitative criteria for bidialectalism reported below focus on Rachel's data alone when it comes to statistical comparisons and assertions that can be made on the basis of those comparisons. This is not to suggest that the bidialectals who dropped out of the study—or even other bidialectals in south central Pennsylvania—do not exhibit the same linguistic features as Rachel or the same frequencies and constraints. This assessment remains a question for future research. The most this chapter can present is linguistic data collected only from recorded interviews with Rachel. Social data gathered from the other informants before they left the study, however, will be considered alongside Rachel's social data when this chapter turns to the development of a profile of a south central Pennsylvania bidialectal in section 7.2.

7.2. CRITERIA FOR BIDIALECTALISM

QUALITATIVE CRITERIA FOR BIDIALECTALISM. Recall that Hazen's (2001, 92–94) requirements for bidialectalism state that, for a person to be deemed a genuine bidialectal, that speaker must...

1. produce the same sets of features as monodialectal speakers of both dialects, without overlap,
2. produce those features in the same "language variation patterns" that monodialectals do, and
3. possess a social motivation for acquiring the second dialect while retaining the first one.

To determine how well Rachel meets these criteria, she was recorded in two different conversations, one a little more than an hour long with friends who speak SCPE and one a little more than an hour long with friends who speak PDE. These conversations were transcribed, coded, and analyzed, and her data will be compared to that of the monodialectal SCPE and PDE speakers who participated in this study.

FEATURE CRITERIA FOR BIDIALECTALISM. Table 7.1 lists the PDE features used by the youngest and middle-aged PDE-speaking monodialectal informants, based on data collected on five phonological features deemed diagnostic of PDE speakers, plus the bilabial fricative. The table also presents the PDE features used by the SCPE-speaking monodialectals (all 30–40 years old at the time of the recording, agemates of the youngest PDE speakers). Table 7.2 lists the features used by Rachel in each recorded conversation.

Recall from chapters 4 and 5 that no PDE speaker in this study uses any PDE feature categorically—the one exception to this being the monophthongization of /a/ before nasals in the middle-aged generation of speakers. SCPE and PDE have been in heavy contact for a long time, and when someone who is deemed a PDE speaker is NOT using a PDE feature in a possible context, then he or she is likely using a realization that overlaps with

TABLE 7.1
PDE Features Used by Monodialectals

PDE Speakers[a]
   Middle Generation
       obstruent devoicing (*bed* as [bɛt])
       bilabial fricative (substituted for /w/ in strong environments in word-initial contexts and in onsets of stressed syllables)
       monophthongization of /aʊ/ to [a] (*house* as [has])
       monophthongization of /aɪ/ to [æ] before liquids (*mile* as [mæl])
       monophthongization of /a/ to [ʌ] before nasals (*bomb* as [bʌm])
       raised [æ]
   Youngest Generation
       obstruent devoicing
       monophthongization of /aʊ/ to [a]
       monophthongization of /aɪ/ to [æ] before liquids
       monophthongization of /a/ to [ʌ] before nasals
       raised [æ]
SCPE Speakers[b]
   obstruent devoicing
   /aʊ/ monophthongization
   raised [æ]

a. Again, recall from the chapter 5 that not every speaker from each group uses every feature. This is particularly true for the youngest generation, where feature use varies widely between speakers

b. One SCPE speaker used a single token of obstruent devoicing (1/374 tokens), and another SCPE speaker used a single token of /aʊ/ monophthongization (1/74 tokens) and a small percentage of PDE raised [æ] (3/60 tokens).

TABLE 7.2
PDE Features Used by Rachel in Her Two Conversations

PDE Conversation
    obstruent devoicing
    bilabial fricative
    monophthongization of /aʊ/ to [a]
    monophthongization of /aɪ/ to [æ] before liquids
    monophthongization of /a/ to [ʌ] before nasals
    raised [æ]
SCPE Conversation
    obstruent devoicing

the SCPE feature for that same segment. Hazen's (2001) criterion that the bidialectal must produce the same sets of features as monodialectal speakers of the two respective dialects seems reasonable, but his stipulation that this be done "without overlap" is an overly restrictive criterion in the face of the kind of intense dialect contact that exists in south central Pennsylvania. In the case of a PDE-SCPE bidialectal, the most that can be done to fulfill this criterion is to reserve uniquely PDE features for PDE discourse and to refrain from using PDE features in SCPE discourse.

This is exactly what Rachel does. Table 7.2 shows that she restricts her use of PDE features, almost exclusively, to her PDE speech. The one exception to this—that is, the one place where there is a small degree of "bleeding" between her two systems with regard to these PDE features—is in her obstruent devoicing. As will be shown below in table 7.3, this is not statistically significant from the SCPE speaker who shows evidence of an insignificant amount of obstruent devoicing as well (a single token). Note also that when speaking PDE Rachel uses the bilabial fricative, a feature used by the middle-aged generation, but not at all by her monodialectal PDE-speaking peers from the youngest generation of PDE speakers.

Rachel is viewed by SCPE speakers as a speaker of SCPE, and it does not appear that the obstruent devoicing "bleed" between her PDE and SCPE systems jeapordizes that status. By her own account, it is less clear whether PDE speakers consider her a fellow speaker of PDE, but she definitely feels that she is seen as "fitting in" with them, and her use of PDE features is no doubt intended to achieve exactly that result. In terms of the phonological features chosen for this study's analysis as diagnostic of the PDE speaker, Rachel succeeds in keeping her PDE features almost entirely out of her SCPE speech with the exception of the small amount of obstruent devoicing discussed above; she simultaneously uses the full complement of PDE features (including the bilabial fricative) when she speaks PDE.

QUANTITATIVE CRITERIA FOR BIDIALECTALISM. Hazen's (2001) second criteria for bidialectalism is that, for a speaker to be considered bidialectal, that speaker must produce features in the same "language variation patterns" that monodialectals do. This means that to qualify as a true bidialectal, Rachel must show evidence of the same language variation patterns as monodialectal speakers in her PDE and SCPE. "Language variation patterns" is a multifaceted concept; certainly it involves frequencies at which features are produced, but it also includes conditioning factors that determine when noncategorical dialect features are produced as well as how features are classified with regard to other features in a speaker's grammar. In other words, to match the language variation patterns of the PDE monodialectals in this study, Rachel will have to show evidence that she uses PDE features with the same frequencies that monodialectal speakers do and that her use of PDE features follows the same grammatical restrictions as the monodialectal speakers follow. Similarly, to match the language variation patterns of SCPE speakers, Rachel must also show evidence that she uses SCPE features with the same frequencies and with the same grammatical restrictions as SCPE monodialectals. However, language variation patterns of SCPE speakers have not been delineated by linguistic researchers or by this particular study, with its focus on PDE. In light of this, the most that can be proven with certainty here is that Rachel does not use PDE features any more often than her SPCE monodialectal peers when speaking SCPE.

Frequencies. First this section compares Rachel's SCPE with that of the SCPE monodialectals. Table 7.3 briefly presents Rachel's frequency data for PDE features when speaking SCPE, alongside frequency data for SCPE speakers from her age group. Data for SCPE speakers JL, RK, and EL (monodialectal SCPE-speaking agemates of Rachel) are given separately, along with their combined frequency for use of the different PDE variants.

The SCPE speakers in this sample are all individuals who, like Rachel, grew up in homes with PDE-speaking parents. Thus, all these individuals would have spoken PDE as their first dialect and then abandoned it at some point in favor of SCPE. In this sense, they are the perfect match for Rachel in this study, because they presumably faced as preteens the same pressure to shift dialects that Rachel faced. Despite the fact that these speakers settled on SCPE as their chosen dialect, some minor residual effect of PDE in their SCPE is still evident for speakers JL and RK: the data for JL show a single token of obstruent devoicing, and RK shows a single token of /aʊ/ monophthongization. Even more notable is RK's relatively high percentage (for an SCPE speaker) of [æ] raising; this may be due to the influence of

TABLE 7.3

Comparison of Rachel's Use of PDE Features When Speaking SCPE
with SCPE Speakers' Use of PDE Features

[β] for /w/		
JL	0/148	(0.0%)
RK	0/344	(0.0%)
EL	0/296	(0.0%)
TOTAL	0/788	(0.0%)
Rachel	0/385	(0.0%)
/aʊ/ monophthongization		
JL	0/71	(0.0%)
RK	1/74	(1.4%)
EL	0/61	(0.0%)
TOTAL	1/206	(0.5%)
Rachel	0/78	(0.0%)
/aɪ/ monophthongization		
JL	0/6	(0.0%)
RK	0/5	(0.0%)
EL	0/20	(0.0%)
TOTAL	0/31	(0.0%)
Rachel	0/4	(0.0%)
/a/ centralization		
JL	0/2	(0.0%)
RK	0/9	(0.0%)
EL	0/6	(0.0%)
TOTAL	0/17	(0.0%)
Rachel	0/9	(0.0%)
[æ] raising		
JL	0/27	(0.0%)
RK	3/60	(5.0%)
EL	0/58	(0.0%)
TOTAL	3/145	(2.1%)
Rachel	0/60	(0.0%)
Obstruent devoicing		
JL	1/374	(0.0%)
RK	0/635	(0.0%)
EL	0/684	(0.0%)
TOTAL	1/1,693	(0.1%)
Rachel	11/905	(1.2%)

$\chi^2 = 14.73; p = .0001$

NOTE: Yates's correction was used when a cell contained fewer than 5 tokens.

her PDE-speaking husband, who has the highest incidence of [æ] raising of any individual who took part in this study. Despite this [æ] raising, RK is considered to be an SCPE speaker by others in the speech community, perhaps because her use of other PDE features is so minimal or perhaps because [æ] raising is not a core feature of the PDE dialect in the minds of either PDE or SCPE speakers.

How does Rachel's PDE feature use when speaking SCPE compare to the SCPE monodialectal feature use? Like her SCPE-speaking peers, she shows no evidence of the PDE bilabial fricative, monophthongized or centralized vowels, or raised [æ] when she is speaking SCPE. As shown in tables 7.2 and 7.3, the only PDE feature Rachel produced in her SCPE speech is obstruent devoicing. Even though her devoicing occurs at a very low rate (1.2%), there is enough deviance from the combined rate of her SCPE-speaking peers to be significant ($p = .0001$, using the Yates's chi-squared correction because one of the cells has fewer than five tokens). However, in comparison with JL, the only SCPE monodialectal who shows any evidence of obstruent devoicing (with a single token), Rachel's deviance is not significant ($p = .199$, with Yates's correction). Evidently Rachel is successful enough at keeping most PDE features in check when speaking SCPE; even for obstruent devoicing, the only PDE feature in her SCPE speech, she is successful at least to the point where her use of the feature falls within an acceptable (i.e., not statistically significant) margin of deviance from the use of that feature by at least some of her SCPE-speaking peers. Rachel acquired SCPE as her second dialect, just as these monodialectals did, and her linguistic behavior conforms to theirs; her degree of avoidance of PDE features meets the requirements (at least for the diagnostic PDE features highlighted in this study) to be considered an authentic speaker of SCPE.

Table 7.4 presents the frequencies at which Rachel uses PDE features when speaking PDE, alongside the frequencies of PDE feature use for her PDE-speaking peers. When comparing the combined results of the PDE speakers with Rachel's results, it would appear at first glance that her frequencies do not match those of her peers:[4] her frequencies are higher than the combined frequencies of her peers for every PDE feature except for /aʊ/ monophthongization, for which her frequency is lower. Moreover, Rachel uses the bilabial fricative, a feature employed by middle-aged speakers of PDE, but not by younger speakers. The measures of statistical significance of the differences between Rachel's frequencies and the combined frequencies of her peers for various features tells a similar story: Rachel's frequencies differ to a statistically significant degree from her peers' combined frequencies for the bilabial fricative (since her peers do not use this

TABLE 7.4
Comparison of Rachel's Use of PDE Features When Speaking PDE
with Young PDE Speakers' Use of PDE Features

[β] for /w/			
DK	0/377	(0.0%)	
DwK	0/298	(0.0%)	
LK	0/326	(0.0%)	
TOTAL	0/1,001	(0.0%)	$\chi^2 = 179.972; p < .001$
Rachel	78/450	(17.3%)	
/aʊ/ monophthongization			
DK	26/65	(40.0%)	
DwK	5/47	(10.6%)	
LK	7/75	(9.3%)	
TOTAL	37/187	(19.8%)	$\chi^2 = 1.341; p = .247$
Rachel	13/92	(14.1%)	
/aɪ/ monophthongization			
DK	0/1	(0.0%)	
DwK	0/7	(0.0%)	
LK	1/7	(14.3%)	
TOTAL	1/15	(6.7%)	$\chi^2 = 0.021; p = .885$
Rachel	1/4	(25.0%)	
/a/ centralization			
DK	2/10	(20.0%)	
DwK	0/12	(0.0%)	
LK	1/13	(7.7%)	
TOTAL	3/35	(8.6%)	$\chi^2 = 0.024; p = .876$
Rachel	1/4	(25.0%)	
[æ] raising			
DK	1/39	(2.6%)	
DwK	17/49	(34.7%)	
LK	3/40	(7.5%)	
TOTAL	21/128	(16.4%)	$\chi^2 = 14.622; p = .0001$
Rachel	26/62	(41.9%)	
Obstruent devoicing			
DK	3/623	(0.5%)	
DwK	17/558	(3.0%)	
LK	89/656	(13.6%)	
TOTAL	109/1,837	(5.9%)	$\chi^2 = 33.736; p < .001$
Rachel	87/671	(13.0%)	

NOTE: Yates's correction was used when a cell contained fewer than 5 tokens.

feature at all) as well as for [æ] raising and obstruent devoicing. Perhaps there is a better way than comparing averages of combined results to evaluate the extent to which Rachel's PDE matches that of other PDE speakers.

Recall from chapter 5 that there is tremendous variability in PDE feature use among the last generation of speakers, Rachel's peers, with some speakers using some features but not others and some speakers using one particular feature more frequently than other speakers in the same data set. This kind of variability among speakers results in combined rates of feature use that do not truly exhibit a central tendency. In this case, looking at how Rachel's frequencies fall within or outside of the range of frequencies exhibited by her peers is a better method for determining whether her frequencies actually match theirs. Table 7.5 lists these ranges for each feature and compares Rachel's results, providing measures of statistical significance of the difference between Rachel's results and the highest frequency exhibited by a monodialectal.

As it turns out, Rachel's frequencies sit solidly with the range of frequencies exhibited by her peers for /aʊ/ monophthongization (14.1%) and obstruent devoicing (13.0%), the two most salient features for PDE speakers. For /aɪ/ monophthongization and /a/ centralization, Rachel's frequencies (25% for each) are higher than any of her peers', but a chi-squared

TABLE 7.5

Range of Frequencies for PDE Feature Use by the Youngest PDE Speakers
Compared with Rachel's Frequencies

PDE Feature	Monodialectal Range	Rachel	Significance
[β] for /w/[a]	0/298 (0.0%) – 0/377 (0.0%)	78/450 (17.3%)	$\chi^2 = 56.552;$ $p < .001$
/aʊ/ monophthongization	7/75 (9.3%) – 26/65 (40.0%)	13/92 (14.1%)	within range
/aɪ/ monophthongization[b]	0/7 (0.0%) – 1/7 (14.3%)	1/4 (25.0%)	$\chi^2 = 0.136;$ $p = .712$
/a/ centralization[b]	0/12 (0.0%) – 2/10 (20.0%)	1/4 (25.0%)	$\chi^2 = 0.265;$ $p = .607$
[æ] raising	1/39 (2.6%) – 17/49 (34.7%)	26/62 (41.9%)	$\chi^2 = 0.605;$ $p = .437$
Obstruent devoicing	3/623 (0.5%) – 89/656 (13.6%)	101/779 (13.0%)	within range

NOTE: Yates's correction was used when cell contained fewer than 5 tokens.

a. The bilabial fricative is not used at all by younger PDE monodialectals, but Rachel uses it.

test with a Yates's correction reveals that even so she does not differ in a statistically significant manner from the peer with the highest frequencies of those features (the *p*-values are greater than .05 in both cases). Even so, only a single token from Rachel of each variant was used to make this assessment, and it is thus impossible to determine whether the lack of statistical significance of her deviance from her peers is because of too little data or because her linguistic behavior is really more like theirs than the numbers indicate. (Given the evidence for her matching her peers in use of some other PDE features, however, I am inclined to accept the latter hypothesis.) Rachel is also high in her use of the PDE raised [æ] (41.9%), but again, using a regular chi-squared test, she differs from her peers with the highest frequency in a way that is not statistically significant (*p* = .437). To sum up, with the exception of her use of the bilabial fricative, Rachel does not differ significantly from her highest-ranking PDE-speaking peers in the use of any of the PDE phonological features that are the focus of this study. She may be a CONSERVATIVE speaker, but her linguistic behavior generally fits with the frequency patterns of her age cohort.

Given Rachel's use of the bilabial fricative and her high frequencies for certain features (/aɪ/ monophthongization and /a/ centralization, both features of which she evidences only one token), one might suspect that she is actually "hypercorrect" in her use of PDE features in an attempt to distinguish between her PDE and SCPE "ways of speaking." One could further hypothesize that she is modeling her frequencies for PDE features after those of the middle-aged generation, who are, of course, more "Dutchified" in both popular conception and in reality, based on their PDE feature use. Table 7.6 tests this idea by comparing the middle-aged generation of PDE speakers and Rachel in terms of the frequencies with which they use PDE features.

Compared to the combined usage rates of the middle-aged PDE speakers, Rachel's rates are lower (sometimes much lower) for every feature except [æ] raising, although she is only a little lower in her use of the bilabial fricative and obstruent devoicing. The chi-squared test shows that her frequencies are not statistically different (*p* > .05) from the overall frequency for the middle-aged speakers for the bilabial fricative, /aɪ/ monophthongization, and obstruent devoicing; she does differ in a statistically significant way (*p* < .05) for /aʊ/ monophthongization, /a/ centralization, and [æ] raising. Table 7.7 shows how Rachel matches up in terms of range of frequencies exhibited by the middle-aged speakers, with *p*-values indicating the statistical level of significance between herself and the middle-aged speaker closest to her in frequency for any feature for which Rachel's frequencies are not in the range exhibited by the other speakers.

TABLE 7.6

Comparison of Rachel's Use of PDE Features When Speaking PDE
with Middle-Aged PDE Speakers' Use of PDE Features

[β] for /w/			
DG	125/452	(27.7%)	
LM	20/80	(25.0%)	
LG	12/222	(5.4%)	
TOTAL	157/754	(20.8%)	$\chi^2 = 2.184; p = .140$
Rachel	78/450	(17.3%)	
/aʊ/ monophthongization			
DG	5/7	(71.4%)	
LM	17/19	(89.5%)	
LG	26/64	(40.6%)	
TOTAL	48/90	(53.3%)	$\chi^2 = 31.378; p < .001$
Rachel	13/92	(14.1%)	
/aɪ/ monophthongization			
DG	5/7	(71.4%)	
LM	2/2	(100.0%)	
LG	0/2	(0.0%)	
TOTAL	7/11	(63.6%)	$\chi^2 = 0.549; p = .459$
Rachel	1/4	(25.0%)	
/a/ centralization			
DG	17/17	(100.0%)	
LM	2/2	(100.0%)	
LG	1/1	(100.0%)	
TOTAL	20/20	(100.0%)	$\chi^2 = 179.972; p < .001$
Rachel	1/4	(25.0%)	
[æ] raising			
DG	1/52	(1.9%)	
LM	6/22	(27.3%)	
LG	18/74	(24.3%)	
TOTAL	25/148	(16.9%)	$\chi^2 = 17.05; p < .001$
Rachel	26/62	(41.9%)	
Obstruent devoicing			
DG	102/746	(13.7%)	
LM	25/144	(17.4%)	
LG	70/451	(15.6%)	
TOTAL	197/1,341	(14.7%)	$\chi^2 = 179.972; p = .271$
Rachel	101/779	(13.0%)	

NOTE: Yates's correction was used when a cell contained fewer than 5 tokens.

TABLE 7.7

Range of Frequencies for PDE Feature Use by the Middle-Aged PDE Speakers
Compared with Rachel's Frequencies

PDE Feature	Monodialectal Range	Rachel	Significance
[β] for /w/	12/222 (5.4%) – 125/452 (27.7%)	78/450 (17.3%)	within range
/aʊ/ monophthongization	26/64 (40.6%) – 17/19 (89.5%)	13/92 (14.1%)	$\chi^2 = 14.13$; $p < .001$
/aɪ/ monophthongization[a]	0/2 (0.0%) – 2/2 (100.0%)	1/4 (25.0%)	within range
/a/ centralization[a]	1/1 (100.0%) – 17/17 (100.0%)	1/4 (25.0%)	$\chi^2 = 9.381$; $p = .002$
[æ] raising	1/52 (1.9%) – 6/22 (27.3%)	26/62 (41.9%)	$\chi^2 = 1.48$; $p = .224$
Obstruent devoicing	102/746 (13.7%) – 25/144 (17.4%)	101/779 (13.0%)	$\chi^2 = 0.165$; $p = .685$

NOTE: Yates's correction was used when a cell contained fewer than 5 tokens.

a. As was discussed in chapter 5, these features have conditioning environments that do not occur frequently in casual conversation, and hence numbers of tokens are low (see table 6.2). By an accident of the data, Rachel's frequencies for these PDE variants are based on single tokens. Likewise, for /a/ centralization, one middle-aged speaker also exhibits categorical use of the PDE variant based on a single token.

As table 7.7 indicates, Rachel's frequencies sit solidly within the range shown by the middle-aged speakers for the bilabial fricative. They do for /aɪ/ monophthongization as well, but this is because of a single middle-aged speaker[5] who does not monophthongize /aɪ/ at all in this data set. In fact, Rachel's frequencies are similar to the middle-aged speakers' frequencies for four of the six PDE features listed here, with /a/ centralization and /aʊ/ monophthongization the two exceptions. For example, Rachel's obstruent devoicing does not differ from the lowest-frequency middle-aged speaker in a statistically signficant way ($p = .685$), nor does her rate of [æ] raising differ significantly from the highest-frequency middle-aged speaker ($p = .224$). The difference in Rachel's frequency for /a/ centralization is statistically significant ($p = .002$), but numbers of tokens are quite low, making it difficult to ascertain whether this result reflects a true difference or is an artifact of the data. The only PDE feature for which Rachel does in fact unqualifiedly differ in a significant way from the middle-aged speakers is /aʊ/ monophthongization ($p < .001$), since the middle-aged speakers use this feature categorically and she does not.

So, is Rachel "hyperdialectal" in the sense that she matches the middle-aged generation's frequencies for her PDE features better than she matches her peers? One could surmise that this is the case since she does not differ significantly from the middle-aged speakers for the majority of PDE features listed here, but it is telling that Rachel does differ from the middle-aged speakers in her use of the salient /aʊ/ monophthongization and that she overuses the nonsalient [æ] raising compared to both middle-aged and younger speakers. If Rachel were truly "hyperdialectal," she would make good use of the highly salient /aʊ/ monophthongization to mark her PDE, and [æ] raising would figure much less prominently in her speech. Perhaps a better explanation for her behavior displayed here is that the data for Rachel were recorded, by her choice, while she was speaking with middle-aged interlocutors and may thus have been accommodating toward their norms; it could be that if Rachel had been speaking with interlocutors of her peer group, her frequencies would not have been as high for any of the features listed here. (Further study of Rachel's behavior should take this factor into account.) For the purposes of ascertaining frequency matching, although the statistics show that Rachel is a conservative speaker—and that she may be skilled at accommodating to the speech of her interlocutors— she is not HYPERCORRECT in her use of PDE features.

Table 7.8 summarizes how her frequencies compared to her PDE-speaking peers and to the middle-aged speakers of PDE, with features indicated for which there are too few tokens to draw strong conclusions. The data provide the kind of evidence demanded earlier to show that Rachel is indeed a bidialectal: these results show that she both produces the same

TABLE 7.8
Overview of Rachel's Rates Compared to Other PDE Speakers

Feature	Rachel Compared to Middle-Aged PDE Speakers	Rachel Compared to Youngest PDE Speakers
[β] for /w/	normal	very high[a]
/aʊ/ monophthongization	very low	normal
/aɪ/ monophthongization	(too few tokens)	(too few tokens)
/a/ centralization	(too few tokens)	(too few tokens)
[æ] raising	high[b]	high[b]
Obstruent devoicing	normal	high[b]

a. Feature was not used at all by the youngest PDE speakers.

b. These are features for which Rachel's frequencies are not statistically significantly different than the highest-frequency or lowest-frequency evidence provided by a monodialectal PDE speaker in that age group.

dialect features monodialectal speakers do and at frequencies that compare favorably with—or at least are not significantly different from—those of her peers for all features (except for her use the biliabial fricative). She produces the same variety of features the middle-aged speakers do, and her frequencies compare favorably with that generation for some, but not all, features. Rachel is unique among her PDE-speaking peers in that she uses the bilabial fricative in her PDE, but her use of the feature cannot be said to be completely idiosyncratic, since she uses it with the frequencies of the middle-aged speakers. In terms of features produced and frequencies of features produced, Rachel's patterns fit with those exhibited by monodialectal PDE speakers.

More Language Variation Patterns. Exactly what does one mean when one says that two speakers have the same "language variation patterns," and how does one go about proving that they do? One method is to show that phonological conditions favoring the use of a certain phonological feature are the same for two sets of speakers. In his article on tests for bidialectalism, for example, Hazen (2001) uses the relative frequencies of /ay/-ungliding among Warren, North Carolina, speakers from a single family, showing how their Appalachian English pattern of ungliding favors unglided /ay/ less before voiceless obstruents than before voiced obstruents, nasals, or liquids, even though their frequencies of ungliding differ across the generations; in other words, Hazen (2001, 93) was able to demonstrate that, even though all three generations of the Warren County family had different frequencies for /ay/ ungliding, they had the same Appalachian English variation patterns.

Auger (2001) went one step further with a probabilistic method to determine the intricate conditioning of language-internal factors behind word-initial vowel epenthesis in Picard, a minority language spoken in northern France, coupled with an Optimality Theory analysis. She drew her data from ten authors who differ both qualitatively and quantitatively in the way they use vocalic epenthesis in their writings and who, therefore, might be expected to have divergent language variation patterns for this feature. Using an Optimality Theory analysis to account for those differences between authors, Auger (2001) shows that they nevertheless share the same basic community grammar, albeit with individual variation. By proposing individual grammars that are more specific than the community grammar, Auger was able to create a predictive model that elegantly accounts for individual differences between their grammars while still keeping in view the part of their grammar that is mutual.

If anyone could be expected to differ from the mainstream community grammar in an individualistic way, it would be a self-proclaimed bidialectal like Rachel, who as a matter of course goes back and forth between grammars to mark her two modes of speaking. To determine how well Rachel's PDE language variation patterns match those of other speakers in the PDE speech community, I will next analyze the factors conditioning /aʊ/ monophthongization and obstruent devoicing, the two features of PDE speakers are most aware and for which sufficient information is available concerning their conditioning (see chapters 4 and 5). Closer analysis of these two features is possible because there are sufficient tokens available in the data; the restricted environments in which other, less-salient features (like /aɪ/ monophthongization and /a/ centralization) occur cause a paucity of tokens in casual speech that makes it difficult to determine from this data set what factors condition their use. In the section below, a probabilistic comparison of the factors that condition Rachel's use of these features with those that condition their use by PDE monodialectals will indicate whether she shares the same grammar as those monodialectal speakers and can thus be considered a "true" speaker of PDE. This section will then compare Rachel's core PDE features to core features evidenced by monodialectal PDE speakers from both generations. Finally, this section will sketch out Rachel's use of nonphonological features of PDE, specifically morphosyntactic features, as further evidence that she is a genuine bidialectal.

Probabilistic Analysis for Monophthongized /aʊ/. As presented in chapter 5 and reiterated in tables 7.4 and 7.6, combined frequencies of use of /aʊ/ monophthongization are drastically different between the middle-aged and youngest generations of PDE speakers. As also was presented in chapter 5, middle-aged speakers favor closed syllables for monophthongization, while the youngest PDE speakers equally favor open and closed syllables. This simplification of phonological processes involved in /aʊ/ monophthongization is evidence in part for the unraveling of the PDE dialect.

For the purposes of this chapter, however, the question is how Rachel's usage compares with that of her parents' generation and her peers. Which generation (if either) does she match in terms of her language variation patterns for /aʊ/ monophthongization? Table 7.9 shows the results of the probabilistic analysis of Rachel's use of this feature. Like her peers, Rachel does not favor monophthongization in either open or closed syllables (i.e., she uses the standard variant more often than the PDE variant), and she does not show a significantly higher rate of monophthongization in either phonological context ($p = .581$). Not only does Rachel match the range of use exhibited by her peers for this feature (see tables 7.4 and 7.5), but with

TABLE 7.9
/aʊ/ Monophthongization Rates for Rachel

Syllable Type	Monophthongized	Not Monophthongized	Significance
Open	5/29 (17.2%)	24/29 (82.8%)	$\chi^2 = 0.304; p = .581$
Closed	8/62 (12.9%)	54/62 (87.1%)	

regard to language variation patterns for /aʊ/ monophthongization, Rachel also matches her peers (but not the middle-aged generation) in that she lacks the phonological conditioning factors that govern the rule for favoring/disfavoring monophthongization based on syllable type.

Probabilistic Analysis for Obstruent Devoicing. As described in chapter 4, obstruent devoicing is the other feature for which the middle-aged and youngest generations of PDE speakers employ different phonological constraints. A probabilistic analysis of the obstruent devoicing of middle-aged speakers using Goldvarb reveals that they use a complex combination of factors to determine where devoicing occurs: devoicing occurs most frequently when there is no segment following the obstruent in question (i.e., when the obstruent is at the end of a phrasal unit), when the obstruent is a /z/ with morphemic status, and when the segment preceding the obstruent in question is a coda consonant. In marked contrast, the youngest speakers of PDE have a simplified set of constraints: /z/ with morphemic and without morphemic status are the only obstruents that favor devoicing.

A Goldvarb analysis of Rachel's devoicing patterns is included in table 7.10. Although Rachel devoices obstruents far more often than the average of her peers in the 30–40-year-old age group (13.0% of the time, compared with the youngest speakers' combined rate of 5.9%), her use of the feature falls solidly within the range of frequencies for individual speakers in the

TABLE 7.10
Factors Influencing Obstruent Devoicing: Rachel
($\chi^2 = 59.6084$; log likelihood $= -249.791$)

Factors	Tokens	Factor Weight
Segment quality		
/z/ with morphemic status	16/77 (20.8%)	0.659
/z/ without morphemic status	40/219 (18.3%)	0.623
/d/ without morphemic status	19/202 (9.4%)	0.434
other fricatives	10/130 (7.7%)	0.381
/d/ with morphemic status	2/43 (4.7%)	0.265
TOTAL	87/671 (13.0%)	

youngest generation, as seen in tables 7.4 and 7.5. A Goldvarb analysis of the phonological conditioning for obstruent devoicing reveals that Rachel, like other speakers of her generation, relies on a simplified grammar to determine where she devoices obstruents: factors like following segment and coda structure—significant for the middle-aged speakers (see chapter 4)—were eliminated in the multivariate analysis here; only segment quality is significant for Rachel, with /z/ (with and without morphemic status) as the only obstruent which favors devoicing. In this regard, Rachel's grammar is exactly like that of her peers. The only place where she deviates from her peers is in her ranking of factors that disfavor devoicing for obstruents: whereas her peers disfavor obstruent devoicing more for other fricatives than for /d/ (with or without morphemic status), Rachel ranks other fricatives in between /d/ without morphemic status and /d/ with morphemic status. Overall, however, Rachel's ranking of conditioning factors is similar to that of her peers. Hazen (2001) stipulated that the authentic bidialectal must match the language variation patterns of monodialectal speakers; Rachel definitely meets this requirement with regard to her grammar for obstruent devoicing, matching the grammar of PDE speakers of her own age cohort.

Determining Language Variation Patterns Based on Feature Prominence. Yet another method for comparing Rachel's language variation patterns to those of monodialectal speakers is to note which PDE features are prominent in her data and theirs. This involves not only a comparison of which PDE features each speaker uses—to any degree at all—but also a determination of which features surface at a rate greater than the 10% threshold of perception and which do not. This 10% figure, while somewhat arbitrary, was suggested by Trudgill (2004, 110) for his study of dialect leveling and new dialect formation in New Zealand English as a line of demarcation for variants that are sufficiently present for children to "notice" and acquire them. In other words, variants present in less than a 10% proportion in a mix of dialect features are unlikely to be passed on to the next generation. Here this percentage will be applied in a similar manner to the feature sets of individual PDE speakers: features which occur above the 10% proportion for a speaker are considered "prominent," while those below the threshold of perception are not. This is useful evidence in discussing the unraveling of PDE as it progresses toward extinction and provides some rationale for discussion of mechanisms behind the fact that speakers younger than 30 do not use the dialect at all (but, rather, speak SCPE).

Recall from tables 7.1 and 7.3 that Rachel does not evidence any PDE features in her SCPE speech, except for a very small (1.2%) degree of obstruent devoicing. Does this pattern of having "just a little" PDE in her SCPE match what her SCPE-speaking peers do as well? Table 7.11 lists the different features used by each SCPE speaker and Rachel (when she is speaking SCPE). As table 7.3 showed earlier, none of the SCPE-speaking monodialectals in this study produces any PDE feature at a rate greater than 10%. Speaker EL produces no PDE variants at all, and JL produces only a single token of obstruent devoicing. RK actually produces the most PDE features in her speech, with a 5% incidence of raised [æ] and a single token of /aʊ/ monophthongization. Thus, when Rachel likewise exhibits a small degree of obstruent devoicing in her SCPE (1.2%), her linguistic behavior actually resembles that of her SCPE-speaking peers.[6] The presence of this small percentage of PDE variants in her SCPE is no different (with regard to PDE features) than the language variation patterns of her SCPE-speaking peers.

Table 7.12 compares the PDE features Rachel uses with the features used by the middle-aged and youngest PDE monodialectal speakers who participated in this study, again broken down by speaker. Features which occur less than 10% of the time in any speaker's data are indicated by parentheses. This comparison reveals again the great variability present in the PDE-speaking community today as the dialect moves toward extinction. For the most part, the middle-aged speakers show evidence of the same features in this study's data set: the only aberrations are that DG uses [æ] raising less than 10% of the time, and LG has a low rate (5.4%) of bidialectal fricative use and no evidence of /aɪ/ monophthongization (although recall from an earlier note in chapter 4 that this speaker was being more careful than usual in her recorded conversation). The youngest generation, as discussed earlier, is in accord in that no speaker uses the bilabial fricative, but they show a great degree of variability among individual speakers for the use of all other features: of the four features DK uses, only two are used more than 10% of the time (/aʊ/ monophthongization and /a/ centralization), and there is no evidence in this data set for him for /aɪ/ monophthongization.[7] DwK uses the fewest PDE features of all—no bilabial fricative, of course,

TABLE 7.11

Prominence of PDE Features: SCPE Monodialectals and Rachel

EL: no PDE features

RK: raised [æ] (3/60 tokens, 5.0%)
     /aʊ/ monophthongization (1/74 tokens, 1.4%)

JL: obstruent devoicing (1/374 tokens, 0.3%)

Rachel (speaking SCPE): obstruent devoicing (11/905 tokens, 1.2%)

TABLE 7.12
Feature Prominence: PDE Monodialectals and Rachel
(less than 10% listed in parentheses)

Middle-Aged Generation
  DG
    /a/ centralization
    /aʊ/ monophthongization
    /aɪ/ monophthongization
    bilabial fricative
    obstruent devoicing
    (raised [æ])
  LM
    /aɪ/ monophthongization
    /a/ centralization
    /aʊ/ monophthongization
    raised [æ]
    bilabial fricative
    obstruent devoicing
  LG:
    /a/ centralization
    /aʊ/ monophthongization
    raised [æ]
    obstruent devoicing
    (bilabial fricative)
    no /aɪ/ monophthongization

Youngest Generation
  DK
    /aʊ/ monophthongization
    /a/ centralization
    (raised [æ])
    (obstruent devoicing)
    no /aɪ/ monophthongization
    no bilabial fricative
  DwK
    raised [æ]
    /aʊ/ monophthongization
    (obstruent devoicing)
    no bilabial fricative
    no /aɪ/ monophthongization
    no /a/ centralization
  LK:
    /aɪ/ monophthongization
    obstruent devoicing
    (/aʊ/ monophthongization)
    (/a/ centralization)
    (raised [æ])
    no bilabial fricative

Rachel (speaking PDE)
  raised [æ]
  /aɪ/ monophthongization
  /a/ centralization
  bilabial fricative
  /aʊ/ monophthongization
  obstruent devoicing

but also no /aɪ/ monophthongization or /a/ centralization—but he uses the most raised [æ] of any speaker in this study, middle-aged or younger; he also uses obstruent devoicing less than 10% of the time. LK appears to be the most balanced speaker, using all the PDE features (except the bilabial fricative, of course), but the only features she uses more than 10% of the time are obstruent devoicing and /aɪ/ monophthongization. Thus there is tremendous variability among the youngest speakers with regard to which features are used and which features—when they ARE used—account for a noticeable proportion of tokens; this is a clear indication of the unraveling of PDE among its last generation of speakers.

Rachel does not really line up with her peers in terms of feature prominence, although exactly what "lining up" with them would entail is questionable, considering the wide degree of variability among them. Rachel is most like the female speaker LK in that she utilizes a range of PDE features, except Rachel also uses the bilabial fricative (which LK does not), and she uses all the PDE features with a frequency higher than the 10% level of perception (LK only uses two features at that higher level of frequency). Rachel actually lines up better with the middle-aged generation because she uses all the features they do (including the bilabial fricative) and uses them all in a sufficiently high proportion to register above the 10% rate for threshold of perception. Again, this may be because Rachel is a conservative speaker of PDE or perhaps because of accommodation toward middle-aged norms in her recorded conversation.

It would appear that Rachel has used the middle-aged generation as her model for determining which PDE features will occur in her speech and for the prominence with which those features should occur. Whereas her peers show great variability between them in the PDE features they utilize, Rachel demonstrates that she has a more accurate sense of which PDE features are prominent in the speech community as a whole, EVEN IN A CONTEXT OF DIALECT UNRAVELING. Rachel is not only a genuine speaker of PDE, but she is (for her age cohort) a linguistically sensitive speaker of the dialect, both in terms of the PDE features she uses and the frequencies at which she uses them. This is not simply a case of hyper-use of PDE features to distinguish her PDE from her SCPE; rather, it is a sophisticated utilization of features that reveals a remarkable sensitivity to the target language models presented to her as she grew up and an ability to discriminate between them.

Determining Language Variation Patterns Based on Morphosyntactic Features. One last method used here to determine whether Rachel's language variation patterns match those of monodialectal PDE speakers is to list the morphosyntactic features of PDE that she utilizes in the recordings of her PDE conversation and in her SCPE conversation. So far, this study has focused exclusively on diagnostic phonological variants of PDE, but of course a speaker with full mastery of a dialect must also be proficient in its morphosyntax. In fact, some researchers have claimed that mastery of a dialect's morphosyntax is proof of being an authentic speaker (see, e.g., Sweetland [2002] and Labov [1980] regarding use of AAVE variants in "authentic" and "inauthentic" ways). Sweetland (2002) presents a young white woman, "Delilah", whom she considers an authentic speaker of AAVE. Delilah actually makes limited use of AAVE phonological features and lexical forms, but, as Sweetland documents, she shows extensive expertise in her use of AAVE morphosyntactic features. Delilah's linguistic behavior contrasts with that of non–African American WANNABES, who mostly focus on imitating a few phonological features and vocabulary. (This is also in sharp contrast to the African American informants described by Linnes [1998] who utilized AAVE phonological rather than morphosyntactic variants to distinguish between their Standard American English and AAVE modes of speaking, see chapter 5.) In interviews with neighborhood associates, Delilah's extensive and intimate ties to AAVE-speaking social networks and intense orientation toward the African American culture of her friends and associates, along with her speech patterns, led to her being identified socially by AAVE speakers in her community as "basically black" (Sweetland 2002, 528, 531). Delilah's use of AAVE morphosyntactic features comes as no surprise to them, and she is accepted as an authentic AAVE speaker by those same community members. At least in Delilah's case, Sweetland claims, morphosyntax trumps phonology in marking her as an authentic speaker of AAVE.

Chapter 3 of this monograph listed several of the morphosyntactic features of PDE, including the following:

> bare form of certain verbs for past tense (*eat, run, come*); *seen* for the past tense of *see*
> *still* as a habitual marker
> remote past *had* + past participle
> tag questions *ain't, not,* and *ai-not*
> *once* as an emphatic particle
> *yet* 'still'
> *what for* 'which'

To show that Rachel's use of morphosyntactic features is like that of PDE-speaking and SCPE-speaking monodialectals, she must use PDE features when she speaks PDE, but not when she speaks SCPE. Table 7.13 presents the morphosyntactic features noted in the naturalistic conversation of this study's data set, along with specific examples from the corpus. This is not to imply that Rachel does not use other morphosyntactic features, but the data in this table are restricted to the conversations recorded. One of the problems inherent in investigating morphosyntactic features is the low frequency of occurrence of tokens; for a more complete picture of Rachel's repertoire of morphosyntactic features, a much larger corpus of data would need to be collected.

TABLE 7.13

Rachel's PDE Morphosyntactic Features with Examples from Her Recording
(in her PDE conversation)

Morphosyntactic Feature	Example
still as a habitual marker	Did you go there still?
bare form of *come* as past tense	They got on a sled and come down the hill on the pipeline…
tag questions *ain't* and *not*	You're coming to the dinner, ain't?; We should drop off the package at the house, not?
yet to mean 'still'	Is that school there yet?
what for for 'which'	What for school did you go to?
remote past *had* + participle	LG: Do you have a bus?
	LM: Yeah. It was made into a camper.
	LG: Oh, is that what you used?
	Rachel: That's what we had used.

None of these PDE forms, however, appear in Rachel's SCPE conversation. Just a few tokens of each of the forms listed here appear in her PDE conversation, and none of them acts as a majority form. Nevertheless, by using these forms in her PDE conversation (but not her SCPE conversation), Rachel shows that in terms of morphosyntax, too, she has two distinct systems that resemble—with regard to use of PDE features, anyway—those used by monodialectal speakers of SCPE and PDE. She also demonstrates through her use of these features that she has a proficient understanding of the morphosyntax of PDE and that her mastery of the dialect goes beyond the phonological. As such, she has both phonological and morphosyntactic resources at her disposal for tailoring her language to meet the expectations of two different "worlds."

Social Motivation Criterion for Bidialectalism. Hazen's (2001, 92–94) final criterion for authentic bidialectalism is that bidialectal speakers must be socially motivated to acquire a second dialect while retaining their first one. Much about Rachel's social motivations for adopting bidialectalism was shared in the sketch of her linguistic history at the beginning of this chapter. To reiterate, while growing up in south central Pennsylvania, she felt pressure from the school system and from SCPE speakers in her peer network to learn to speak SCPE; at the same time, her sense of pride in her heritage and the desire to gain the approval of older PDE-speaking family members led her to retain PDE. This social motivation, to navigate successfully two different "worlds," has led Rachel and others like her to master two distinct dialects. Rachel successfully meets this criterion for bidialectalism, just as she does the other two.

In summary, then, recall Hazen's (2001, 92–94) requirements for bidialectalism: for a person to be deemed a genuine bidialectal, that speaker must...

1. produce the same sets of features as monodialectal speakers of both dialects, without overlap,
2. produce those features in the same "language variation patterns" that monodialectals do, and
3. possess a social motivation for acquiring the second dialect while retaining the first one.

This section has demonstrated, at least regarding her use or nonuse of PDE features, that Rachel has solidly and successfully met all these criteria and can rightly be considered an "authentic bidialectal."

7.3. ON THE HUNT FOR THE BIDIALECTAL

Where does one find bidialectals like Rachel to study? Chapter 6 has already pointed out the difficulties encountered by Hazen and his colleagues as they examined the speech of children of parents born outside the West Virginia area (Hazen and Hall 1999) and college students (some of them self-proclaimed bidialectals) who had moved to Morgantown from other parts of the state (Hazen 2001). However, other researchers, while not focused on bidialectalism, may have uncovered evidence of bidialectal speakers. Rex O'Neal, a fisherman and carpenter from Ocracoke on the Outer Banks of North Carolina, who enjoys "performing" his dialect for tourists and linguistic researchers (Schilling-Estes 1998, 56), would seem at first glance to be "hyperdialectal," not an authentic bidialectal. Yet, Schilling-Estes (1998) remarks that, at one point in a linguistic interview, Rex's brothers came into the room, and Rex turned from the interviewer to them and altered his use of the diagnostic vowel /aɪ/ in a way that is more the norm in the Ocracoke dialect. Noah, mentioned in chapter 6, demonstrated a degree of accuracy in his "imitation" or "performance" speech that warrants a closer look at him as a possible bidialectal (Evans 2002). Also discussed in the last chapter, Sjöström et al. (2008) mention their use of a bidialectal Scanian Swedish–Stockholm Swedish speaker as a source of recordings for a perception task that investigated whether familiarity of a speaker's dialect had any effect on the listener's ability to accurately identify speakers' voices. Therefore, despite the paucity of literature on bidialectalism, it would appear that bidialectals do indeed exist.

So where should the linguist interested in bidialectalism begin to search for bidialectal speakers? The empirical study of individuals who have moved from one dialect area to another has traditionally been a fertile field for the study of dialect acquisition and accommodation; examples of such research include Chambers's (1992) study of Canadians who moved to the United Kingdom as children and teens; Auer, Barden, and Grosskopf's (1998, 2002) examination of East German speakers of Upper Saxonian who migrated to West Germany, mentioned in chapters 4 and 5; and Tagliamonte and Molfenter's (2007) chronicle of British English features acquired by three children who had moved from Toronto to the United Kingdom. However, the focus of such studies is normally the abandonment of native dialect features in favor of features of the new area's dominant dialect, and there is little indication in any of these studies that any of the speakers show bidialectal tendencies. To locate bidialectals in a migratory linguistic context, researchers would need to investigate features from the native dialect that are retained even as speakers acquire features from the new dialect area. For the moment it is unclear whether dialect contact situations like these are conducive to bidialectalism. Areas of heavy (community-wide) long-term dialect contact like that in south central Pennsylvania are perhaps more promising places to look.

Even so, true bidialectals are, as Hazen and the West Virginia Dialect Project team discovered, notoriously difficult for linguistic researchers to locate (Hazen 2001, 95). By the very nature of their speech habits, bidialectals blend in with whichever dialectal group they are with, and unless a researcher happens to observe them in two different contexts or with two different kinds of interlocutors in a single context—situations that would merit switching on the part of the bidialectal between their two dialects in a natural manner—their bidialectal abilities will go unnoticed. Even the friends, family, and associates of bidialectals rarely recognize their ability to alternate between two dialects. This may be due to a certain "blindness" that comes with familiarity with the bidialectal, or it may be that the switching itself is—although rare—a "normal enough" behavior in the context of the intense-language contact speech community that most people simply never notice what the bidialectal is doing.

In light of these challenges, it would be helpful to researchers both to know the characteristics of speech communities conducive to bidialectalism and to understand what kinds of speakers are predisposed toward becoming bidialectal. This section discusses first the sociohistorical and sociolinguistic characteristics of a speech community in which one might find bidialectals. It then uses the linguistic histories of individual speakers to create a profile for the SCPE-PDE bidialectals in south central Pennsylvania, with components taken from general interviews with Rachel and the other self-professed bidialectals who could not complete this study. Speaker age, social network, motivations, career aspirations, and linguistic awareness all play a role in distinguishing the south central Pennsylvania bidialectals from other speakers of PDE and SCPE. Not all of these profile components will necessarily apply to other speakers in other places and in other types of language variety contact situations, but they at least serve as a starting point for discovering bidialectals in contexts outside south central Pennsylvania. Le Page and Tabouret-Keller (1985, 182) have stated that

We can only behave according to the behavioural patterns of groups we find it desirable to identify with to the extent that:

    i. we can identify the groups

    ii. we have both adequate access to the groups and ability to analyse their behavioural patterns

    iii. the motivation to join the groups is sufficiently powerful, and is [...] reinforced [...] by feedback from the groups

    iv. we have the ability to modify our behaviour.

The next several paragraphs describe a series of situations potentially conducive to bidialectalism, based on Le Page and Tabouret-Keller's (1985) observations and on what is known about language behavior in Pennsylvania from this study, as well as the study of speakers like Rex (Schilling-Estes 1998), Noah (Evans 2002), and the Swedish speaker described by Sjöström et al. (2008):

1. Bidialectalism arises in contexts in which heavy dialect contact has taken place on the societal level for a lengthy period (i.e., more than one generation). In heavy dialect contact situations (where there are many speakers of each dialect), potential bidialectals are exposed to input from both target dialects to a sufficient degree that some of them are able to master both dialects and to keep them distinguished from each other as two coherent systems; as shown in this study, this heavy dialect contact has been the case in the PDE-SCPE speech communities of south central Pennsylvania. On the other hand, speakers who have moved into another dialect area (where only the second dialect is predominant) as children may have difficulty finding sufficient exposure to models of their first dialect to learn what makes it distinct from the dialect they are surrounded by, at least to the degree necessary to master two coherent systems and not just end up

with a mixed set of features taken from both dialects (as Hazen and Hall [1999] found in the speech of the children they studied). In terms of social motivation for learning a new dialect while maintaining a native one, the composition and attitudes of speakers' social networks in heavy dialect contact situations (where social networks commonly contain speakers of both dialects) are also more likely to provide the necessary environment and impetus for a speaker to master two dialects. In contrast, migrants to a new area (like those studied by Auer et al. 1998) may find that their social networks are soon composed primarily of people from the new area, speakers of the second dialect, and this network composition may cause a waning of motivation to retain the first dialect. Based on the data from this study, it also appears that finding sufficient opportunities to use both dialects is also important to becoming a bidialectal: heavy dialect contact, unlike many migratory situations, provides opportunities for bidialectal speakers to engage in daily or near-daily use of both dialects and thereby constantly practice managing their feature sets as distinct systems. This is what the self-proclaimed bidialectals in south central Pennsylvania and Sjöström et al.'s (2008) Stockholm Swedish–Scanian Swedish speaker do. Speakers who have migrated to an area where there are not many speakers of their native dialect, however, may rarely need to use their native dialect, or they may resort to using it only when they interact with speakers who still reside in the home area (as when they travel home or talk on the phone with friends and family from the home area). This particular combination of factors— sufficient exposure to target models of both dialects, composition of social networks, motivations, and opportunities for using both dialects—are all characteristics of an area of extended dialect contact and are not readily applicable to areas with one overwhelmingly dominant dialect. Therefore, it makes sense for researchers to look for bidialectals in a linguistic context of heavy dialect contact.

2. Bidialectalism arises when speakers have been exposed to two dialects since childhood, in the generation of speakers that has had sufficient target models for both dialects available for acquisition. Even when speakers have been exposed to a dialect since childhood, they still may not be motivated to acquire it all, or may not be able to totally acquire its more complex features (see Payne's [1980] child informants who had moved into the King of Prussia area as children but still had not totally mastered the Philadelphia tensed [æ] pattern). The chances are presumably much greater, however, that children exposed to a second dialect early will more completely acquire both its features and its variable rules (Chambers 1992). For this study's cohort of PDE-SCPE speakers in their 30s and 40s in south central Pennsylvania,

exposure to PDE began at home and exposure to SCPE began when they started school at age 5. Given this bit of language contact history, then, this would be exactly the generation in which bidialectals would be expected to develop: the oldest generation of PDE speakers who served as informants for this study (who learned Pennsylvania German as a first language and only later acquired PDE at school as a second language) presumably did not have enough exposure to models of SCPE to have acquired that dialect, although nearly every individual in their age cohort did become bilingual in English and Pennsylvania German. Given the prevalence of small local schoolhouses in northern Lebanon County, acquisition of SCPE (and subsequent development of bidialectalism) as children was not possible for most of this age group, since social networks were dominated by PDE speakers. The middle-aged generation of PDE speakers in this study acquired PDE in the home as a first dialect of English (a few acquired bilingual proficiency in Pennsylvania German as well); they did not encounter SCPE speakers to any large degree until they went off to find employment as young adults, so these individuals remained monodialectal speakers of PDE. The youngest generation of PDE speakers in this study, the 30–40-year-olds, learned PDE in the home as a first dialect just as their parents had, but their schooling took place in consolidated schools that exposed them to enough SCPE from classmates and teachers that two models of English were actually available to them during their language acquisition period. As discussed earlier, many PDE speakers in this age group opted to acquire SCPE and abandon PDE; those who remained PDE speakers have ended up with a PDE that is marked by dialectal unraveling, characterized by high variability between speakers in use of PDE features (see chapters 4 and 5). It is from the context of this "multiple model" language variety situation that bidialectals have arisen in south central Pennsylvania, in the generation that represents the last of the PDE speakers.

Thus, a potential context in which to find bidialectals for further linguistic research is a dialect contact situation with speakers exposed to two dialects since childhood. If bidialectals have arisen from that dialect contact, they will most likely be part of whatever generation(s) of speakers would have had multiple language variety target models available to them for input to a sufficient degree to make acquisition possible.

3. Bidialectalism arises in situations where the attitudes in a speech community are complex enough that prestige is accorded not only to the dominant language variety, but also to the minority language variety, at least by some of the minority variety's speakers. Language attitudes in communities

that result in individuals with two modes of speaking can be complex for a number of reasons: social factors, economics, concern about identity, and so on. Data from interviews show that language attitudes toward PDE and SCPE in south central Pennsylvania—both those of the older PDE-speaking members of their social networks and of their SCPE-speaking peers and teachers—have definitely been a deciding factor in the dialect choices of many of the 30–40-year-olds who took part in this study. Each of the bidialectals interviewed for this study reported spending (and having spent) a significant amount of time with older PDE-speaking relatives, and for some of the bidialectals interviewed in this study, a simple desire to identify in a linguistic way with these relatives led to the maintenance of their PDE even after they had acquired SCPE in the school context. For some of these bidialectals, however, the deciding factor for maintaining PDE was the desire to please those who constituted for them an overcritical social network who held to the covert prestige of PDE; as discussed earlier, some older speakers who took pride in their dialect (but also criticized the youngsters if they were perceived as "uppity" or "disloyal") exerted pressure on young speakers to continue speaking PDE. Bidialectals in this kind of social network may have chosen to maintain PDE to gain some modicum of approval from their PDE-speaking older relatives and parents and thereby avoid censure.

At the same time, however, these same young bidialectal speakers felt pressure from teachers and members of their social networks who spoke SCPE to conform linguistically to the mainstream in order to sound intelligent, be more successful in life, and so on. The language attitudes involved in such a complex dual-dialect situation provided certain individuals with the social motivation to develop two modes of speaking to cope with the demands of being part of two kinds of social networks. Thus, a dialect contact situation with sufficient numbers of speakers of each dialect, who accord prestige of some sort to their respective dialects, and a social situation where individuals are likely to have speakers of each dialect in their social networks, seems like a reasonable linguistic context in which to look for bidialectals.

4. Bidialectalism arises where there is sufficient motivation for some speakers to identify with two dialects. This motivation, stipulated by Hazen (2001, 94) as a necessary requirement for authentic bidialectalism, comes into play in tracking down bidialectals for research as well. For Rachel and the other bidialectals in south central Pennsylvania, this interacts with the social situation described in (3) above. For these particular bidialectals, the choice of maintaining PDE has been motivated in part by their social network com-

position, but also by their own individual career aspirations, ambitions that made it seem desirable to identify linguistically with the community that uses SCPE.

The three 30–40-year-old bidialectals in this study had (as teenagers) and have (today, as adults) social networks composed of many SCPE- and PDE-speaking friends.[8] This social network composition is unarguably one reason these speakers were motivated to acquire SCPE in the first place. The bidialectals' abilities in two dialects arise at least in part from feeling it necessary to match the linguistic varieties of those in their social networks with whom they have strong ties.

At the same time, the bidialectals interviewed also felt the need to learn SCPE in order to fulfill career aspirations. An examination of their backgrounds reveals a marked tendency for them to be academically successful and to "speak well." Of the three bidialectals interviewed for this study, two have obtained master's degrees and are currently teaching. The other, a Mennonite, was singled out as a teacher's assistant when she was completing her eleventh and twelfth grade years in school[9] and then went off to a Mennonite school for teacher training; up until she married and had children, she too taught, in a Mennonite school.

It is noteworthy that all the bidialectal informants pursued careers in education because it runs counter to the sentiments of many in these speakers' social networks, who hold that education is totally impractical and that the everyday common sense of an uneducated person is vastly superior to whatever one might learn in the classroom. Tension arises from this mismatch of opinions about education and between the two "worlds" (academic and nonacademic) the speaker wishes to inhabit. Becoming bidialectal was seen by all the bidialectal speakers in this study as one way of increasing the likelihood of successfully functioning in both. Thus, a dialect contact situation with speaker motivations related to both careers and social network that prompt them to identify with speakers of two dialects seems like a promising context in which to look for bidialectals.

5. Bidialectalism may arise when speakers are linguistically astute enough to understand differences between the two dialects. Linguistic sensitivity may not be a requirement for bidialectalism, but it is striking that, in the sample of south central Pennsylvania bidialectals interviewed for this study, all three demonstrated a level of linguistic awareness much greater than that of the monodialectals interviewed. While they may not be cognizant of any more PDE features than the average PDE speaker,[10] each is able to talk at length about whom they speak which dialect with, where, and why. Each self-proclaimed bidialectal also spoke of strategies for deciding what dialect

to use with someone they encounter for the first time (i.e., when they are uncertain if the other person is a speaker of PDE or SCPE). These speakers have the remarkable ability to assess social situations and determine whether PDE or SCPE is the most appropriate code to use; they quite consciously wield their codes in ways that accomplish social tasks and project various identities.

South central Pennsylvania bidialectals are not unique in this ability, of course: Rex, the potential bidialectal speaker from Ocracoke described by Schilling-Estes (1998), is similarly able to talk about how tourists react to his performances of island speech in which he uses stereotypical Ocracoke English features, and Sjöström et al.'s (2008) Swedish speaker delineated interlocutors with whom he used Scanian versus Stockholm Swedish. At the very least, it seems that self-proclaimed bidialectals report having made a conscious choice at some point in their lives to learn a second dialect while maintaining their first one, and that act itself requires a certain degree of linguistic awareness. Bidialectal speakers may not have any more detailed knowledge of dialectal features than their monodialectal counterparts, but they appear to have more insights or opinions about the nature and use of those features than most of their family and peers. Thus, one place where researchers could reasonably look for bidialectals is among the ranks of linguistically astute individuals in a context of dialect contact.

6. Bidialectalism may arise as a fleeting phenomenon, the culmination of the linguistic history of a geographic region before a minority language variety breathes its last. From a completely probabilistic viewpoint—setting all matters of identity, language attitudes, and social motivation aside—it would appear that, when more than one model of language becomes pervasive enough in a community, a process of leveling simplifies the numbers and quality differences in the feature sets available to children for acquisition (see Trudgill et al. [2000] for a similar situation—albeit with more dialects involved—in the formation of New Zealand English). If this is the case, then the time frame for the development of bidialectalism can be quite short, depending on how quickly leveling takes place between dialects or how long the minority dialect holds out against pressures from the majority dialect. In south central Pennsylvania, it would appear that bidialectalism appears exclusively among speakers in their 30s and 40s in nonsectarian communities, and today's children (even children of two PDE-speaking parents) do not speak PDE at all. Complete language variety shift may not be the case for every dialect contact situation, but researchers should be aware that time frame may play a large part in the ability to find bidialectal speakers. If south central Pennsylvanians are representative in this regard,

the place to look for bidialectal speakers may be in the last generation of speakers of an obsolescing dialect.

The preceding list of possible characteristics of the bidialectal "habitat" is, of course, neither exhaustive nor definitive, but it is a starting point from which to develop more informed notions about the contexts in which bidialectalism can arise. Perhaps a more sustained effort on the part of dialect contact researchers to locate bidialectals will result in a broader range of linguistic contexts.

7.4. DISCUSSION: CRITIQUE OF HAZEN'S CRITERIA FOR BIDIALECTALISM

Reiterating yet again what was presented in the first part of this chapter concerning criteria for bidialectalism, Hazen (2001, 92–94) has claimed that a truly bidialectal speaker must...

1. produce the same sets of features as monodialectal speakers of both dialects, without overlap,
2. produce those features in the same "language variation patterns" that monodialectals do, and
3. possess a social motivation for acquiring the second dialect while retaining the first one.

Given that so many speakers in areas of dialect contact show evidence of intermediate dialectal forms (Chambers and Trudgill 1980; Auer, Barden, and Grosskopf 1998) and that children in these areas often acquire a mixed set of dialect features (Hazen and Hall 1999), it is not surprising that researchers like Hazen (2001) might conclude that true bidialectalism is impossible. However, this chapter has carefully examined PDE feature frequencies and linguistic patterns exhibited by Rachel when she speaks PDE and when she speaks SCPE and has determined that she meets Hazen's criteria for bidialectalism in all respects. Regarding the PDE features she uses and the frequencies and patterns with which she uses those features, her linguistic behavior does not differ from monodialectal speakers of her own age group in any significant manner, with the exception of her use of the bilabial fricative, a feature prevalent among middle-aged speakers of PDE but abandoned by younger PDE monodialectals. Her SCPE differs from that of her SCPE-speaking peers only in her small incidence of obstruent devoicing; however, even where her SCPE is "tinged" by her PDE obstruent devoicing, it is to a degree consistent with the appearance of PDE features in the SCPE of her peers. Rachel is clearly a speaker of SCPE and of PDE and is able to switch between them as two coherent systems. Her linguistic history, shared earlier in this chapter, relates her social motivations for maintaining two dialect systems. Rachel meets all of Hazen's (2001, 92–94) criteria for bidialectalism and is thus an "authentic bidialectal"; as such, she provides a direct counterexample to combat Hazen's (2001) claim that bidialectals cannot exist.

Despite Rachel's success at fulfilling these criteria, the bidialectalism criteria themselves deserve further critical examination. Especially in light of the unique issues that arise in contexts of intense dialect contact, this study raises five issues that challenge Hazen's (2001) reasoning.

DIALECT FEATURE OVERLAP. Hazen (2001, 8–10) stipulates that the true bidialectal must produce all the features of the two dialects WITHOUT OVERLAP, as two distinct systems of dialect features. On the surface, this seems to make sense because an authentic bidialectal speaker cannot just make use of a mixed set of features. But heavy dialect contact often results in a great degree of overlap between dialectal systems, which makes it difficult for individuals with two modes of speaking to meet Hazen's stringent requirement. In south central Pennsylvania, for instance, there is enough overlap between PDE and SCPE that PDE speakers use variants in their speech that can be designated as either "PDE" or "SCPE." (No PDE feature is used categorically by all speakers, with the exception of /a/ centralization, which the middle-aged speakers use 100% of the time.) For the purposes of this study, a working definition of SCPE was developed that delineated SCPE as anything "not PDE," but this is inadequate as well for an in-depth description of the entire linguistic situation in south central Pennsylvania. The boundaries between dialects in a heavy contact situation are not always discrete, and this needs to be taken into account when developing testable criteria for bidialectalism.

DIALECT FEATURE MATCHING. Regarding Hazen's (2001, 8–10) insistence that bidialectals match the dialect features used by monodialectal speakers of the two varieties in question, this study of PDE as a dying dialect points out that what seems at first like a totally logical notion may not be defined well enough to act as a testable criterion, not without qualification. In other words, in order to determine whether a speaker meets the feature matching requirement for bidialectalism, exactly whose feature set is the target for the bidialectal? The speakers' peers? Parents? It seems most logical that an authentic bidialectal's language patterns would mirror those of his/her contemporaries in the speech community, but, then, which peers must the

bidialectal match? Situations of heavy dialect contact that give rise to bidialectalism also give rise to dialect obsolescence, and this chapter has provided evidence that bidialectalism can co-occur with dialect unraveling that
results in extreme variability in feature use by the bidialectal's peers. Moreover, WHICH features does a bidialectal speaker need to match? Phonological features? Morphosyntactic features? What if a speaker shows evidence
for some or all phonological features of a dialect, but not the morphosyntactic? Or vice versa? Even in healthy language varieties, the notion of the
"ideal speaker" is fraught with problems, and the situation worsens consid-
erably when language obsolescence (Dorian 1994) and dialect unraveling
are added to the mix.

Another difficulty in Hazen's (2001, 8–10) requirement for individuals with two modes of speaking to match monodialectals is the question of
HOW WELL a speaker has to match those targets. What if an individual with
two modes of speaking uses all but one feature out of the set of all possible
features employed by speakers of a dialect? Does that fact render the individual an inauthentic user of a dialect and, therefore, make his or her two
modes of speaking out to be something less than dialect differences? Labov
(1980) asserted as much when he commented on a case study by Hatala
(1976) of a white student who was identified blindly by African American
listeners as an authentic user of AAVE because of her use of AAVE morphosyntax; Labov (1980) noted that the speaker lacked the usual AAVE tense/
aspect features and could not therefore be considered an authentic user of
AAVE, no matter how she was categorized by native AAVE-speaking listeners.
In stark contrast, Sweetland (2002, 531) insists that her white informant,
Delilah, shows that she is indeed a true speaker of AAVE since she uses
morphosyntactic rather than surface-level phonological features of the dialect and, moreover, is likewise identified by members of the AAVE-speaking
speech community in which she lives and works as "basically black." Linnes
(1998) reports great variability among her speakers in the use of AAVE
morphosyntactic features, but considers all her speakers to be authentic.
So, again, which monodialectal speakers must an individual with two modes
of speaking match to be considered bidialectal?

Hazen's (2001, 92–94) insistence that bidialectals match monodialectals in their feature use creates an unfortunate disjunct between the linguist's assessment of speaker abilities and the sociopsychological reality
of how such speakers see themselves in their own linguistic contexts and
how other speakers see them. As "right" as trained linguists may be in their
assessment of the situation it is definitely true that speakers can and do over-
estimate or underestimate their language abilities and classify the behaviors
of themselves and others in ways that do not match the realities uncovered

by in-depth linguistic investigation. The fact that speakers see themselves as bidialectal reflects at least some kind of folk linguistic reality (Preston 1996) about the linguistic context in which they live, the linguistic challenges that they face, and the linguistic strategies they have developed for dealing with those challenges. These speakers, whether technically bidialectal or not, nevertheless incorporate the notion of bidialectalism into their language identities and, in response to that, exhibit rather sophisticated awareness of what distinguishes one dialect from another and remarkable levels of pragmatic strategizing in determining when to use one dialect versus the other. An ideal assessment of who is a true bidialectal would rest not soley on researchers' assessments, but would take into account these kinds of speaker attitudes, behaviors, and abilities.

LANGUAGE VARIATION PATTERN MATCHING. Hazen's (2001) criterion that bidialectals match the "language variation patterns" of monodialectal speakers seems intuitive on the surface, but the difficulties in testing it are similar to those described in the previous section: Whose "patterns" are bidialectals expected to match? Peers'? Parents'? And which mode of assessment should the linguist use to determine whether "language patterns" are being matched or not? Frequencies for feature use? The weights of factors influencing feature use? The prominence of features used by speakers? Every form of linguistic analysis has its limitations—this is particularly apparent when the dialect sliding toward extinction has reached a disordered state. Nor do all dialectal variants lend themselves to the kinds of statistical analysis that sociolinguists commonly use to determine the role of different language-external and language-internal factors in predicting feature use: in this study, for example, only obstruent devoicing yielded enough tokens in the corpus of real speech to make a multivariate regression analysis possible, and only /aʊ/ monophthongization occurred in phonological settings varied enough to facilitate even a simple chi-squared analysis of language-internal features. Even in cases where statistical analyses like Varbrul and chi-squared tests can be used, what can be concluded about the individuals with two modes of speaking when they are compared to generations of speakers who themselves show inconsistency in relative weights for language-internal and language-external factors? This is the kind of analytical challenge that can be encountered in a heavy dialect contact situation, the most fruitful context for finding bidialectals.

COGNITIVE DEMAND OF HAVING DISTINCT SYSTEMS. Hazen's (2001, 92–94) strict criteria address neither issues of cognitive demand that bidialectal speakers grapple with nor strategies that such speakers develop to distinguish efficiently between their two modes of speaking. Such cognitive demand issues have received the attention of researchers of bilingualism, who recognize that bilinguals do not maintain discrete boundaries between their language systems and that there is bidirectional influence between bilinguals' two language systems (e.g., Romaine 1995). If bidialectalism is analogous to bilingualism, why should bidialectals be expected to meet standards that bilinguals themselves do not meet? A less stringent set of criteria that does not simply view a bidialectal as a composite of two mono-dialectals—like a bilingual is not simply a composite of two monolinguals—would undoubtedly open the path to learning much about the processes that bidialectals use in managing the cognitive demand of linguistically navigating two separate "worlds."

SPEECH COMMUNITY IDENTIFICATION OF THE BIDIALECTAL. A final criticism of Hazen's (2001, 92–94) criteria is that they do not take into consideration how the speech community sees the bidialectal speaker. If a speech community with a history of intense dialect contact accepts an individual as an authentic speaker of a particular dialect—or of two dialects—is it the prerogative of the linguist to deny that status completely based on the data collected from a sample of monodialectal speakers that have been studied? As a researcher, one hopes, of course, that the frequencies and "language variation patterns" of the sample speakers accurately reflect the norms of a speech community, but what if a speaker falls outside those norms and yet is considered a member of that same speech community by that language variety's speakers (e.g., Sweetland's [2002] informant Delilah)? If that acceptance simply means that the speech community is responding to superficial extralinguistic cues from the speaker that make that person appear to be an authentic part of the speech community, then that is a matter that Hazen's (2001) criteria—rightly so—cannot address. However, if the speech community's response to the bidialectal reflects that its members consider what the bidialectal produces to fall within the acceptable range of productions deemed to be part of each dialect in question, then the ideas of the speech community will indeed have to be taken into consideration as a criteria for measuring "authentic" bidialectalism.

Despite the shortcomings of Hazen's bidialectalism criteria, it seems appropriate to conclude this chapter by presenting the questions Hazen himself listed concerning bidialectalism at the end of his own article (2001, 96), in testament to the significance of his development of testable criteria for the study of bidialectalism. Following each question listed below is an answer—at least a partial one—based on what this study has discovered in the examination of a single bidialectal and the current linguistic status of PDE in south central Pennsylvania.

1. *"Can a speaker fully acquire a second dialect and maintain the language varia-tion patterns of the first dialect?"* (Hazen 2001, 96). Rachel would seem to be strong evidence that this is indeed possible: she successfully mastered SCPE in school, and she continues, even now that she is much older, to maintain mastery of PDE, her first dialect. Rachel not only regularly uses the same features of PDE that her peers and middle-aged speakers of PDE do, with frequencies and an understanding of grammar that proves that she does not simply "throw in" a feature here and there to sound "Dutchified," but her language variation patterns for those PDE features are also very similar to those of her monodialectal peers in terms of frequency of feature use, language-internal constraints on feature use, and prominence of features used. While Rachel was the focus of this chapter as the bidialectal who com-pleted this particular study, it is certain that she is not simply an anomaly; a more sustained effort to identify bidialectal behavior, in favorable linguistic contexts and among favorable groups of speakers, would undoubtedly find more bidialectal speakers in south central Pennsylvania and farther afield.

2. *"Can a speaker who has acquired a second dialect in another region come back to the home region and continue to convince native speakers that the first dialect is authentic?"* (Hazen 2001, 96). Although the data for Rachel presented above do not directly answer this particular question (she did not acquire her sec-ond dialect in another region), it does suggest—along with self-reported language habits of the bidialectal Swedish speaker described by Sjöström et al. (2008)—that growing up and living in an area where two dialects are spoken may contribute to opportunities and motivation to maintain one's first dialect, as opposed to shifting to the second dialect in another region. Perhaps the daily "practice" of keeping two dialects distinct (recall that Sjöström et al.'s [2008] speaker uses one dialect with his children and colleagues and another with his wife) that can occur in an area like south central Pennsylvania helps the would-be bidialectal maintain a firmer hold on the first dialect than would have been the case if that person had moved to another region.

3. *"If a speaker produces D[ialect] 1 and then acquires features of D[ialect] 2, will that speaker acquire those features with the same qualitative and quantitative con-straints as a native speaker?"* (Hazen 2001, 96). The data presented in this chapter show how well Rachel has acquired SCPE, at least in terms of lack of PDE features. The data presented earlier show that she has mastered it with the same quantitative constraints as her SCPE-speaking peers, at least with regard to PDE features not "tainting" her SCPE beyond an acceptable degree. Presumably, she has mastered the qualitative constraints of SCPE as

well, although that was not investigated in this particular study. Due to the nature of this study and the composition of the speech community in south central Pennsylvania, however, it is necessary to add a disclaimer here: this study compared Rachel to SCPE speakers who likewise grew up in households where PDE was spoken; in fact, it is difficult even today to find an SCPE speaker in the 30–40-year-old age range, native to Lebanon County, Pennsylvania, who did not have at least one PDE-speaking parent. If data were collected from an individual who was native to Lebanon County but had grown up in a household with two SCPE-speaking parents—in other words, who themselves had not learned a second dialect as a child—the results of a comparison with Rachel might well differ from what was presented in this chapter.

4. *"Will the speaker be able to switch between sets of dialect features instead of mixing linguistic features from two dialects in a single production?"* (Hazen 2001, 96). Whether or not Rachel can switch between two dialects in a single production—it is a little unclear what kind of production unit Hazen is suggesting here—is also not a matter that the data presented in this chapter can completely address given that her recorded SCPE conversation was with SCPE speakers and her recorded PDE conversation was with PDE speakers. Rachel herself feels that the question seems to impose an artificial constraint on language choice: if bidialectal speakers choose which dialect's features to employ based on context and on interlocutor, using two dialects in a single production would have to occur only in a contrived situation, when demonstrating or imitating dialect features, for example. That said, Rachel is able to turn from speaking PDE or SCPE with someone in person, speak on the phone with someone in the other dialect, and then revert back to the original dialect with the original interlocutor. The situation is much more complex, however, if there are both PDE and SCPE speakers present in person in a single conversation; in that case, Rachel reports that she often defaults to SCPE, unless one of the interlocutors is an older person to whom she wishes to show respect by sticking with PDE. For Rachel, switching between SCPE and PDE is uncomfortable within the bounds of a single sentence or conversational unit.

5. *"Can the speaker produce both sets of language variation patterns in unpracticed conversation? Even in practiced conversation?"* (Hazen 2001, 96). It is unclear exactly what Hazen means here by "practiced conversation"; but perhaps he is referring specifically to demonstrations of bidialectal ability like that he investigated in his study of self-proclaimed dialectals who were asked to "perform" their abilities while being recorded (95). Again, this is an

extremely artificial context, and as such stands in direct contrast to the kind of natural, unpracticed, daily use of two sets of language variation patterns that Rachel engages in. Practice does not help the bidialectal who "lives" two sets of patterns, and the artificiality that such "practice" requires would indeed dampen it: in south central Pennsylvania anyway, if people ask a speaker to produce his or her dialect on demand to be recorded, that speaker usually reasons that the interviewers are most likely educated people with whom one would use the regional standard, SCPE, and therefore to utilize any other form with them is awkward. Such a bidialectal may be able to "perform" some language features for the recorder, but overall it is an artificial situation that destroys any guarantee of matching the language variation patterns of monodialectals in the same circumstances.

6. *"Can a speaker switch more than linguistic stereotypes? Can the speaker switch less salient markers or indicators?"* (Hazen 2001, 96). Again, the data presented for Rachel show that she is capable of producing the full range of phonological features of PDE, not just the highly salient stereotypical ones of obstruent devoicing and /aʊ/ monophthongization. Whether or not she produces less-salient features with the same language variation patterns as her fellow PDE speakers has not been tested in this chapter, since scarcity of tokens for most PDE features (caused by the restriction of those features to relatively rare phonological environments) did not make it possible in this study to determine patterns of variation for those features for either Rachel or the monodialectal speakers.

TOWARD ANOTHER DEFINITION OF BIDIALECTALISM. The determination of Rachel's bidialectalism shows that these methods developed by Hazen (2001, 92–94) can, despite their shortcomings, indeed establish that a speaker has mastery of two internally consistent dialect systems and that the speaker uses those systems in ways that are comparable to the linguistic behaviors of monodialectal speakers of both dialects. Besides pointing out concerns about the applicability of these criteria in situations of intense language variety contact, this study does not here propose specific changes to these stated criteria; more research and thought are needed to craft the most effective tools to account for individuals who have two modes of speaking.

In response to this need, this chapter concludes by proposing an expanded and modified definition of bidialectalism that builds on Hazen's (2001) criteria but also takes into consideration the assessment of the bidialectal by the speech community. According to my proposed new definition, a bidialectal speaker will exhibit...

1. ability to use two modes of speaking that constitute separate, internally consistent systems of speech patterns and that correspond at multiple (but not necessarily all) linguistic levels with dialects used by members of the speech community of which they are an accepted part; and

2. fluency in both dialects (i.e., the ability of the bidialectal to speak unselfconsciously and with enough native-like competence to be accepted as a member of the community of speakers who speak a certain dialect) (see Johnstone 1999).

The first criterion is, of course, based directly on Hazen's (2001) assessments of a speaker's linguistic behavior, but the second adds a layer of assessment of that linguistic behavior by members of the bidialectal's speech community. Many factors enter into the development of "fluency" for speakers of any language variety, but here the term focuses entirely—in this context of developing a test of bidialectalism—on the fit between bidialectal behaviors and the speech community expectations that cause that speaker either to be seen as part of the speech community in question or not. Johnstone (1999, 506) used a similar definition in her study of Texas women's linguistic identities, stating that her four subjects used "Southern speech" fluently "in the sense that their uses of [that variety] sound native, as well as in the sense that they are members of or at least on the margins of the group whose usage defines fluency." For a speaker to fulfill the fluency criteria, then, requires two key elements:

1. Speaker communicative competence that is native-like in both grammatical and sociopragmatic knowledge of two dialect systems, and

2. Recognition from monodialectal speakers of both dialects that the speaker is a member of the groups that use each respective dialect and is, moreover, an authentic user of each of those codes.

Demonstrating mastery of communicative competence in its linguistic and sociopragmatic forms makes it possible for the speaker to receive recognition from the monodialectal speech communities as an authentic user of the dialect. As Chambers (2002, 11) puts it, "for social interaction to work, both the context of the speech and its form must be appropriate to the speakers and the interlocutors in the particular social context." When social interaction works, it paves the way for speakers to be accepted as part of the group. Thus, individuals with two modes of speaking may not be the most "extreme" or "prototypical"—or even "average"—users of their two dialects, but they are accepted as genuine members of the speech communities with which they interact.

Benefits of This Definition for the Study of Bidialectalism. In this version of a definition for bidialectalism, the first criterion (the need for native-like behavior) isolates the linguistic correlates of an individual's two modes of speaking. It is attractive, despite its limitations, because it sets these speakers' linguistic behavior apart, in a verifiable and measurable manner, from language variety contact behaviors such as those discussed in chapter 6: style shifting (Baugh 2001; Labov 2001), performance speech (Schilling-Estes 1998), accommodation (Giles, Taylor, and Bourhis 1973), language crossing (Rampton 1995), extreme personal pattern variation (Dorian 1994; Wolfram and Beckett 2000), and so on. By insisting that the bidialectal exhibit evidence of use of two separate systems of dialectal features, this definition eliminates speakers who show evidence of having a mixed set of dialect features (see Hazen 2001, 96). However, unlike Hazen's formulation of this type of criterion, this definition allows there to be overlap between the dialects, a situation that is part of the linguistic reality of the PDE-SCPE context in Pennsylvania today and presumably in other intense language variety contact environments. The key for the bidialectal is that the overlap is part of each dialect's SYSTEM of features and language variation patterns; in other words, even when a feature is shared between the two dialects, that feature's use is conditioned—for the true bidialectal—by different factors determined by the rules of the dialect being spoken.

Another difficulty remedied by this first criterion is how one distinguishes between the true dialect speaker and the imitator. The requirement for native-like behavior from a bidialectal requires such speakers to exhibit masterful ability in two dialects at levels of language beyond the surface level and to do so in a way that fits within the range of what native speakers of each respective dialect do. In other words, simple phonological substitutions and use of a few inserted lexical items are not enough to make someone a true speaker of a dialect (Sweetland 2002); an authentic speaker must show evidence of native-like skill at a more foundational level of the dialect—for example, in lower-level phonological processes, morphosyntactic features, or pragmatic strategies. This thereby eliminates from consideration bidialectals as both imitators, who rely on such surface-level devices as voice quality, speech tempo, and intonation (Preston 1992, 1996; Labov 1994), and WANNABES, speakers who imitate a dialect in order to project a certain image of themselves (Sweetland 2002).

The second criterion in this definition is fluency, defined here as the recognition of the authenticity of a speaker's linguistic behavior by the speech community (Johnstone 1999). Using the intuitions of the speech community in determining who is an authentic speaker solves several of the problems inherent in Hazen's (2001, 92–94) criteria for bidialectals. One such problem for Hazen's criteria in the context of an intense language variety contact situation is the determination of which monodialectal target models a bidialectal must match to be considered a true speaker of a dialect. Chapters 5 and 7 of this study have shown how difficult it can be to settle on one model when an obsolescing dialect is in the process of unraveling and where interspeaker variation can be much higher than in a nonobsolescent situation. Relying on the speech community's acceptance or nonacceptance of the speaker as authentic allows for the bidialectal to fall within the RANGE of feature use and language variation patterns that the speech community considers acceptable—rather than on what the linguist determines is acceptable from some sample of speakers—without the bidialectal being required to match precisely any one group of speakers. In this way also, if a speaker relies on low-level language features but not on surface-level features—like Sweetland's (2002) Delilah, for example, who was considered "basically black" by her Cincinnati AAVE-speaking speech community—then that speaker's mastery of the dialect can be recognized and that individual can be deemed an authentic speaker whose language attitudes and linguistic behaviors can contribute to the study of what speakers do in dialect contact and obsolescing dialect situations. Moreover, the use of fluency rather than monodialectal target matching as a criterion allows individuals with two modes of speaking to differ from each other in their particular use of language features, yet still be grouped into the same class of bidialectals, another great advantage to closer examination of their behavior, particularly within a variationist framework (which relies on sufficient sample sizes to conduct appropriate analyses).

Perhaps the greatest benefit, however, for the use of fluency instead of target matching in making interspeaker comparisons is that it provides a method of fitting the behavior of these individuals into linguistic theory as a whole, thus permitting the linguist to draw parallels: between the linguist's definition of bidialectalism and the sociopsychological reality of speaker behavior and subsequent identification by other speakers as members of a monodialectal speech community, as well as between models of bilingualism (native-like competence in the use of two grammars that are distant enough from each other to be called separate languages) and bidialectalism (native-like competence in two varieties of a single language). The ability to draw such parallels can serve to enlighten research on bidialectalism and investigation into other outcomes of contact between language varieties.

Fluency and the Bilingualism-Bidialectalism Parallel. One advantage to linguistic researchers of using fluency as an indicator of bidialectalism is that it allows for similar standards to be applied to bilinguals and bidialectals in the scope of linguistic research. Martin-Jones and Romaine (1986) note that a remarkably popular perception among the general public is that people who speak two languages are, in fact, semilinguals, with complete mastery of neither language. This belief is usually based on the comparison of the productions of such speakers with an assortment of textbook ideas about what is grammatical or "correct," usually with a focus on highly noticeable surface features (like vocabulary, pronunciation, and grammar); sometimes it is in condemnation of the fact that such speakers often do poorly on written tests of their languages even when their speaking abilities are fluent. Linguists, of course, reject this narrow perspective out of hand because it does not account for many aspects of speech behavior: native-like ability that a speaker may have in terms of communicative competence, the dynamics with which language use changes, intergenerational variation, or the "reshuffling" of a language's repertoire in a community and its resultant "redefinition of codes and communicative norms" (Martin-Jones and Romaine 1986, 33). Grosjean (1995) underscores these sentiments in his assertion that bilinguals are competent in their respective languages to the point that is demanded by the changing linguistic situations in which they find themselves:

Bilinguals are not the sum of two complete or incomplete monolinguals, but have a unique and specific linguistic configuration. They have developed competencies in their languages to the extent required by their needs and those of the environment. [...] Levels of fluency in a language will depend on the need for that language and will be domain-specific. [...] New situations, new environments, new interlocutors will involve new linguistic needs and will therefore change the language configuration of the person involved. [Grosjean 1995, 259–60]

So even though the general public may entertain the notion of a "full" or "balanced" bilingual, linguists agree that speakers such as those Grosjean (1995) describes are indeed truly bilingual, even if they cannot match targets set by older speakers or by speakers who live outside of the bilingual community in question.

This more flexible view of bilingualism needs to be applied as well to bidialectalism. If fluency (acceptance by the speech community as authentic) rather than mere monodialectal target matching is adopted as a requirement for bidialectalism, it then opens the door for investigating bidialectalism in a manner similar to how bilingualism has recently been investigated (e.g., Grosjean 1995; Romaine 1995; Martin-Jones and Romaine 1986), for example, with regard to what constitutes triggers or switches between dialects, how separate or integrated dialect grammars are in the speaker's mind, how perception and production modes operate for each dialect, what strategies speakers use in dialect processing, how cognitive demand affects speaker code choice, and so on.

Authentic bidialectals may be rare, but—given the right linguistic context and sustained effort on the part of the linguist—not impossible to find. From the point of view of the sociolinguist, it is remarkable how such speakers rise to the challenge of learning and actively maintaining two dialects in response to motivations of identity, showing solidarity with other speakers, and so on. From the point of view of the researcher of language variety obsolescence, it is amazing that such sophisticated language use can occur in the context of the linguistic (and social) disorder that arises as a variety slides toward extinction. There is much more about how humans use language that linguists can learn from these bidialectal masters of acquisition.

8. CONCLUSION

Sociolinguistics has always been interested in both the grammatical and communicative competence of speakers, and places where language varieties come into contact offer tremendous opportunities for investigating what the range of those competencies can be. South central Pennsylvania is one such place where language varieties have come together in long-term contact; the development and use of Pennsylvania German, Pennsylvania Dutchfied English, and South Central Pennsylvania English simultaneously in this geographic area has created a linguistic environment in which speakers of various sorts use the different codes available to fulfill a variety of communicative and pragmatic functions.

However, as often happens in situations where more than one language variety is present, one variety is winning out over the others. In sectarian (specifically, Amish and Mennonite) communities, Pennsylvania German is still spoken as one of the language varieties of the home and community, but all speakers are fluent in PDE and/or SCPE as well. In nonsectarian communities, the shift from Pennsylvania German-PDE bilingualism to PDE monolingualism was more or less complete 30–40 years ago. At about that same time, those same nonsectarian communities began a shift from PDE to SCPE as well. As a result, PDE is now an obsolescing dialect and is expected to be extinct in nonsectarian communities within the next 50–60 years. However, in the last phase of its life cycle, bidialectal speakers of both PDE and SCPE have emerged from PDE's last generation of speakers, a development not documented in the literature on dialect contact until now.

This study's two goals have been to document the unraveling of the PDE dialect taking place among PDE speakers in this last stage of the dialect's life and to document the rise of bidialectalism that has also occurred. This volume has accomplished these goals by presenting an account of how PDE developed, a description of the traditional features of PDE, an analysis of how PDE has changed over the generations of speakers, and the results of a more detailed investigation of PDE-SCPE bidialectal linguistic behaviors.

What began as the leveling of German dialects into Pennsylvania German as immigrants from various parts of the German-speaking world flooded into William Penn's colony in the late seventeenth and eighteenth centuries eventually yielded one more new English dialect: Pennsylvania Dutchified English. As PDE has succumbed over the decades to pressure from the regional standard, SCPE, monodialectal speakers of PDE have become more rare; many 30–40-year-olds who grew up speaking PDE have now shifted completely to SCPE, and none of the children and younger adults in nonsectarian communities today speaks the dialect.[1] Reasons for this shift have been discussed, particularly chapter 7. In less than 100 years, the linguistic climate of south central Pennsylvania has therefore transitioned in nonsectarian communities from one of Pennsylvania German monolingualism to Pennsylvania German-PDE bilingualism to PDE monolingualism to a mixed context in which both PDE and SCPE are spoken. In another 50–60 years, only SCPE will be spoken.

In many ways this progression is quite similar to that seen in many immigrant language communities throughout the United States, where the original generation of monolingual speakers of the immigrant language gave birth to a generation of speakers who were bilingual in English and the immigrant variety. By the third generation, the shift to English was often complete, and the speakers of that generation were overwhelmingly monolingual. In south central Pennsylvania, the high concentration of Pennsylvania Germans, even in nonsectarian communities, made it possible for Pennsylvania German to enjoy an extended life, spanning many generations, and for PDE itself to span three generations (at least in northern Lebanon County); once school consolidation began in earnest, exposing PDE-speaking children to SCPE, the demographic balance was tipped, and PDE began its decline. As members of PDE's last generation of speakers—all of whom had learned PDE as their first dialect—were confronted as children with both PDE and SCPE models and negative attitudes toward PDE, many chose to shift completely to SCPE. Even those who remained PDE speakers ended up with an "unraveling" variety of PDE that shows evidence of interspeaker inconsistency. Faced with such inconsistent PDE models, children of this last generation of PDE speakers have acquired SCPE instead, even when growing up in households with one or even two PDE-speaking parents. A detailed description of the inconsistencies in the PDE dialect as it is spoken today was presented in chapters 4 and 5, along with an in-depth explanation of the results of this "unraveling" and a description of how that "unraveling" may have come about.

In the last generation of PDE speakers, there has also arisen a group of bidialectal speakers of PDE and SCPE. Confronted with PDE and SCPE as they acquired language as very young and school-aged children, these individuals established an identity for themselves in the larger speech community that revolves around authentic use of both PDE and SCPE. The linguistic backgrounds, attitudes, and motivations of three south central Pennsylvania bidialectals were sketched out in chapter 7; specific linguistic data from one of those bidialectals, Rachel, was presented in an effort both to prove that bidialectals exist and to highlight the actual outcomes of this bidialectalism in terms of use of dialectal features, the grammars behind those features, and so on.

Rachel is a SCPE-PDE bidialectal speaker, not just according to her own designation, but also according to her fulfillment of the testable criteria for bidialectalism set out by Hazen (2001, 92–94), that a speaker who is truly bidialectal will...

1. produce the same sets of features as monodialectal speakers of both dialects, without overlap,
2. produce those features in the same "language variation patterns" that monodialectals do, and
3. possess a social motivation for acquiring the second dialect while retaining the first one.

As chapter 7 clearly showed, Rachel successfully met all of these criteria. Nevertheless, these criteria reveal some weaknesses when put to the test in an intense language variety contact situation like that of south central Pennsylvania, and they reveal the need for careful modification. A modified definition of bidialectalism was proposed at the conclusion of chapter 7 that includes as a key component the notion of "fluency" with regard to the uses of dialects and speakers estimation by the speech community in a dialect contact situation.

The days of Pennsylvania Dutchified English as a viable dialect are numbered, but this study has demonstrated how much there is to be learned from a study of such an obsolescing dialect in the sociolinguistic context of its last generation of speakers. The generation in which these speakers were born is a unique one in south central Pennsylvania's linguistic history: PDE and SCPE speakers alike grew up in households with PDE-speaking parents but were then exposed to SCPE through school teachers and friends. This "generation of choice" made three distinct kinds of decisions regarding language use, with some retaining PDE, some acquiring and shifting completely to SCPE, and a few choosing bidialectalism in PDE and SCPE. This "generation of choice" has also taken part in the unraveling of the PDE dialect as PDE's last speakers have lost consistency between themselves with regard to which features they use and how they use them. This inconsistent state of the PDE dialect, in addition to continued pressure from the dominant SCPE (and the language attitudes, identity issues, etc. associated with it), has sealed PDE's fate, as the children of those last PDE speakers have turned from the inconsistent target models of PDE available to them and acquired SCPE instead of PDE.

This study has also provided a look into the behaviors of bidialectal speakers of PDE and SCPE, proving not only that such speakers can and do exist, but that they present a fascinating opportunity to study unique combinations of social motivations and attitudes and interesting combinations of linguistic strategies to distinguish between their two dialects. In light of information gained from this look at bidialectals in an intense language variety contact situation, this volume has also proposed a more comprehensive definition of bidialectalism than has been previously developed, based on determining bidialectal status through the identifying speaker characteristics of (1) use of two separate sets of internally consistent speech patterns that correspond to separate dialects, and (2) fluency in those two dialects based on communicative competence with membership in the groups whose usage defines fluency. It is hoped that this monograph will prove helpful to those studying the outcomes of dialect contact, language variety obsolescence and death, and bidialectalism/bilingualism as a whole.

APPENDIX

1. SAMPLE TOKENS FROM YOUNGEST MONODIALECTAL PDE SPEAKERS (DK, DwK, AND LK)

Tokens with Environments for Obstruent Devoicing

	Voiced	*Not Voiced*
DK	leagues, says, Amber's, was, because	job, horrible, probably, remember, number, Amber, maybe, Bible, able, probably, incredible, Lebanon, girlfriend, side, find, word, understand, said, did, find, schooled, old, played, was, cause, kids, kinds, years, cells, have, give, love, believe, live
DwK	dad, said, wood, ahold, said, kid, backwards, have, raised, classes, was, years, days	could, good, had, head, would, said, grandpa, Ed, grandparents, they'd, dead, United, around, we'd, budge, charge, friends, George, kids, God's, words, range, biggest, begin, big, other, bother, even, levels, we've, have, lived, relatively, everything, every, have, love, give
LK	dad, said, wood, ahold, said, kid, backwards, have, raised, classes, was, years, days	could, good, had, head, would, said, grandpa, Ed, grandparents, they'd, dead, United, around, we'd, budge, charge, budge, friends, George, kids, God's, words, range, biggest, begin, big, other, bother, even, levels, we've, have, lived, relatively, everything, every, have, love, give

Tokens with Environments for /aʊ/ Monophthongization

	Monophthongized	*Not Monophthongized*
DK	now, how, sounds, wow, down, about, out	now, how, down, downstairs, around, Jonestown's, houses, out, about, without, outside
DwK	around, how	how, now
LK	now, how	how, now, about, allowing, found, discount

Tokens with Environments for /a/ Centralization

	Centralized	*Not Centralized*
DK	John, comment	Mom
DwK	mom	conversation, John's, John, concrete, mom, constantly, bomb
LK	comments	comment, combination, mom, honor, responsible, misconduct, conferences, responded

Tokens with Environments for /aɪ/ Monophthongization

	Monophthongized	*Not Monophthongized*
DK	wire, while	
DwK		miles, miles, while
LK	Palmyra	fired, child, Palmyra

Tokens with Environments for Raised [æ]

Raised	*Not Raised*
half, class, laugh, bad	staff, camping, afterwards, laugh, planning, understand, can't, pastor, asked, last, has

NOTE: Only *yeah* was coded for, but other words provided appropriate environments for this feature as well. These tokens are samples taken from all three of the youngest PDE speakers.

Tokens with Environments for [β]

[β]	[w]
we, were wanna, word, Watergate, anywhere, when, won't, wasn't, well, which, way, went, woulda	well, we, what, one, working, Oswald, always, watched, anywhere, weekend, war, winning, we're, went

NOTE: The youngest PDE monodialectals did not use the bilabial fricative at all. These tokens are gathered from the data collected from the middle-aged PDE monodialectals.

2. EXCERPTS FROM RACHEL'S CONVERSATIONS

CONVERSATION 1 (with an SCPE speaker, talking about the TV show *Where in the World Is Carmen San Diego?*, music, and childhood memories)

R: I can't remember. J— was so small that I can't remember if we actually watched
E:

R: it, the whole thing, or   Did they have a game show, and also an animated
E: Mmhmm.

R: kind of thing?
E: I think there was– there were two different shows. Like two

R: OK.   I can't put
E: different takes of it maybe.   Or two   takes on the same show. I can't

R: it together. That's why I, I'm thinking that maybe I never watched a whole
E:

R: episode, cause I'm having trouble.   'Cause I
E: Yeah, I can't put it togther now either.

R: could see it as an animated thing, but then like it has this real-live part that
E:

R: kinda hooks the episodes together. And I seem to remember kids being asked
E: Yeah.

R: questions, but I might be mixing it up. But I do remember these three jazz
E: That might be it actually.

R: guys, and I still remember the thing that would always make me laugh was when
E:

R: they said "The Loot!" I don't know!   So, oh, goodness.   Does she?
E: Yes.   Yeah.   Emily really enjoys jazz.   Like on

R:
E: the piano   like the jazz books. So do you, are you familiar with any– Do you

R: I love jazz!
E: like jazz? Are you familiar with some good jazz groups or something? It would

R: Yeah, actually!
E: be fun to get her a CD of jazz or something, but I don't how what to get

R: Yeah, I don't actually– I'm not very good in terms of that. I know like the old
E:

R: timer, I know like the old– There's different styles of jazz, and I'm more
E:

R: familiar with the old-timers, you know, so like Duke Ellington, Louis Armstrong,
E: Mmhmm.

R: a little more recent Mile Davis. We have a couple of CDs of his stuff, and that's
E: Yeah.

R: fun, but yeah, I'm not– Jon know so much more that I do about Jazz. Yeah, he
E:

R: kinda introduced me to it– I didn't know anything about it until I met him.
E: Oh, interesting.

R: Well, my parents always listened to country music   So like on rare
E: Yeah, that makes sense.

R: occasions I would get to hear like classical music once in a while– very rare,
E:

R: very, very rare. And I still remember, like a very vivid memory– We would–
E: Uhhuh

R: We didn't own a VCR, but sometimes on New Year's Eve Mom would rent a
E: Ah

R: VCR from Redner's? And I still remember like one New Year's Eve, like
E:

R: everyone else had fallen asleep, and I watched Amadaeus, the movie Amadaeus,
E:

R: by myself, and just, it wasn't even the movie– I could have cared less about the
E:

R: movie itself– although it's always fun to see a period piece with the beautiful
E: Uhhuh.

R: dresses and everything– But the music! I just was like– I just sat there until like
E: Yeah.

R: the last credit had finished because I was like But I just had no, I just
E: Oh, how neat!

R: didn't, except for band, you know– except for what we did in band, I just had
E:

R: very little exposure with classical music
E: Yeah! That's a neat story.

CONVERSATION 2 (with middle-aged PDE speakers, talking about significant historical events that impacted life)

R: Well, since you saw so many people shot, G—, does that mean you were in on
G:
L:
LM:

R: it, like Dad said? Well, if you think
G: Yeah. (laugh)
L:
LM: I'm beginning to wonder.

R: about it, youse did see a lot of people shot, though.
G: Yeah. Well, a lot of stuff in our
L:
LM:

R: But how did that make you feel,
G: lifetime, I'm getting at, that we seen.
L:
LM:

R: I guess is what I'm trying to ask, cause you know
G:
L:
LM: Well, it made him feel good

R: Well (laugh) Well, that's G—f's
G:

L:
LM: because he wanted to bump them off anyway!

  R: Mafia connections! But I guess what I mean is, um, like a lot of time, for
  G:
  L:
LM:

  R: your generation, when they would say like what is something you remember,
  G:
  L:
LM:

  R: they would say "Well, I remember when John F. Kennedy got shot."
  G:
  L:
LM:

  R: Yeah.   But then all this other stuff happened with it, it wasn't
  G: Right. Right.   Right.
  L:
LM:

  R: just that. Now how did you feel– compare how you felt with that, compared
  G:
  L:
LM:

  R: to like when, well, like when 9-11 happened.   Was it the same kinds of
  G: Huh.
  L:
LM:

  R: feelings, like the world's going cr– I mean, what were you thinking when it
  G:
  L:
LM:

  R: happened?
  G: I don't know what we were thinking. Well, you know, when they
  L:
LM:

  R: Mmhmm.   Oh, you mean, for 9-11.
  G: announced it on the radio, they said "Terrorists."   For
  L:
LM:

  R: How can that be?
  G: 9-11. I thought "Naaaw."   I thought, they're not just gonna take a

L:
LM:

R:
G: plane and fly it into the Empire State, but then when they said there was a
L:
LM:

R: (to LM) And you
G: second one, I thought, "Oh my goodness, this is for real?"
L:
LM:

R: seen it on television, right?
G: And I was going up 81, in the car,
L: Yeah, I did too.
LM:

R: Oh, my gosh!
G: going to a camper show.   And that camper show, when I got in there,
L:
LM:

R: Oh, yeah?
G: everybody was exactly in chaos!   All the business– I mean– all the
L:
LM:

R: You mean like "Buzz-buzz-buzz" chaos? Or do you mean dead silence?
G: Cause the airports were all shut
L:
LM:

R: Oh, right.
G: down. All the businessmen had people coming in. They couldn't get out.
L:
LM:

NOTES

CHAPTER 3

1. Use of *had* + Verb for remote past has been discovered only in the speech of PDE monodialectal speakers and the study's bidialectal. However, unelicited occurrences of this feature are very rare, and further investigation may determine that this feature is shared by both PDE and SCPE.

CHAPTER 4

1. From another point of view, /d/ may be seen as the "normal" stop because it does not devoice in obstruent-liquid onset clusters in the "strong" position at the beginning of a stressed syllable, whereas /b/ and /g/ do. This conservative PDE devoicing of /b/ and /g/ in such environments can by accounted for if a certain ranking of PDE phonological constraints is adopted, as in the Optimality-Theoretic analysis of this problem by Anderson and Davis (2003, 2013).

2. This ratio is not the only acoustic correlate that has been examined with regard to obstruent voicing/devoicing, however. Other researchers have pointed instead to spectral properties of the preceding vowel, perhaps in combination with temporal properties or burst release (Dinnsen 1985), quantity ("duration"), intensity, duration of voicing through a closure (Kraehenmann 2001), and so on. In the end it may indeed be that one of these effects better illuminates the complexities of obstruent voicing/devoicing in PDE, but for this study, the ratio of vowel to obstruent duration will be the focus of investigation.

3. Port and O'Dell (1985) and others have shown that devoiced stops are in fact longer than their voiceless counterparts, by as much as 10% (Dinnsen 1985), but voiceless stops are not the focus of this particular study.

4. Despite its popularity and genuine usefulness in examining many kinds of sociolinguistic data, the VARBRUL program was not utilized because it depends on discrete values. The duration and ratio values in this study are scalar and do not lend themselves to accurate analysis with such programs.

5. Note that a simple *t*-test could also have performed the same function for this data, at least for the comparison of means of groups of speakers according to language status and sex. Because of the three-way division in groups according to age, however, it was necessary to use both the ANOVA program and its corresponding post hoc tests (in this study, a Tukey HSD and a Bonferroni test) to determine if significant differences between the groups exist.

6. This is in contrast to General American English, which uses both consonant durations and vowel-to-consonant duration ratios to distinguish devoicing of /z/ (see José 2010).

7. Actually, there were sufficient tokens of the bilabial fricative as well. Since the youngest speakers do not use that feature at all, however—the feature has been totally abandoned by them—an in-depth analysis of conditioning factors favoring its use would not have informed the discussion of feature loss across the generations.

8. Each of the language-internal factors included in this analysis were used by José (2010) in his examination of the devoicing of the obstruent /z/ in Midwestern American English. The results of his study will be discussed at the end of this section on obstruent devoicing.

9. Because tokens of /d/ and /z/ dominated the corpus and /b/ and /g/ were never devoiced by any speaker in the data set, all other obstruents (all fricatives) were grouped together to give their category enough weight to add meaningfulness to the analysis.

10. There were few tokens of individual phonemes or even more defined groups (like nasals, liquids, etc.). These were, therefore, grouped together to make categories with enough tokens to make analysis possible.

CHAPTER 5

1. As an example of hindrance to comprehensibility caused by monophthongization of /aʊ/ to [a], many people not native to the northern Lebanon County area in south central Pennsylvania are surprised when they find out that the town just across Gold Mine Mountain to the north of the Lebanon-Schuykill County border is really Tower City and not "Tar City," since so many local residents (even SCPE speakers) pronounce the name with the PDE variant.

2. One could conjecture that this is an example of females tending toward more "standard" speech, as well as females leading the way in terms of language change. However, the limited amount of data available here does not allow this to go beyond mere speculation at this point, and it may simply be that the informant was being "careful" in her speech since she knew she was being recorded and thus used this stigmatized PDE variant less frequently.

3. In the case of *iron*, two PDE processes work together to turn it into a monosyllabic word with a monophthong for the syllable nucleus. First the monophthongization process changes the /ai/ to [æ]. Then the tendency in PDE to reduce unstressed syllables at the ends of words (a feature also attested in Philadelphia English) results in the pronunciation of *iron* as a single syllable, [ærn]. This tendency to reduce word-final unstressed syllables sometimes results in the dropping of those final syllables in colloquial speech, as in *tomorrow* [tə.már], *wheelbarrow* [wil.bǽr], and even place-names such as *Palmyra* [pal.mǽr].

4. A particularly humorous illustration of this hindrance to comprehensibility occurred one afternoon when my uncle's girlfriend, a PDE speaker in her 50s, tried to engage my husband (a non-PDE speaker born and raised in Indiana) in conversation about the then-current problems with pirates taking over ships in the Gulf of Aden. The exchange started out something like this:

> PDE SPEAKER: So did you hear about the pirates ([pærəts]) in Somalia?
> NON-PDE SPEAKER: Parrots? In Somalia? I had no idea there were parrots in Somalia!
> PDE SPEAKER: Didn't you hear about them in the news?
> NON-PDE SPEAKER: No, I didn't! Are they endangered?
> PDE SPEAKER: Well, yeah, I hope so...

This misunderstanding continued for several minutes before my husband realized that my uncle's girlfriend was talking about robber sailors instead of exotic birds!

5. One could conjecture that this is a case of male-female differences in PDE feature use, but there is not enough data here to come to such a conclusion. Besides, in the youngest generation the situation is exactly reversed: the female informant uses the feature, while the two male informants do not.

6. Nevertheless, it must be kept in mind that these 30–40-year-old PDE speakers are from the last generation of speakers of PDE, and despite its robustness across the generations, raised [æ] too will disappear when PDE is extinct: PDE raised [æ] has not been observed in the speech of the 30–40-year-olds' (non-PDE-speaking) children.

7. Or at least she does not in this data set; she has been noted to monophthongize /ai/ in unrecorded conversation contexts.

8. And PDE is seeing the end of its life span, definitely in Lebanon County, and, I suspect, elsewhere. None of the children of the 30–40-year-old age group of PDE speakers speaks PDE, at least in nonsectarian (non-Amish, non-Mennonite) households. This may be true in sectarian households as well. Personal observation of Mennonite and Amish people (a great many of whom are bilingual in Pennsylvania German and English) from daily life in south central Pennsylvania—e.g., at the store, at the post office—reveals that, even for those sectarians, those in the 30–40-age range may speak English with a Dutchified accent, but those who are younger do not. It has likewise been anecdotally noted that Amish farmers who bring produce in to the central market in Philadelphia (a place where many stands are manned by Amish farmers who live outside the city limits) and Amish contractors/builders who travel to do construction work also do not speak English with a "Dutchified" accent, at least to non-Pennsylvania German speakers. The Pennsylvania German language has shown much decline over the generations, but linguists have assumed that the sectarian households of Pennsylvania (and other states as well, as Amish and Mennonites move to farmland outside the Keystone State) would keep it alive. No such hope exists for the continuation of PDE.

CHAPTER 7

1. At least some of the 30–40-year-old informants interviewed in the course of this study indicated that "Dutchified" is the only way they can talk now, or ever could talk. At the time that they were preteens or young teenagers, they may not have felt like it was possible for them to learn to speak SCPE.

2. In a preliminary study on social network and use of PDE conducted in 1993–95, the only social factor that correlated with degree of "Dutchifiedness" of PDE-speaking informants was career aspirations.

3. Rachel's grandmother had lost a leg due to complications of diabetes and was mostly confined to bed. Rachel would spend summer days with her while her uncle (who lived with her grandmother) was at work, and during the school year, she would get off the bus at her grandmother's house to do the same every day after school (when she wasn't involved in school activities).

4. Of course, three speakers is a very small sample to begin with.

5. This is a likely an effect of the Observer's Paradox (Labov 1972, 209): this female speaker has been heard to use this feature in normal casual conversation; however, despite efforts to help her relax during recording, it was obvious that she was careful in her speech, either because of the tape recorder's presence or the fact that this recording was destined to be part of an academic investigation.

6. Recall that each of these speakers came from a home with PDE-speaking parents. Speaker RK is also married to a PDE speaker.

7. This may be due to the carefulness of speech during recording, as was discussed in an earlier note for middle-aged speaker LG, or an accident of the data, since there are so few tokens of this feature. In casual conversation, I have heard DK monophthongize /ai/, even repeating the monophthongized variant for a single word again and again in one conversation.

8. In my M.A. thesis (Anderson 1995), I did not find a correlation between "Dutchifiedness" and whether the people with whom the speaker spent the most time were also PDE speakers; however, that study considered all generations of PDE speakers together as one group. It is possible that, if the results were compiled again today with only the 30–40-year-olds (who were then 20-somethings), there would be a strong correlation between "Dutchifiedness" and social network composition.

9. Typically children who attend Mennonite schools in south central Pennsylvania only remain in school until tenth grade, when they reach the age of 16, at which time the state allows them to drop out of school. They then typically work on the family farm or in the family business (construction, for example). For a student—even a female—to finish school is a rarity, thus such individuals are in high demand as teachers for Mennonite schools. (Males who are willing to work as teachers and supervisors are in even higher demand as principals for Mennonite schools, typically taking on teaching duties for the children in the

highest grades.) For a student to be singled out as having teaching ability, as this female informant was, is quite remarkable.

10. In other words, the two features of PDE for which they express the greatest awareness are obstruent devoicing and /aʊ/ monophthongization, and they show little awareness of any other features, just like other PDE and SCPE speakers.

CHAPTER 8

1. Younger speakers in sectarian communities are also shifting to SCPE, but those in northern Lebanon County seem to be, at least for the moment, lagging behind nonsectarian communities. This may partially be the result of the continued influence of Pennsylvania German in their linguistic environment, although Kopp (1999) reports that the Pennsylvania German–English bilinguals he studied speak a standard variety of English, not PDE.

REFERENCES

The American Heritage Dictionary of the English Language. 2006. 4th ed. Boston: Houghton Mifflin.

Anderson, Vicki Michael. 1995. "How Now Brown Cow? A Look at Sociolinguistic Variables Affecting the Use of Pennsylvania Dutchified English in Green Point, Pennsylvania." M.A. thesis, Ball State University.

———. 2001. "The Problem with 'Sabrina': An OT Analysis of Obstruent Devoicing in Pennsylvania Dutchified English." Unpublished MS.

Anderson, Vicki, and Stuart Davis. 2013. "Where American English Meets German: Devoicing in Pennsylvania Dutchified English." *Journal of the Phonetic Society of Japan* 17.1: 18–25.

Auer, Peter, Birgit Barden, and Beate Grosskopf. 1998. "Subjective and Objective Parameters Determining 'Salience' in Long-Term Dialect Accommodation." *Journal of Sociolinguistics* 2.2: 163–88. doi:10.1111/1467-9481.00039.

———. 2000. "Long-Term Linguistic Accommodation and Its Sociolinguistic Interpretation: Evidence from the Inner-German Migration after the *Wende*." In *Dialect and Migration in a Changing Europe*, edited by Klaus Mattheier, 79–98. Frankfurt am Main: Lang.

Auger, Julie. 2001. "Phonological Variation and Optimality Theory: Evidence from Word-Initial Vowel Epenthesis in Vimeu Picard." *Language Variation and Change* 13.3: 253–303. doi:10.1017/S0954394501133016.

Aurand, A. Monroe, Jr. 1939. *Quaint Idioms and Expressions of the Pennsylvania Germans: A Delightful Bit of Entertainment.* Rev. ed. Lancaster, Pa.: Aurund Press.

Bao, Zhiming, and Lionel Wee. 1999. "The Passive in Singapore English." *World Englishes* 18.1: 1–11. doi:10.1111/1467-971X.00117.

Bardovi-Harlig, Kathleen. 1987. "Markedness and Salience in Second-Language Acquisition." *Language Learning* 37.3: 385–407. doi:10.1111/j.1467-1770.1987.tb00577.x.

Baugh, John. 2001. "A Dissection of Style-Shifting." In *Style and Sociolinguistic Variation*, edited by Penelope Eckert and John R. Rickford, 109–18. Cambridge: Cambridge University Press.

Bethin, Christina Y. 2010. "Perceptual Salience in Dialect Contact: The Okan'e/Akan'e Dialects of East Slavic." *Journal of Slavic Linguistics* 18.1: 7–54. doi:10.1353/jsl.0.0033.

Blom, Jan-Petter, and John J. Gumperz. 1972. "Social Meaning in Linguistic Structures: Code-Switching in Norway." In *Directions in Sociolinguistics: The Ethnography of Communication*, edited by John J. Gumperz and Dell Hymes, 407–34. New York: Holt, Rinehart and Winston.

Boas, Hans C. 2009. *The Life and Death of Texas German.* Publication of the American Dialect Society 93. Durham, N.C.: Duke University Press.

Boeree, C. George. 2004. "Dialects of English." http://webspace.ship.edu/cgboer/dialectsofenglish.html.

Britain, David. 2002. "Diffusion, Levelling, Simplification and Reallocation in Past Tense BE in the English Fens." *Journal of Sociolinguistics* 6.1: 16–43. doi: 10.1111/1467-9481.00175.

Brown, Becky. 2003. "Code-Convergent Borrowing in Louisiana French." *Journal of Sociolinguistics* 7.1: 3–23. doi:10.1111/1467-9481.00208.

Chambers, J. K. 1992. "Dialect Acquisition." *Language* 68.4: 673–705. doi:10.2307/416850.

———. 2002. "Studying Language Variation: An Informal Epistemology." In *The Handbook of Language Variation and Change*, edited by J. K. Chambers, Peter Trudgill, and Natalie Schilling-Estes, 4–14. Maldan, Mass.: Blackwell.

Chambers, J. K., and Peter Trudgill. 1980. *Dialectology*. Cambridge: Cambridge University Press.

Charles-Luce, Jan. 1985. "Word-Final Devoicing in German: Effects of Phonetic and Sentential Contexts." *Journal of Phonetics* 13.4: 309–24.

Clopper, Cynthia, and David Pisoni. 2003. "Free Classification of Regional Varieties of American English." Poster presented at the 32nd annual meeting on New Ways of Analyzing Variation in English (NWAVE 32), Philadelphia, Pa., Oct. 9–12. Abstract at http://www.ling.upenn.edu/NWAVE32/abs-pdf/clopper.pdf.

Clyne, Michael. 2003. *Dynamics of Language Contact: English and Immigrant Languages*. Cambridge: Cambridge University Press.

Connell, Bruce. 2002. "Phonetic/Phonological Variation and Language Contraction." *International Journal of the Sociology of Language* 157: 167–85. doi:10.1515/ijsl.2002.038.

Davis, Stuart. 2010. "On the analysis of aspiration in American English." Paper presented at Indiana University, LTC Colloquium Series, Apr. 8, 2010.

Davis, Stuart, and Vicki Anderson. 2003. "The Prosodic Alignment of Laryngeal Features in Two Dialects of English." Talks presented at the Meertens Instituut, Amsterdam, Oct. 2003.

Dinnsen, Daniel A. 1985. "A Re-examination of Phonological Neutralization." *Journal of Linguistics* 21.2: 265–79. doi:10.1017/S0022226700010276.

Dorian, Nancy C. 1994. "Varieties of Variation in a Very Small Place: Social Homogeneity, Prestige Norms, and Linguistic Variation." *Language* 70.4: 631–96. doi: 10.2307/416324.

Dubois, Sylvie, and Barbara M. Horvath. 1999. "When the Music Changes, You Change Too: Gender and Language Change in Cajun English." *Language Variation and Change* 11.3: 287–313. doi:10.1017/S0954394599113036.

Dyer, Judy. 2002. "'We All Speak the Same Round Here': Dialect Levelling in a Scottish-English Community." *Journal of Sociolinguistics* 6.1: 99–116. doi:10.1111/1467-9481.00179.

Escobar, Anna María. 2001. "Semantic and Pragmatic Functions of the Spanish Diminutive in Spanish in Contact with Quechua." *Southwest Journal of Linguistics* 20.1: 135–49.

Evans, Betsy E. 2002. "An Acoustic and Perceptual Analysis of Imitation." In *Handbook of Perceptual Dialectology*, vol. 2, edited by Daniel Long and Dennis R. Preston, 95–112. Amsterdam: Benjamins.

Fasold, R. W. 1980. "The Conversational Function of Pennsylvania Dutch Intonation." Paper presented at the ninth annual meeting on New Ways of Analyzing Variation in English (NWAVE 9), Ann Arbor, Mich, Oct. 31.

Flege, James Emil. 1987. "The Production of 'New' and 'Similar' Phones in a Foreign Language: Evidence for the Effect of Equivalence Classification." *Journal of Phonetics* 15.1: 47–65.

Fries, Charles C. 1964. "On the Intonation of Yes-No Questions in English." In *In Honour of Daniel Jones: Papers Contributed on the Occasion of His Eightieth Birthday, 12 September 1961*, edited by David Abercrombie, D. B. Fry, P. A. D. MacCarthy, N. C. Scott, and J. L. M. Trim, 242–54. London: Longmans, Green.

Gates, Gary. 1987. *How to Speak Dutch-ified English, Volume 1 (Vun): An "Inwaluable" Introduction to an "Enchoyable" Accent of the "Inklish Lankwitch."* Intercourse, Pa.: Good Books.

———. 1998. *How to Speak Dutch-ified English, Volume 2 (Twoah): An "Advanced Version" of the "Enchoyable" Accent of the "Inklish Lankwitch."* Intercourse, PA: Good Books.

George, Darren, and Paul Mallery. 2000. *SPSS for Windows Step by Step: A Simple Guide and Reference, 9.0 Update.* 2nd ed. Boston: Allyn and Bacon.

Gibbons, Phebe Earle. 1869. "Pennsylvania Dutch." *Atlantic Monthly* 24.144 (Oct.): 473–87.

Giles, Howard, Donald M. Taylor, and Richard Bourhis. 1973. "Towards a Theory of Interpersonal Accommodation through Language: Some Canadian Data." *Language in Society* 2.2: 177–92. doi:10.1017/S0047404500000701.

Goblirsch, Kurt Gustav. 1994. "Fortis and Lenis in Standard German." *Leuvense Bijdragen* 83: 31–45.

Grosjean, François. 1995. "A Psycholinguistic Approach to Code-Switching: The Recognition of Guest Words by Bilinguals." In *One Speaker, Two Langauges: Cross-Disciplinary Perspectives on Code-Switching*, edited by Lesley Milroy and Pieter Muysken, 259–75. Cambridge: Cambridge University Press.

Guy, Gregory, and Laureen Lim. 2005. "Diglossia, Code-Switching, Style-Shifting: A Field Theory of Variety Alternation." Paper presented at the 34th annual meeting on New Ways of Analyzing Variation (NWAV 34), New York, Oct. 20–22.

Hatala, Eileen M. 1976. "Environmental Effects of White Students in Black Schools." M.A. thesis, University of Pennsylvania.

Hazen, Kirk. 2001. "An Introductory Investigation into Bidialectalism." In "Selected Papers from NWAV 29," edited by Tara Sanchez and Daniel Ezra Johnson. *University of Pennsylvania Working Papers in Linguistics* 7.3: 85–100.

Hazen, Kirk, and Laine Hall. 1999. "Dialect Shifts in West Virginia Families." Paper presented at the 60th Southeastern Conference on Linguistics (SECOL 60), Norfolk, Va., Apr. 8–10.

Heeringa, Wilbert, and John Nerbonne. 2001. "Dialect Areas and Dialect Continua." *Language Variation and Change* 13.3: 375–400. doi: 10.1017/S09543945011 33041.

Hinskens, Frans, Peter Auer, and Paul Kerswill. 2005. "The Study of Dialect Convergence and Divergence: Conceptual and Methodological Considerations." In *Dialect Change: Convergence and Divergence in European Languages*, edited by Peter Auer, Frans Hinskens, and Paul Kerswill, 1–48. Cambridge: Cambridge University Press.

Huffines, Marion Lois. 1980. "English in Contact with Pennsylvania German." *German Quarterly* 53.3: 352–66. doi:10.2307/404912.

Hulsen, Madeleine, Kees de Bot, and Bert Weltens. 2002. "'Between Two Worlds.' Social Networks, Language Shift, and Language Processing in Three Generations of Dutch Migrants in New Zealand." *International Journal of the Sociology of Language* 153: 27–52. doi:10.1515/ijsl.2002.004.

Iverson, Gregory K., and Joseph C. Salmons. 2006. "On the Typology of Final Laryngeal Neutralization: Evolutionary Phonology and Laryngeal Realism." *Theoretical Linguistics* 32.2: 205–16. doi:10.1515/TL.2006.014.

Jessen, Michael. 1998. *Phonetics and Phonology of Tense and Lax Obstruents in German*. Amsterdam: Benjamins.

Jessen, Michael, and Catherine Ringen. 2002. "Laryngeal Features in German." *Phonology* 19.2: 189–218. doi:10.1017/S0952675702004311.

Johnstone, Barbara. 1999. "Uses of Southern-Sounding Speech by Contemporary Texas Women." In "Styling the Other," edited by Ben Rampton. Special issue, *Journal of Sociolinguistics* 3.4: 505–22. doi:10.1111/1467-9481.00093.

Johnstone, Barbara, Jennifer Andrus, and Andrew E. Danielson. 2006. "Mobility, Indexicality, and the Enregisterment of 'Pittsburghese.'" *Journal of English Linguistics* 34.2: 77–104. doi:10.1177/0075424206290692.

José, Brian. 2010. "The Apparent-Time Construct and Stable Variation: Final /z/ Devoicing in Northwestern Indiana." *Journal of Sociolinguistics* 14.1: 34–59. doi:10.1111/j.1467-9841.2009.00434.x.

Keiser, Steven Harman. 2012. *Pennsylvania German in the American Midwest*. Publication of the American Dialect Society 96. Durham, N.C.: Duke University Press.

Kerswill, Paul, and Ann Williams. 2000. "Creating a New Town Koine: Children and Language Change in Milton Keynes." *Language in Society* 29.1: 65–115. doi:10 .1017/S0047404500001020.

Kirchner, Robert. 1995. "Contrastiveness Is an Epiphenomenon of Constraint Ranking." *Proceedings of the Annual Meeting of the Berkeley Linguistics Society* 21: 198–208. http://elanguage.net/journals/bls/article/view/3110.

Kopp, Achim. 1999. *The Phonology of Pennsylvania German English as Evidence of Language Maintenance and Shift*. Selinsgrove, Pa.: Susquehanna University Press.

Kraehenmann, Astrid. 2001. "Swiss German Stops: Geminates All over the Word." *Phonology* 18.1: 109–45. doi:10.1017/S0952675701004031.

Kuha, Mai. 1998. "Competing Motivations for NP Order in Kenyan English." *World Englishes* 17.1: 61–70. doi:10.1111/1467-971X.00082.

Labov, William. 1966. *The Social Stratification of English in New York City*. Washington, D.C.: Center for Applied Linguistics.

———. 1972. *Sociolinguistic Patterns*. Philadelphia: University of Pennsylvania Press.

———. 1980. "Is There a Creole Speech Community?" In *Theoretical Orientations in Creole Studies*, edited by Albert Valdman and Arnold Highfield, 369–88. New York: Academic Press.

———. 1994. *Principles of Linguistic Change*. Vol. 1, *Internal Factors*. Oxford: Blackwell.

———. 2001. "The Anatomy of Style-Shifting." In *Style and Sociolinguistic Variation*, edited by Penelope Eckert and John R. Rickford, 85–108. Cambridge: Cambridge University Press.

Labov, William, Sharon Ash, and Charles Boberg. 2006. *The Atlas of North American English: Phonetics, Phonology, and Sound Change*. Berlin: Walter de Gruyter.

Ladefoged, Peter. 2001. *A Course in Phonetics*. 4th ed. Fort Worth, Texas: Harcourt College Publishers.

Le Page, R.B., and Andrée Tabouret-Keller. 1985. *Acts of Identity: Creole-Based Approaches to Language and Ethnicity*. Cambridge: Cambridge University Press.

Linnes, Kathleen. 1998. "Middle-Class AAVE versus Middle-Class Bilingualism: Contrasting Speech Communities." *American Speech* 73.4: 339–67. doi:10.2307/455582.

Llamas, Carmen, Dominic Watt, and Daniel Ezra Johnson. 2009. "Linguistic Accommodation and the Salience of National Identity Markers in a Border Town." *Journal of Language and Social Psychology* 28.4: 381–407. doi:10.1177/0261927X09341962.

Lombardi, Linda. 1999. "Positional Faithfulness and Voicing Assimilation in Optimality Theory." *Natural Language and Linguistic Theory* 17.2: 267–302. doi:10.1023/A:1006182130229.

Louden, Mark L. 1997. "Linguistic Structure and Sociolinguistic Identity in Pennsylvania German Society." In *Languages and Lives: Essays in Honor of Werner Enninger*, edited by James Dow and Michèle Wolff, 79–91. New York: Peter Lang.

Mæhlum, Brit. 1996. "Codeswitching in Hemnesberget—Myth or Reality?" *Journal of Pragmatics* 25.6: 749–61. doi:10.1016/0378-2166(95)00027-5.

Mallinson, Christine, and Walt Wolfram. 2002. "Dialect Accommodation in a Biethnic Mountain Enclave Community: More Evidence on the Development of African American English." *Language in Society* 31.5: 743–75. doi:10.1017/S0047404502315021.

Martin-Jones, Marilyn, and Suzanne Romaine. 1986. "Semilingualism: A Half-Baked Theory of Communicative Competence." *Applied Linguistics* 7.1: 26–38. doi:10.1093/applin/7.1.26.

Milroy, Lesley. 1987. *Language and Social Networks*. 2nd ed. Oxford: Blackwell.

Mitleb, Fares. 1984. "Voicing Effect on Vowel Duration Is Not an Absolute Universal." *Journal of Phonetics* 12: 23–27.

Murray, Thomas E., and Beth Lee Simon. 2002. "At the Intersection of Regional and Social Dialects: The Case of *like* + Past Participle in American English." *American Speech* 77.1: 32–69. doi:10.1215/00031283-77-1-32.

Myers-Scotton, Carol. 2002. *Contact Linguistics: Bilingual Encounters and Grammatical Outcomes.* Oxford: Oxford University Press.

O'Dell, Michael, and Robert Port. 1983. "Discrimination of Word-Final Voicing in German." *Journal of the Acoustical Society of America* 73, supp. 1: S31. doi: 10.1121/1.2020331.

Oswald, Victor A., Jr. 1943. "'Voiced T'—A Misnomer." *American Speech* 18.1: 18–25. doi:10.2307/487263.

Page, Eugene R. 1937. "English in the Pennsylvania German Area." *American Speech* 12.3: 203–6. doi:10.2307/452428.

Payne, Arvilla C. 1980. "Factors Controlling the Acquisition of the Philadelphia Dialect by Out-of-State Children." In *Locating Language in Time and Space*, edited by William Labov, 143–78. Orlando, Fla.: Academic Press.

Plichta, Bartek, and Dennis R. Preston. 2003. "The /ay/s Have It: Stereotype, Perception, and Region." Paper presented at the 32nd annual meeting on New Ways of Analyzing Variation in English (NWAVE 32), Philadelphia, Pa., Oct. 9–12.

Port, Robert F., and Jonathan Dalby. 1982. "Consonant/Vowel Ratio as a Cue for Voicing in English." *Perception and Psychophysics* 32.2: 141–52. doi:10.3758/BF03204273.

Port, Robert, Fares Mitleb, and Michael O'Dell. 1981. "Neutralization of Obstruent Voicing in German Is Incomplete." *Journal of the Acoustical Society of America* 70, supp. 1: S13. doi:10.1121/1.2018716.

Port, Robert, and Michael L. O'Dell. 1985. "Neutralization of Syllable-Final Voicing in German." *Journal of Phonetics* 13.4: 455–71.

Preston, Dennis R. 1992. "Talkin' Black and Talkin' White: A Study in Variety Imitation." In *Old English and New: Studies in Language and Linguistics in Honor of Frederic G. Cassidy*, edited by Joan H. Hall, Nick Doane, and Dick Ringler, 327–55. New York: Garland.

———. 1996. "Where the Worst English Is Spoken." In *Focus on the USA*, edited by Edgar W. Schneider, 297–360. Amsterdam: Benjamins.

Purnell, Thomas, Joseph Salmons, and Delara Tepeli. 2005. "German Substrate Effects in Wisconsin English: Evidence for Final Fortition." *American Speech* 80.2: 135–64. doi:10.1215/00031283-80-2-135.

Rakerd, Brad, and Bartek Plichta. 2003. "More on Perceptions of /a/ Fronting." Paper presented at the 32nd annual meeting on New Ways of Analyzing Variation in English (NWAVE 32), Philadelphia, Pa., Oct. 9–12.

Rampton, Ben. 1995. "Language Crossing and the Problematisation of Ethnicity and Socialisation." *Pragmatics* 5.4: 485–513. http://elanguage.net/journals/pragmatics/article/view/474/406.

Roesch, Karen A. 2012. *Language Maintenance and Language Death: The Decline of Texas Alsatian.* Amsterdam: Benjamins.

Romaine, Suzanne. 1995. *Bilingualism.* 2nd ed. Oxford: Blackwell.

Sancier, Michele L., and Carol A. Fowler. 1997. "Gestural Drift in a Bilingual Speaker of Brazilian Portuguese and English." *Journal of Phonetics* 25.4: 421–36. doi:10.1006/jpho.1997.0051.

Sankoff, D., S. A. Tagliamonte, and E. Smith. 2005. *GoldVarbX: A Multivariate Analysis Application.* http://individual.utoronto.ca/tagliamonte/goldvarb.htm.

Schilling-Estes, Natalie. 1997. "Accommodation versus Concentration: Dialect Death in Two Post-Insular Island Communities." *American Speech* 72.1: 12–32. doi:10.2307/455606.

———. 1998. "Investigating 'Self-Conscious' Speech: The Performance Register in Ocracoke English." *Language in Society* 27.1: 53–83. doi:10.1017/S0047404500019722.

Schirmunski, Viktor. 1930. "Sprachgeschichte and Siedlungsmundarten." *Germanistisch-Romanistische Monatsschrift* 18: 113–22, 171–88.

Sjöström, Maria, Erik J. Eriksson, Elisabeth Zetterholm, and Kirk P. H. Sullivan. 2008. "A Bidialectal Experiment on Voice Identification." *Lund Working Papers in Linguistics* 53: 145–58. http://journals.lub.lu.se/index.php/LWPL/article/view/2278/1853.

Slowiaczek, Louida M., and Helena J. Szymanska. 1989. "Perception of Word-Final Obstruents in Polish." *Journal of Phonetics* 17: 213–37.

Struble, George G. 1935. "The English of the Pennsylvania Germans." *American Speech* 10.3: 163–72. doi:10.2307/451873.

Sturtevant, E. H. 1917. *Linguistic Change: An Introduction to the Historical Study of Language.* Chicago: University of Chicago Press.

Sweetland, Julie. 2002. "Unexpected but Authentic Use of an Ethnically-Marked Dialect." *Journal of Sociolinguistics* 6.4: 514–38. doi:10.1111/1467-9481.00199.

Tagliamonte, Sali A., and Sonja Molfenter. 2007. "How'd You Get That Accent? Acquiring a Second Dialect of the Same Language." *Language in Society* 36.5: 649–75. doi:10.1017/S0047404507070911.

Trudgill, Peter. 1986. *Dialects in Contact.* Oxford: Blackwell.

———. 1996. "Dialect Typology: Isolation, Social Network and Phonological Structure." In *Towards a Social Science of Language: Papers in honor of William Labov,* vol. 1, *Variation and Change in Language and Society,* edited by Gregory R. Guy, Crawford Feagin, Deborah Schiffrin, and John Baugh, 3–18. Amsterdam: Benjamins.

———. 2004. *New Dialect Formation: The Inevitability of Colonial Englishes.* Oxford: Oxford University Press.

Trudgill, Peter, Elizabeth Gordon, Gilliam Lewis, and Margaret Maclagan. 2000. "Determinism in New-Dialect Formation and the Genesis of New Zealand English." *Journal of Linguistics* 36.2: 299–318. doi:10.1017/S0022226700008161.

Van Bree, C. 1992. "The Stability of Language Elements in Present-Day Eastern Standard Dutch and Eastern Dutch Dialects." In *Dialect and Standard Language: Seventeen Studies in English and German,* edited by J. A. van Leuvensteijn and J. B. Bern, 178–203. Amsterdam: Royal Netherlands Academy of Arts and Sciences.

Van Rooy, Bertus. 2002. "Stress Placement in Tswana English: The Makings of a Coherent System." *World Englishes* 21.1: 145–60. doi:10.1111/1467-971X.00237.

Wassink, Alicia Beckford, and Judy Dyer. 2004. "Language Ideology and the Transmission of Phonological Change: Changing Indexicality in Two Situations of Language Contact." *Journal of English Linguistics* 32.1: 3–30. doi:10.1177/0075424203261799.

Wiese, Richard. 1996. *The Phonology of German*. Oxford: Clarendon.

Wilkerson, Miranda E., and Joseph Salmons. 2012. "Linguistic Marginalities: Becoming American without Learning English." *Journal of Transnational American Studies* 4.2. http://escholarship.org/uc/item/5vn092kk.

Wolfram, Walt. 2002. "Language Death and Dying." In *The Handbook of Language Variation and Change*, edited by J. K. Chambers, Peter Trudgill, and Natalie Schilling-Estes, 764–87. Oxford: Blackwell.

———. 2004. "Urban African American Vernacular English: Morphology and Syntax." In *A Handbook of Varieties of English*, edited by Bernd Kortmann and Edgar W. Schneider, 319–40. Berlin: Mouton de Gruyter. doi:10.1515/9783110175325.2.319.

Wolfram, Walt, and Dan Beckett. 2000. "The Role of the Individual and Group in Earlier African American English." *American Speech* 75.1: 3–33. doi:10.1215/00031283-75-1-3.

INDEX

AAVE. *See* African American Vernacular English
 (AAVE)
acoustic analysis, obstruent devoicing (PDE),
 52; ANOVA program and, 57–62; *bedcovers*,
 duration ratio, 52, 53; Cool Edit program, 54;
 first step, 52; methodology, 52–53; procedure,
 54–57; raw vowel durations, 55; tokens of /d/,
 54–55, 55
adjectives, PDE, 39–40
affricate [ʤ], PDE, 28–29
African American Vernacular English (AAVE), 13,
 125–26, 151–52, 164, 172
age groups, obstruent devoicing, 57
American Midwest, 17
Amish people, 187n8
ANOVA program, 185n5; consonant durations,
 analysis of, 58, 58–59; vowel durations, analysis
 of, 59, 59–60
areal distribution, lack of: consonantal features
 for [w] for /v/ and [β] for /w/, 93, 95; monophthongization of /aʊ/ to [a], 75; obstruent
 devoicing, PDE, 63; PDE raised [æ], 89;
 preliquid monophthongization of /aɪ/ to [æ],
 81; prenasal /a/ centralization, 85–86
articulatory distance: consonantal features for
 [w] for /v/ and [β] for /w/, 92, 95; monophthongization of /aʊ/ to [a], 75; prenasal /a/
 centralization, 85
Ash, Sharon, 33, 114
Asian English, 122
Atlantic Monthly, 15
The Atlas of North American English, 20–21
Auer, Peter: adult migration, study on, 9–10; on
 bidialectalism, 119, 155, 157; consonantal
 features for [w] for /v/ and [β] for /w/, 93,
 95–96; monophthongization of /aʊ/ to [a],
 74–76, 78; obstruent devoicing, unraveling
 of, 62, 64; PDE raised [æ], 90; preliquid
 monophthongization of /aɪ/ to [æ], 82–83;
 prenasal /a/ centralization, 86; salience,
 predictive power of, 96–97, 102–5
Auger, Julie, 145
Barden, Birgit: adult migration, study on, 9–10;
 on bidialectalism, 119, 155, 157; consonantal
 features for [w] for /v/ and [β] for /w/, 93,
 95–96; monophthongization of /aʊ/ to [a],
 74–76, 78; obstruent devoicing, unraveling
 of, 62, 64; PDE raised [æ], 90; preliquid
 monophthongization of /aɪ/ to [æ], 82–83;
 prenasal /a/ centralization, 86; salience,
 predictive power of, 96–97, 102–5
Bardovi-Harlig, Kathleen, 105, 111

Baugh, John, 124
bedcovers, duration ratio, 52, 53
Beech Bottom, North Carolina, long-term dialect
 contact situations, 13
Berwick-upon-Tweed, salience, 99, 103
bidialectalism, 19–42, 113–2, 177–78; African
 American Vernacular English (AAVE), 125–26,
 151–52, 164, 172; bilingualism-bidialectalism,
 parallel, 173–74; case study (*see* "Rachel,"
 case study on bidialectalism); comparison to
 other dialect contact phenomena, 120–25;
 constraint references, dialect differences and,
 118; contexts for, 156–57; controversy, 114–16;
 criteria for, 133–54; definition of, proposed
 modified and expanded, 169–74; "Delilah,"
 153, 164, 172; dialect differences, low-level,
 117–18; dialect feature matching, 163–65;
 dialect feature overlap, 163; discussion of
 in literature, 5, 113–14, 125–27; ephemeral
 phenomenon, 129; extensive personal
 pattern variation compared, 123–24; feature
 criteria for, 134–35, *134–35*, *137*, *138*; as
 fleeting phenomenon, 161–62; fluency
 and, 171–74; frequencies, 136, 138–45,
 140; Hazen's criteria for, critique of, 129,
 162–74; "hyperdialectical," 144; identification
 with two dialects, 159–60; imitation/
 performance speech compared, 120–22;
 incidental references to in literature, 126–27;
 interpersonal accommodation compared,
 123; interspeaker comparison tests for
 comparing monodialectals, 120; intraspeaker
 comparison tests for distinctiveness between
 two modes of speakers, 117–20; King of
 Prussia (Philadelphia), migrant children, 8–9,
 118–19, 157–58; language crossing compared,
 122–23; language migration pattern
 matching, 165; language variation patterns,
 145–54; Levenshtein Principle, 119–20;
 linguistic astuteness and, 160–61; linguistic
 behavior, assessments of, 170; middle-aged
 speakers, 141–45, *142–43*, 149–51, 158;
 migration and, 114; monophthongized
 /aʊ/, probabilistic analysis for, 146–47, *147*;
 multiple generations living side by side, 114;
 Optimality Theory analysis, 145; phonological
 processes, complexity, 118–19; prestige and,
 158–59; productive bidialectalism, defined,
 115; profile of bidialectal speaker, 129;
 quantitative criteria, 136–54; research subjects
 as "bidialectals," 125–26; salient features,
 119; social motivation criterion for, 153–54;

social networks and, 159; speech community identification of bidialectical, 166–69; style-shifting compared, 124–25; tests for, 177–20; two dialects, exposure to since childhood, 157–58; West Virginia Dialect Project, 115–16, 155; where to find bidialectals, 154–62; younger speakers, *140*, 147–51

bilabial fricative [β], PDE, 29–30

bilingualism-bidialectalism, parallel, 173–74

Blom, Jan-Petter, 126–27

Boberg, Charles, 33, 114

Boeree, 22

Bourhis, Richard, 123

Britain, David, 12–13

British Fens, 12–13

Brown, Becky, 110

Cajun identity, obstruent devoicing (PDE), 61–62

calques, 40

Cambap, 123–24

case study on bidialectalism. *See* "Rachel" (case study on bidialectalism)

Catalan, obstruent devoicing (PDE), 51

centralization of /aʊ/ to [a], PDE, 31

Chambers, J. K., 73, 81, 104, 155

code alternation: consonantal features for [w] for /v/ and [β] for /w/, 93, 95; obstruent devoicing, PDE, 63; PDE raised [æ], 90; preliquid monophthongization of /aɪ/ to [æ], 82; prenasal /a/ centralization, 86

cognitive demand of having distinct systems, bidialectalism, 165–66

comprehensibility, hindrance to: consonantal features for [w] for /v/ and [β] for /w/, 93, 95; obstruent devoicing, PDE, 64; PDE raised [æ], 90, *91*; preliquid monophthongization of /aɪ/ to [æ], 82–83

Connell, Bruce, 123–24

consonantal features for [w] for /v/ and [β] for /w/, 92–94; areal distribution, lack of, 93, 95; articulatory distance, 92, 95; bilarial fricative for /w/, *94*, 94–96; code alternation, 93, 95; comprehensibility, hindrance to, 93, 95; dichotomy, 93, 95; lay writing, representation in, 93, 95; lexicalization, 93, 95; mimicking, 93, 95; objective (linguistic) criteria, 92–93, 95; phonemicity, 93, 95; stereotyping, 93, 95; subjective (perceptual) criteria, 93–96

consonants (phonemic and phonological features), PDE: affricate [ʤ], 28–29; bilabial fricative [β], 29–30; obstruent devoicing, 30

constraint references, dialect differences and, 118

Cool Edit program, 54

Corby, Great Britain, long-term dialect contact situations, 14

Creole English, 122

Dalby, Jonathan, 50

Davis, Stuart, 48, 66

"Delilah," bidialectalism, 153, 164, 172

dialect contact (PDE), 7–15; long-term dialect contact situations, 13–15; migrations of speakers, 10–13; Morgantown, West Virginia, 9; New Zealand English, 10–12; Philadelphia, migrant children, 8–9

dialect feature matching, bidialectalism, 163–65

dialect feature overlap, bidialectalism, 163

dichotomy: consonantal features for [w] for /v/ and [β] for /w/, 93, 95; monophthongization of /aʊ/ to [a], 75; PDE raised [æ], 89; preliquid monophthongization of /aɪ/ to [æ], 82; prenasal /a/ centralization, 86

Dorian, Nancy C., 110

Dubois, Sylvie, 62

"Dutchifiedness," 28, 38, 40, 72

Dyer, Judy, 14

East German Speakers of Upper Saxonian, 155

East Sutherland Gaelic speakers, 110, 123–24

English lexical items, overlap between PDE and SCPE, 26–27

European Americans, long-term dialect contact situations, 13

Evans, Betsy E., 9, 121

extensive personal pattern variation, 123–24

feature complexity, loss of, 66–71

fluency, bidialectalism and, 171–74

"folk linguistics," 21

foods, dialects and, 22, 27

fortis/lenis, obstruent devoicing (PDE), 50

frequency, obstruent devoicing (PDE), *64*

Gates, Gary, 38, 63

Gibbons, Phebe Earle, 15

Giles, Howard, 123

glottal pulsing, 50

Goldvarb analysis, 67–70, 147

Grosskopf, Beate: adult migration, study on, 9–10; on bidialectalism, 119, 155, 157; consonantal features for [w] for /v/ and [β] for /w/, 93, 95–96; monophthongization of /aʊ/ to [a], 74–76, 78; obstruent devoicing, unraveling of, 62, 64; PDE raised [æ], 90; preliquid monophthongization of /aɪ/ to [æ], 82–83; prenasal /a/ centralization, 86; salience, predictive power of, 96–97, 102–5

Gumperz, John J., 126–27

Guy, Gregory, 118

habitual *still*, PDE, 35–36

Hatala, Eileen M., 164

Hazen, Kirk: on bidialectalism, 113, 118, 129, 135–36; bidialectalism definition, proposed modified and expanded, 169–74; critique of criteria for bidialectalism, 162–74; language variation patterns, bidialectalism, 145; linguistic behavior, assessments of, 170; social motivation criterion for bidialectalism, 153–54; West Virginia Dialect Project, 115–16, 155

"Holy Experiment," 15

Horvath, Barbara M., 62

"how now brown cow," 74–80

"hyperdialectical," 144

imitation/performance speech, 120–22

Indiana, obstruent devoicing (PDE), 63

individualized speakers, extreme variability among, prenasal /a/ centralization, 87–88, *87–88*

interpersonal accommodation, 123

intraspeaker comparison tests for distinctiveness between two modes of speakers, 117–20; constraint references, dialect differences and, 118; dialect differences, low-level, 117–18; Levenshtein Principle, 119–20; phonological processes, complexity, 118–19; salient features, 119

IO-DO-PP word order, PDE, 34–35

"I wonder as I wander," 85–88

Jessen, Michael, 44–45

Johnson, Daniel Ezra, 99, 103, 106

Johnstone, Barbara, 126, 170

José, Brian, 71

Keiser, Steven Herman, 32

Kerswill, Paul, 98, 106

Keynes, J. M., 96

King of Prussia (Philadelphia), migrant children, 8–9, 118–19, 157–58

Labov, William: on bidialectalism, 114, 117, 124; New York City Department store study, 118; New York City, tensed [æ], 33

Lancaster, Pennsylvania, monophthongization of /aɪ/ before liquids, 32

language crossing, 122–23

language-external factors, obstruent devoicing (PDE), 67

language-internal factors, obstruent devoicing (PDE), 67

language migration pattern matching, bidialectalism, 165

language variation patterns, bidialectalism, 145–54; feature prominence, determining variation patterns based on, 148–51, *149–50*; monophthongized /aʊ/, probabilistic analysis for, 146–47, *147*; morphosyntactic features, based on, 151–53, *153*; obstruent devoicing, probabilistic analysis for, *147*, 147–48; social motivation criterion for bidialectalism, 153–54

lay writing, representation in: consonantal features for [w] for /v/ and [β] for /w/, 93, 95; obstruent devoicing, PDE, 63–64; PDE raised [æ], 90; preliquid monophthongization of /aɪ/ to [æ], 82; prenasal /a/ centralization, 86

leave and let, 23, 27

Lebanon County, Pennsylvania, 18

bidialectalism, 20, 158

data from, 3–5, 27–28

obstruent devoicing, 52–53

Le Page, R. B., 156

Levenshtein Principle, 119–20

lexical items, PDE, 38–40; adjectives, 39–40; nouns, 39; verbs, 39

lexicalization: consonantal features for [w] for /v/ and [β] for /w/, 93, 95; obstruent devoicing, PDE, 63; PDE raised [æ], 90; preliquid monophthongization of /aɪ/ to [æ], 82; prenasal /a/ centralization, 86

Lim, Laureen, 118

Linnes, Kathleen, 125–26

listener perception, obstruent devoicing (PDE), 51

Llamas, Carmen, 99, 103, 106

localization, monophthongization of /aʊ/ to [a], 75

long-term dialect contact situations, 13–15

Louden, Mark L., 32

Louisiana, obstruent devoicing (PDE), 61–62

Lumbee Indians, long-term dialect contact situations, 13

Mæhlum, Brit, 126–27

Mallinson, Christine, 13–15

Mennonite people, 187n8, 188n9

Meyers-Scotton, Carol, 2

Mid-Atlantic tensed [æ], 33

Mid-Atlantic vowel quality–PDE raised [ae], 88

middle-aged speakers: bidialectalism, 141–45, *142–44*, 149–51, 158; monophthongization of /aʊ/ to [a], 78–80, *79–80*; obstruent devoicing, PDE, 44, 60, 66, *68*, 69–71, *70*; PDE raised [æ], *91*, 91–92; prenasal /a/ centralization, 87–88, *87–88*; profile of PDE, developing, 106–7, *108*, 110

Midwestern Pennsylvania German-English, 32

migration: bidialectalism and, 114; of speakers, various dialects, 10–13

mimicking: consonantal features for [w] for /v/ and [β] for /w/, 93, 95; monophthongization of /aʊ/ to [a], 75–76; obstruent devoicing, PDE, 64; PDE raised [æ], 90; preliquid monophthongization of /aɪ/ to [æ], 82; prenasal /a/ centralization, 86

Mitleb, Fares, 50

monodialectical speakers: obstruent devoicing, PDE, *68–69*; youngest speakers, sample tokens, 179–80

monophthongization of /aɪ/ before liquids, PDE, 31–32

monophthongization of /aʊ/ to [a], 74–80; areal distribution, lack of, 75; articulatory distance, 75; , bidialectalism, 146–47; code alternation, 75; comprehensibility, hindrance to, 76; dichotomy, 75; feature complexity, loss of, 79–80; generations of speakers, 76–78, *77*; lay writing, representation in, 75; localization, 75; middle-aged speakers, 78–80, *79–80*; mimicking, 75–76; objective criteria, 75; obstruent devoicing, extreme variability among individualized speakers, 78–79, *79*; PDE, 30–31; phonemicity, 75; stereotyping, 75–76; subjective criteria, 75–76; unraveling, evidence of, 78; younger speakers, 78–80, *79–80*

Morgantown, West Virginia, dialect contact (PDE), 9

morphosyntactic features (PDE), 33–38; determining language variation patterns based on, 151–53, *153*; habitual *still*, 35–36; IO-DO-PP word order, 34–35; *once*, 35; prepositional phrases, placement of direct and indirect objects with regard to, 34–35; remote past, 36–37; tag questions, 37–38, *what for...?* for *which?* or *what kind of*, 37

morphosyntax of PDE and SCPE, overlap, 24–25

National Broadcasting Corporation of New Zealand, 11

neutralization rules, obstruent devoicing (PDE), 51

New York City: department store study, 118; Puerto Ricans, 1; raised [æ], 33; vowel quality–PDE raised [æ], 88

New Zealand English, 10–12, 148

"Noah," 9, 15, 121, 154, 155

North Carolina: bidialectalism, 154; language variation patterns, bidialectalism, 145; long-term dialect contact situations, 13–14

Northern Midwestern-style dialect, 121

"Northern Subject Rule," 12

Norwegians, bidialectalism, 126–27

nouns, PDE, 39

objective (linguistic) criteria, obstruent devoicing (PDE), 62–63

Observer's Paradox, 188n5

obstruent devoicing, PDE, 30, 43–72; acoustic analysis of (*see* Acoustic analysis, obstruent devoicing [PDE]); across generations, decline of, 43–44; age groups, 57; areal distribution, lack of, 63; *bedcovers*, duration ratio, 52, *53*, /b/ stop, 47–48; Cajun identity, 61–62; Catalan, 51; code alternation, 63; composite linguistic system, obstruent devoicing at phonetic level as, 49–62; composite linguistic system, obstruent devoicing at phonological level as, 44–49; comprehensibility, hindrance to, 64; dichotomy, 63; /d/ pronunciation, 47–48; environments for, 46; evidence of unraveling, 65–70; extreme variability of use, 66, *66*; feature complexity, loss of, 66–71; fortis/lenis, 50; frequency, *64*; glottal pulsing, 50; Goldvarb analysis, 67–70; /g/ stop, 47–48; informants interviewed, characteristics of, 53, *54*; language-external factors, 67; language-internal factors, 67; language variation patterns, bidialectalism, 147; lay writing, representation in, 63–64; lexicalization, 63; listener perception, 51; loss of obstruents in devised sets, 65–66; mean consonant /d/, 56, *56*, 58; middle-aged PDE speakers, 44, 60, 66, *68*, 69–71, *70*; mimicking, 64; monodialectical speakers, *68–69*; monophthongization of /aʊ/ to [a], 78–79, *79*; neutralization rules, 51; objective (linguistic) criteria, 62–63; overview, 43–49; phonemicity, 63; phonetic level obstruent devoicing as composite linguistic

system, 49–62; phonological level, obstruent devoicing at as composite linguistic system, 44–49; preliquid monophthongization of /aɪ/ to [æ], 84, *84*; rates of, *44*; retention rates, *64*; salience of, 62–65; stereotyping, 64; stops, 47–48; strength, 50; "strong" and "weak" positions, 45–46; subjective (perceptive) criteria, 63–65; syllable-final devoicing, 45; tens/lax, 50; tokens of /d/, 54–55, *55*; /t/ pronunciation, 47; triad of voice, aspiration and duration, 50; unraveling of, 62–71; vowel duration, 51–52, *53*; vowel-to-obstruent durations, 57, *57*; Watertown, Wisconsin, 50; Wisconsin German, 50, 60; youngest speakers, 66, *71*

O'Dell, Michael, 185n3

Okracoke, 154, 161

older generation, bidialectalism. *See* Bidialectalism

once, PDE, 35

O'Neal, Rex, 154, 161

Optimality Theory analysis, bidialectalism, 145

Oswald, Victor A., 46; overlap between PDE and SCPE, 24–27, 40, *41*, 42; English lexical items, 26–27; morphosyntax of PDE and SCPE, 24–25; question intonation pattern, 25–26

"parrots in Somalia," 80–84

participants in study, 3–5, *4*

Payne, Arvilla C., 8–9, 33, 118–19, 157–58

PDE. *See* Pennsylvania Dutchified English (PDE)

PDE raised [æ], 88–92; areal distribution, lack of, 89; code alternation, 90; comprehensibility, hindrance to, 90, *91*; dichotomy, 89; frequency, changes in, *91*; individualized speakers, extreme variability among, *91*, 91–92; lay writing, representation in, 90; lexicalization, 90; middle-aged speakers, *91*, 91–92; mimicking, 90; objective (linguistic) criteria, 89–90; phonemicity, 89; retention rates, changes in, *91*; stereotyping, 90; subjective (perceptual) criteria, 90–92; younger speakers, *91*, 91–92

Pennsylvania Dutchified English (PDE): bidialectalism (*see* Bidialectalism); calques, 40; consonants (phonemic and phonological features), 28–30; development of, 5, 7–18; dialect contact, 7–15; dialect, list of features making up, 5; distinguishing features of, 27–40; "Dutchifiedness," 28, 38, 40, 72; informants participating in study, 3–5, *4*; lexical items, 38–40; morphosyntactic features, 33–38; obstruent devoicing (*see* Obstruent devoicing); shift to SCPE, 2–3, 5; South Central Pennsylvania English (SCPE), overlap, 24–27, 40, *41*, 42; unraveling of (*see* Unraveling of PDE); vowels (phonemic and phonological features), 30–33

Pennsylvania Germans, school-aged, 16–17

Pennsylvania, University of, Linguistics Laboratory, 20–21

Penn, William, 15, 175

performance speech, 120–22

Philadelphia: migrant children, 8–9; raised [æ], 33; vowel quality–PDE raised [ae], 88

Philadelphia English, 5, 23–24

phonemicity: consonantal features for [w] for /v/ and [β] for /w/, 93, 95; monophthongization of /aʊ/ to [a], 75; obstruent devoicing, PDE, 63; PDE raised [æ], 89; preliquid monophthongization of /aɪ/ to [æ], 82; prenasal /a/ centralization, 86

Pittsburgh/Southwestern Pennsylvania English, 5, 23–24

Port, Robert F., 50, 185n3

preliquid monophthongization of /aɪ/ to [æ], 80–84; areal distribution, lack of, 81; code alternation, 82; comprehensibility, hindrance to, 82–83; dichotomy, 82; lay writing, representation in, 82; lexicalization, 82; mimicking, 82; objective (linguistic) criteria, 81–82; obstruent devoicing, extreme variability among individualized speakers, 84, *84*; phonemicity, 82; rates of /aɪ/ to [æ], *83*; stereotyping, 82; subjective (perceptual) criteria, 82–83

prenasal /a/ centralization, 85–88; areal distribution, lack of, 85–86; articulatory distance, 85; code alternation, 86; dichotomy, 86; individualized speakers, extreme variability among, 87–88, *87–88*; lay writing, representation in, 86; lexicalization, 86; middle-aged speakers, 87–88, *87–88*; mimicking, 86; objective criteria, 85–86; phonemicity, 86; stereotyping, 86; subjective (perceptual) criteria, 86–88; younger speakers, 87–88, *87–88*

prepositional phrases, placement of direct and indirect objects with regard to, PDE, 34–35

prestige, bidialectalism and, 158–59

Preston, Dennis R., 114

productive bidialectalism, defined, 115

profile of PDE, developing, 106–11; middle-aged generation, 106–7, *108*, 110; younger generation, 106–7, *108*, 109

Puerto Ricans, New York, 1

Punjabi English, 122

Purnell, Thomas, 50, 60

question intonation pattern, overlap between PDE and SCPE, 25–26

"Rachel" (case study on bidialectalism), 113, 129–74, 176–77; bidialectalism definition, proposed modified and expanded, 169–74; cognitive demand of having distinct systems, 165–66; comparison with other PDE speakers, *144*, 144–45; criteria for bidialectalism, 133–54; dialect feature matching, 163–65; dialect feature overlap, 163; excerpts from conversation, 180–84; feature prominence, determining variation patterns based on, 148–51, *149–50*; features used by, *135*,

137, *138*; frequencies, 136, 138–45, *140*; as "hyperdialectical," 144; identification with two dialects, 159–60; language migration pattern matching, 165; language variation patterns, 145–54; monophthongized /aʊ/, probabilistic analysis for, *147*; morphosyntactic features, determining language variation patterns based on, 151–53, *153*; obstruent devoicing, probabilistic analysis for, *147*, 147–48; overview, 130–33; social motivation criterion for bidialectalism, 153–54; speech community identification of bidialectical, 166–69

raised [æ], PDE, 32–33

Rampton, Ben, 122–23

Reading, Michigan

salience, predictive power of, 96

remote past, PDE, 36–37

retention rates, obstruent devoicing (PDE), *64*

Ringen, Catherine, 44–45

Roaring Creek, North Carolina, long-term dialect contact situations, 13

salience, predictive power of, 96–106; definition of salience, 97; degree of salience, 102; PDE data and, 99, *100*, 101–5; simple and complex rules, 104; speaker awareness, 105–6; summary of information for features, *101*

Salmons, Joseph, 50, 60

Scanian Swedish, 127. *See also* Stockholm Swedish–Scanian Swedish

Schilling-Estes, Natalie, 122, 154, 161

Schirmunski, Victor, 9–10, 62

school-aged Pennsylvania Germans, 16–17

SCPE. *See* South Central Pennsylvania English (SCPE)

Sjöström, Maria, 127, 154–56, 161

Slowiaczek, Louida M., 51

social motivation criterion for bidialectalism, 153–54

social networks, bidialectalism and, 159

South Central Pennsylvania English (SCPE): bidialectalism (*see* Bidialectalism); complexity, 15; informants participating in study, 3–5, *4*; King of Prussia (Philadelphia), 8–9, 118–19, 157–58; long-term dialect contact situations, 14–15; map of South Central Pennsylvania, *21*; Pennsylvania Dutchified English (PDE), overlap, 24–27, 40, *41*, *42*; shift to, 2–3, 5; working description of, 20–24

South Central Pennsylvania, map of, *21*

"Southern English," 126

speech community identification of bidialectical, 166–69

stereotyping: consonantal features for [w] for /v/ and [β] for /w/, 93, 95; monophthongization of /aʊ/ to [a], 75–76; obstruent devoicing, PDE, 64; PDE raised [æ], 90; preliquid monophthongization of /aɪ/ to [æ], 82; prenasal /a/ centralization, 86

Stockholm Swedish, 127

Stockholm Swedish-Scanian Swedish, 154–55, 157, 161
stops, obstruent devoicing (PDE), 47–48
strength, obstruent devoicing (PDE), 50
"strong" and "weak" positions, obstruent devoicing (PDE), 45–46
Sturtevant, E. H., 109
style-shifting, 124–25
subjective (perceptive) criteria, obstruent devoicing (PDE), 63–65
Sweetland, Julie, 172
syllable-final devoicing, 45
Szymanska, Helena J., 51
Tabouret-Keller, Andrée, 156
tag questions, PDE, 37–38
Taylor, Donald M., 123
TELSUR project, 20–21
tens/lax, obstruent devoicing (PDE), 50
Tepeli, Delara, 50, 60
"Texan English," 126
triad of voice, aspiration and duration, 50
Trudgill, Peter: on bidialectalism, 119; monophthongization of /aʊ/ to [a], 76, 78; New Zealand English, study on, 10–12; obstruent devoicing, 72; PDE raised [æ], 90; salience, predictive power of, 96–97, 106; unraveling of obstruent devoicing, 62
Tukey, 59
U.K. teens, salience among, 99
unraveling of PDE, 5, 73–111, 176; consonantal features for [w] for /v/ and [β] for /w/, 92–94; evidence of unraveling, 65–70; "how now brown cow," 74–80; "I wonder as I wander," 85–88; monophthongization of /aʊ/ to [a], 74–80; obstruent devoicing, PDE, 62–71; "parrots in Somalia," 80–84; preliquid monophthongization of /aɪ/ to [æ], 80–84; prenasal /a/ centralization, 85–88; profile of PDE, developing, 106–11; salience, predictive power of, 96–106; vocalic features, 73–92

Upper Saxon vernacular speakers, 103, 105
Van Bree, C., 98
VARBRUL program, 185n4
verbs, PDE, 39
vocalic features, unraveling of PDE, 73–92; "how now brown cow," 74–80; "I wonder as I wander," 85–88; monophthongization of /aʊ/ to [a], 74–80; "parrots in Somalia," 80–84; PDE raised [æ], 88–92; preliquid monophthongization of /aɪ/ to [æ], 80–84; vowel quality–PDE raised [æ], 88–92
vowel duration, obstruent devoicing (PDE), 51–52, 53
vowels (phonemic and phonological features), PDE, 30–33; centralization of /aʊ/ to [a], 31; monophthongization of of /aɪ/ before liquids, 31–32; monophthongization of /aʊ/ to [a], 30–31; raised [æ], 32–33
vowel-to-obstruent durations, 57, 57
Watertown, Wisconsin, obstruent devoicing, PDE, 50
Watt, Dominic, 99, 103, 106
West Germany, Upper Saxon vernacular speakers, 103, 105
West Virginia Dialect Project, 115–16, 155
what for…? for which? or what kind of, PDE, 37
Williams, Ann, 98, 106
Wisconsin German, obstruent devoicing (PDE), 50, 60
Wisconsin, obstruent devoicing (PDE), 63
Wolfram, Walt, 13–15
Yates, 141
younger speakers: bidialectalism, 140, 147–51; monodialectical speakers, sample tokens, 179–80; monophthongization of /aʊ/ to [a], 78–80, 79–80; obstruent devoicing, PDE, 66, 71; PDE raised [æ], 91, 91–92; prenasal /a/ centralization, 87–88, 87–88; profile of PDE, developing, 106–7, 108, 109